Hiking the Absaroka-Beartooth Wilderness

Books by Bill Schneider

Where the Grizzly Walks, 1977
Hiking Montana, 1979
The Dakota Image, 1980
The Yellowstone River, 1985
Best Hikes on the Continental Divide, 1988
The Flight of the Nez Perce, 1988
The Tree Giants, 1988
Hiking the Beartooths, 1995
Bear Aware, A Quick Reference Bear Country Survival Guide, 1996
Hiking Carlsbad Caverns & Guadalupe Mountains National Parks, 1996
Best Easy Day Hikes Yellowstone, 1997
Exploring Canyonlands & Arches National Parks, 1997
Hiking Yellowstone National Park, 1997
Backpacking Tips, coauthor, 1998
Best Easy Day Hikes Beartooths, 1998
Best Easy Day Hikes Grand Teton, 1999
Hiking Grand Teton National Park, 1999
Hiking Montana 20th Anniversay Edition, coauthor, 1999
Best Backpacking Vacations Northern Rockies, 2002
Hiking the Absaroka-Beartooth Wilderness, 2003
Where the Grizzly Walks, 2003

Learn more about Bill Schneider's books at www.billschneider.net

A **FALCON** GUIDE®

Hiking the Absaroka-Beartooth Wilderness

Bill Schneider

Updated Fishing Information by Richard K. Stiff, former High Mountain Lakes Survey Coordinator, Montana Department of Fish, Wildlife & Parks

Second Edition

FALCON®

GUILFORD, CONNECTICUT
HELENA, MONTANA
AN IMPRINT OF THE GLOBE PEQUOT PRESS

A **FALCON** GUIDE ®

ISBN 0-7627-2238-X
ISSN 1544-0850

Manufactured in the United States of America
Second Edition/First Printing

Contents

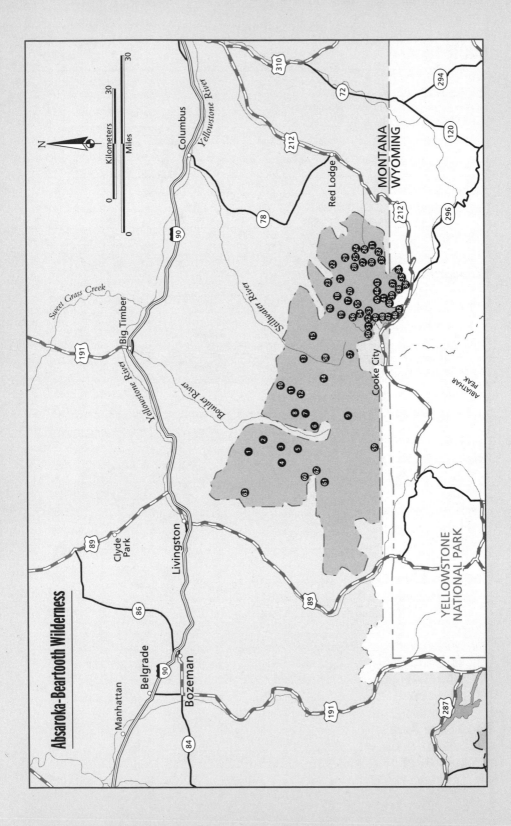

The Beartooth Highway

Absaroka Range

Map Legend

START

🚶 Featured trail start

🚶 Trailhead

═══⬭90═══ Limited access highway

══⬭2══ U.S. highway

──⬭18── State highway

────── Paved road

══════ Gravel road

= = = = = Unimproved road

--------- Trail

━ ━ ━ ━ Featured trail

— · — · Park boundary

— — — — Wilderness boundary

⋈ Bridge

⬥ Campground

)(Pass

▲ Peak or butte

∥ Waterfall

Acknowledgments

No book, especially a hiking guide, gets into print without lots of help from lots of people. In this case, I received invaluable help from many people.

First, I must thank my hiking partners, Mike Cannon and Jim Melstad, who survived some major "power hiking" to cover those last miles before the snow fell, and my family who not only spent some long days on the trail with me but withstood many nights away from home, tight schedules, and the long process of writing the book on nights and weekends.

I also gathered vital information from other hikers—Ann Boyd, Cathy Wright, Dick Krott, and Mike Sample. And as you can see, Mike also provided many of the photos for the book.

My friends in the Forest Service (Allie Wood, Frank Cifala, Dan Tyers, and Lyle Hancock) helped me gather all those details and reviewed the draft manuscript. I also learned much during those long talks on the hiking trail with wilderness rangers Dorothy Houser and Susan Nicholas.

And of course, I owe a big thank you to the staff at Falcon, who endured my distraction with the original book and helped me in a thousand ways to make it happen—especially Randall Green, guidebook editor, Will Harmon, who edited the original manuscript, and graphic artists Eric West and Chris Stamper, who did the maps and charts for the first edition. Now, an equal thank you goes to the staff at Globe Pequot Press, the current owner of Falcon Publishing, especially Jeff Serena, Gillian Belnap, Nancy Freeborn, and Julie Marsh.

Driving the Beartooth Highway—getting to the trailhead can be more exciting and scenic than the trip itself. Photo: Michael S. Sample

Introduction: A Tale of Two Wildernesses

The Absaroka-Beartooth Wilderness isn't a national park. It's even better. It's a national treasure.

This guidebook outlines trips of varying lengths, including day hikes and overnighters. But most people quickly discover that a day or two in the Absaroka-Beartooth isn't enough. Actually, it's probably impossible to get enough of this place, so I've also included several multiday backpacking adventures to help you get your fill of paradise.

The 943,377-acre Absaroka-Beartooth Wilderness is one of the most visited wilderness areas in the United States. This is surprising considering that snow usually covers the area until July and often reclaims the highland again in early September. This book covers both the high-elevation, lake-strewn uplift, commonly called the Beartooth Plateau or more simply, the Beartooths, and the gentler, forested mountains of the Absaroka.

In this wilderness the vast majority of activity occurs in the Beartooths. Even though the Beartooths attract lots of visitors, the area can absorb this use in a way that can give you the feeling you have the wilderness to yourself. Instead of competing for designated campsites or huts, backcountry travelers can camp anywhere. And anywhere is a big place in the Beartooths.

Almost all use on the Beartooth Plateau occurs from July through September. During July, snow may still stick to some sections of trail, and in September, winter can come early and with a vengeance, so most use is concentrated into a six-week period from mid-July through August.

In the Absaroka and lower-elevation sections of the Beartooths, the season can be slightly longer, but the winter snows still don't give up some trails until at least late June. In September and October, large numbers of hunters and outfitters head into the Absaroka Mountains and more or less take over the area.

Most people admire the Beartooth Mountains for their sheer, unbridled beauty. But many geologists marvel at this range for a different reason. A band of igneous rock rich in rare minerals lies along the northern edge of these mountains, often called the Beartooth Front. The uplifted granite that comprises most of the range dates back more than three billion years and contains some of the oldest rocks on Earth. The Beartooths also boast the highest mountain in Montana: Granite Peak, at 12,799 feet. From the top of Granite or many other peaks in the range, the view is dizzying.

With 944 lakes and nine major drainages, the Beartooths are also an angler's paradise. Rainbow, cutthroat, brook, golden, and lake trout thrive in the waterways of the plateau. About 350 lakes have stocked or naturally reproducing trout populations. Though the area is extremely popular, a persistent angler can usually find an unoccupied lake or stream to call his or her own for a day or two. Conversely, the Absaroka has limited fishing opportunities, and the streams, not lakes, offer the best fishing.

Hiking above treeline on the Beartooth Plateau. Photo: Michael S. Sample

Much of the Beartooth Plateau rests at about 10,000 feet and is covered with delicate alpine tundra. Because of the high use, zero-impact camping practices are essential to the preservation of this fragile ecosystem. Actually, most people visiting the Beartooths nowadays take great care to leave no trace of their visit. This is, of course, one reason this great masterpiece of the national forest system still seems pristine and uncrowded. It's the responsibility of all future visitors to carry on this tradition.

The Absaroka could be compared to the second child, a quieter, less aggressive sibling. Fans of the Absaroka must put up with the "first-born" getting all the fanfare and friends and fame and fortune while they sulk in obscurity. The Absaroka is like that—wild and magnificent but almost forgotten next to its big sister, the Beartooths.

Unlike the Beartooths, the Absaroka is a more stereotypical western mountain range with fewer lakes and alpine areas, but more streams. The Absaroka is a quiet wilderness, less rock but more greenery. And if you want to get up to 10,000 feet, you have to climb up there. You aren't parking your vehicle at 10,000-foot trailheads and hiking all day at that elevation as you can in the Beartooths.

Also, unlike the Beartooths, the Absaroka has great trails begging for hikers—with the exception of a few hot spots like Passage Falls, Pine Creek Lake, and Elbow Lake that get heavy use. When you get tired of people but still want a pristine wilderness, try the Absaroka.

Not all Absaroka trails are included in this guidebook. Some are only outfitter trails, leading more or less nowhere, unless you're looking for a spike (hunters') camp. Others are little used and with no real destination such as a mountaintop or lake that might test an experienced hiker's route-finding skills. For this reason, this guidebook covers only selected routes in the Absaroka Range, not the entire trail system.

Using This Guidebook

This guidebook won't answer every question you have concerning your planned excursions into the Absaroka-Beartooth. But then, most people don't want to know everything before they go, lest they remove the thrill of making their own discoveries while exploring this magnificent wilderness. This book does provide the basic information needed to plan a successful trip.

Types of Trips

Loop: Starts and finishes at the same trailhead, with very little retracing of your steps. Sometimes the definition of a loop is stretched to include trips that involve a short walk on a road at the end of the hike to get back to your vehicle. Mileage given is trailhead to trailhead.

Shuttle: A point-to-point trip that requires two vehicles or an arrangement to be picked up at a designated time. The best way to manage the logistical problems of shuttles is to arrange for another party to start at the other end of the trail, meet in the middle and trade keys, and when finished, drive each other's vehicles home.

Out-and-Back: Traveling to a specific destination such as a lake or mountaintop and then retracing your steps back to the trailhead.

Base Camp: An out-and-back trip involving a multinight stay to enjoy short day trips from a base camp.

Distances

It's almost impossible to get precisely accurate distances for most trails. The distances used in this guidebook are based on a combination of actual experience hiking the trails, distances stated on USDA Forest Service signs, and estimates from topographic maps. In some cases, distances may be slightly off, so consider this when planning a trip. Keep in mind that distance is often less important than difficulty—a rough, 2-mile cross-country trek can take longer than 5 or 6 miles on a good trail. Also, keep mileage estimates in perspective because they are all at least slightly inaccurate. How many signs have you seen saying it's 2 miles or 5 miles to a lake, but what's the chance that it's exactly 2 or 5 miles? Or should we really worry about it?

Taking a break during a day hike from base camp on the Lake Plateau.

Ratings

The estimates of difficulty should serve as a general guide only, not the final word. What is difficult to one person may be easy to the next. In this guidebook, difficulty ratings take into account both how long and how strenuous the route is, but they do not consider your physical condition. Here are general definitions of the ratings.

Easy: Suitable for any hiker, including small children or the elderly, without serious elevation gain, no off-trail or hazardous sections, and no places where the trail is faint.

Moderate: Suitable for hikers who have some experience and at least an average fitness level; probably not suitable for small children or the elderly unless they have an above-average level of fitness; perhaps with some short sections where the trail is difficult to follow; and often with some hills to climb.

Difficult: Suitable for experienced hikers with an above-average fitness level; often with some sections of the trail that are hard to follow or some off-trail sections that could require knowledge of route-finding with topo map and compass; often with serious elevation gain; and possibly with some off-trail hiking and hazardous conditions such as difficult stream crossings, snowfields, or cliffs.

In a few sidebars, the ratings have more colorful definitions of Human, Semi-human, and Animal. These ratings roughly equal the definitions of easy, moderate, and difficult, although the Animal rating could be described as very difficult.

Special Regulations

The USDA Forest Service (FS) has special regulations for hikers and backcountry horsemen. In some cases, the regulations apply throughout the wilderness, while in other cases they apply to specific trails or ranger districts. Check with the FS before you leave on your trip, and be sure to read and follow any special regulations posted at the trailhead. The FS doesn't come up with these regulations to inconvenience backcountry visitors. Instead, the regs are designed to promote sharing and preservation of the wilderness.

Inconsistent Names

Some names of places and features used in this guidebook may not match the names found on some maps and in other books. In some cases, lakes named in this book are unnamed on some maps. The USGS maps, for example, list only officially approved names, but many lakes, streams, and mountains have common names that appear on other maps and trail signs and in guidebooks, including, in some cases, this book.

Trails Only

As mentioned several times in this guidebook, off-trail travel is the essence of the Beartooths. However, this guidebook does not, with a few exceptions, cover off-trail travel. Even those exceptions are cases where there has been so much off-trail travel on a certain unofficial route that it has resulted in a definable trail. Off-trail travel should be tried only after you've gained enough experience to feel confident with your abilities. Perhaps the best way to achieve this experience is to go on a few trips with an experienced off-trail hiker.

Following Faint Trails

Trails that receive infrequent use often fade away in grassy meadows, on ridges, or through rocky sections. Don't panic. These sections are usually short, and you can look ahead to see where the trail goes. Often the trail is visible going up a hill or through a hallway of trees ahead. If so, focus on that landmark and don't worry about being off the trail for a short distance.

Also watch for other indicators that you are indeed on the right route, even if the trail isn't clearly visible. Watch for cairns, blazes, downfall cut with saws, and trees with the branches whacked off on one side. Follow only official Forest Service blazes, which are shaped like an upside-down exclamation point, and don't follow blazes made by hunters, outfitters, or other hikers.

Sharing

We all want our own wilderness area all to ourselves, but that happens only in our dreams. Lots of people use the Absaroka-Beartooth Wilderness, and to make everyone's experience better, we all must work at politely sharing the wilderness.

For example, hikers must share trails with backcountry horsemen. Both groups have every right to be on the trail, so please do not let it become a confrontation. Keep in mind that horses and mules are much less maneuverable than hikers, so it becomes the hiker's responsibility to yield the right-of-way. All hikers should stand on the downhill side of the trail, well off-trail for safety's sake, and let the stock quietly pass.

Another example of politely sharing the wilderness is choosing your campsite. If you get to a popular lake late in the day and all the good campsites are taken, don't crowd in on another camper. This is most aggravating, as these sites rightfully go on a first-come, first-served basis. If you're late, you have the responsibility to move on or take a less desirable site a respectable distance away from other campers.

Elevation Profiles

All hikes have elevation profiles to give you a general idea of the elevation gain and loss on the route. Be sure to check the scale on the axis of the profiles to get a better picture of the route's difficulty.

Rating the Hills

In the process of publishing dozens of FalconGuides, we have been working to develop a consistent rating system to help hikers determine how difficult those "big hills" really are. Such a system would help hikers decide how far they wanted to hike that day or even whether they wanted to take that trail at all. In the past, guidebook authors have described hills to the best of their ability, but subjectively. What is a big hill to one hiker might be a slight upgrade to the next.

Also, it isn't only going up that matters. Some hikers hate going down steep hills and the knee problems that go with descending with a big pack. These "weak-kneed" hikers might want to avoid Category 1 and Category H hills.

This new system combines the elevation gain and the length of that section of trail in a complicated mathematical formula to come up with a numerical hill rating similar to the system used by cyclists. The system only works for climbs of 0.5 mile or longer, not short, steep hills.

Here is a rough description of the categories, listed from easiest to hardest.

Category 5: A slight upgrade.

Category 4: Usually within the capabilities of any hiker.

Category 3: A well-conditioned hiker might describe a Category 3 climb as "gradual," but a poorly conditioned hiker might complain about the steepness. It's

FalconGuide Hill Rating Chart

ELEVATION GAIN (in feet)	DISTANCE (in miles)											
	0.5	1.0	1.5	2.0	2.5	3.0	3.5	4.0	4.5	5.0	5.5	6.0
200	4.2	5.0	5.4	5.5	5.6	5.6	5.7	5.7	5.7	5.7	5.7	5.7
300	3.3	4.5	4.9	5.2	5.3	5.4	5.5	5.5	5.5	5.5	5.6	5.6
400	1.8	4.0	4.5	4.8	5.1	5.2	5.3	5.3	5.4	5.4	5.4	5.4
500	1.0	3.5	4.2	4.5	4.7	5.0	5.1	5.2	5.2	5.2	5.3	5.3
600	H	3.0	3.8	4.2	4.4	4.6	4.9	4.9	5.0	5.1	5.1	5.1
700	H	2.5	3.4	3.9	4.2	4.3	4.5	4.8	4.9	4.9	4.9	5.0
800	H	1.4	3.1	3.6	3.9	4.1	4.2	4.3	4.7	4.7	4.8	4.9
900	H	H	2.7	3.3	3.6	3.9	4.0	4.1	4.2	4.6	4.7	4.7
1,000	H	H	2.3	2.9	3.4	3.6	3.8	3.9	4.0	4.1	4.5	4.6
1,100	H	H	1.9	2.7	3.1	3.4	3.6	3.7	3.8	3.9	3.9	4.5
1,200	H	H	H	2.4	2.8	3.1	3.4	3.5	3.6	3.7	3.8	3.9
1,300	H	H	H	2.1	2.6	2.9	3.2	3.3	3.5	3.5	3.6	3.7
1,400	H	H	H	1.8	2.3	2.7	2.9	3.1	3.3	3.4	3.5	3.5
1,500	H	H	H	1.6	2.1	2.4	2.7	2.9	3.1	3.2	3.3	3.3
1,600	H	H	H	H	1.9	2.2	2.3	2.7	2.9	2.9	3.1	3.2
1,700	H	H	H	H	1.7	1.9	2.3	2.5	2.7	2.8	2.9	3.0
1,800	H	H	H	H	1.5	1.8	2.0	2.3	2.5	2.6	2.7	2.8
1,900	H	H	H	H	1.3	1.7	1.9	2.1	2.3	2.4	2.6	2.6
2,000	H	H	H	H	H	1.5	1.7	1.9	2.1	2.2	2.4	2.5
2,100	H	H	H	H	H	1.3	1.6	1.8	1.9	2.0	2.2	2.3
2,200	H	H	H	H	H	1.2	1.4	1.6	1.8	1.9	1.9	2.1
2,300	H	H	H	H	H	1.0	1.3	1.5	1.7	1.8	1.9	1.9
2,400	H	H	H	H	H	H	1.2	1.4	1.5	1.6	1.8	1.8
2,500	H	H	H	H	H	H	1.0	1.2	1.4	1.5	1.6	1.7
2,600	H	H	H	H	H	H	H	1.1	1.3	1.4	1.5	1.6
2,700	H	H	H	H	H	H	H	H	1.1	1.3	1.4	1.5
2,800	H	H	H	H	H	H	H	H	H	1.1	1.3	1.4
2,900	H	H	H	H	H	H	H	H	H	1.0	1.2	1.3
3,000	H	H	H	H	H	H	H	H	H	H	1.0	1.1

definitely not steep enough to deter you from hiking the trail, but these climbs will slow you down.

Category 2: Most hikers would consider these "big hills," steep enough, in some cases, to make hikers choose an alternative trail, but not the real lung-busting, calf-stretching hills.

Category 1: These are among the steepest hills in the park. If you have heart or breathing problems or simply dislike climbing big hills, you might look for an alternative trail.

Category H: These are hills that make you wonder if the person who laid out the trail was on drugs. Any trail with a Category H hill is steeper than any trail should be. (Incidentally, "H" stands for "Horrible.")

The hills in this book are rated according to the accompanying chart. Some climbs are rated in the hike descriptions of this book, but if not included (or to use this formula in other hiking areas), get the mileage and elevation gain off the topo map and look them up on rating chart.

Finding Maps

Good maps are easy to find, and they are essential to any wilderness trip. For safety reasons, maps are essential for finding routes and for "staying found." For non-safety reasons, most people would not want to miss out on the unending joy of mindlessly whiling away untold hours staring at a topo map and wondering what the world looks like here and there.

For trips into the Absaroka-Beartooth, there are three good choices for maps:

- U.S. Geological Survey (USGS) topographic maps;
- An excellent Absaroka-Beartooth Wilderness map published by the U.S. Department of Agriculture (USDA) Forest Service;
- A series of six topo maps published by Rocky Mountain Survey (RMS), a private company in Billings, Montana, especially for hikers and anglers.

Ranger district maps are available from the various Forest Service offices in the region. The large wilderness map, however, includes the same information at a smaller scale.

Which maps do you need? The well-prepared wilderness traveler will take all three. Look for maps at the following locations:

USGS: Check sporting goods stores in the Absaroka-Beartooth area or write directly to the USGS at the following address and refer to the specific quad you need. Note the grid on page 9.

Map Distribution
U.S. Geological Survey
Box 25286, Federal Center
Denver, CO 80225
303–202–4700

USGS Topographic Map Index

	COLUMBUS EAST	SHANE RIDGE	COONEY RESERVOIR	ROBERTS	RED LODGE EAST	TOLMAN FLAT	CLARK
	COLUMBUS WEST	WHITEBIRD SCHOOL	ROSCOE NE	CASTAGNE	RED LODGE WEST	MOUNT MAURICE	NORTH BENNETT CREEK
	SPRINGTIME	ASBAROKEE	ROSCOE NW	ROSCOE	BARE MOUNTAIN	BLACK PYRAMID MTN.	DEEP LAKE
	REED POINT	SANDBORN CREEK	FISHTAIL	MACKAY RANCH	SYLVAN PEAK	SILVER RUN PEAK	BEARTOOTH BUTTE
	WORK CREEK	COW FACE HILL	BEEHIVE	EMERALD LAKE	ALPINE	CASTLE MOUNTAIN	MUDDY CREEK
GREYCLIFF	PACKSADDLE BUTTE	WILDCAT DRAW	NYE	MOUNT WOOD	GRANITE PEAK	FOSSIL LAKE	JIM SMITH PEAK
BIG TIMBER	BOSS CANYON	SLIDEROCK MOUNTAIN	MEYER MOUNTAIN	CATHEDRAL POINT	LITTLE PARK MOUNTAIN	COOKE CITY	PILOT PEAK
CARNEY	MCLEOD	SQUAW PEAK	PICKET PIN MOUNTAIN	TUMBLE MOUNTAIN	PINNACLE MOUNTAIN	CUTOFF MOUNTAIN	ARIATHAR PEAK
KELLY HILLS	SPRINGDALE	MCLEOD BASIN	CHROME MOUNTAIN	MOUNT DOUGLAS	HAYSTACK PEAK	ROUNDHEAD BUTTE	MOUNT HORNADAY
ELTON	MOUNT RAE	WEST BOULDER PLATEAU	THE NEEDLES	IRON MOUNTAIN	HUMMINGBIRD PEAK		LAMAR CANYON
MISSION	LIVINGSTON PEAK	MOUNT COWEN	THE PYRAMID	MOUNT WALLACE	SPECIMEN CREEK		TOWER JUNCTION
LIVINGSTON	BRISBIN	DEXTER POINT	KNOWLES PEAK	MINERAL MOUNTAIN	ASH MOUNTAIN		BLACKTAIL DEER CREEK
HOPPERS	CHIMNEY ROCK	PRAY	EMIGRANT	MONITOR PEAK	GARDINER		MAMMOTH
BOZEMAN PASS	BALD KNOB	BIG DRAW	DAILEY LAKE	DOME MOUNTAIN	ELECTRIC PEAK		QUADRANT MOUNTAIN
KELLY CREEK	MOUNT ELLIS	FRIDLEY PEAK	LEWIS CREEK	MINER	SPORTSMAN LAKE		JOSEPH PEAK
BOZEMAN	WHEELER MOUNTAIN	MOUNT BLACKMORE	THE SENTINEL	RAMSHORN PEAK	BIG HORN PEAK		DIVIDE LAKE
BOZEMAN HOT SPRINGS	GALLATIN GATEWAY	GARNET MOUNTAIN	HIDDEN LAKE	LONE INDIAN PEAK	SUNSHINE POINT		UPPER TEPEE BASIN

ABSAROKA BEARTOOTH WILDERNESS

YELLOWSTONE NATIONAL PARK

MONTANA / WYOMING

Forest Service: The Absaroka-Beartooth Wilderness map is also available at sporting good stores around the Beartooths, or call, stop by, or write to any of these Forest Service offices:

Custer National Forest
Forest Supervisor's Office
2602 First Avenue South
P.O. Box 2556
Billings, MT 59103
(406) 657-6361

Shoshone National Forest
Forest Supervisor's Office
808 Meadow Lane
Cody, WY 82414
(307) 527-6241

Gallatin National Forest
Forest Supervisor's Office
P.O. Box 130, Federal Building
Bozeman, MT 59715
(406) 587-6701

RMS: Again, look for RMS maps at sporting goods stores near the Absaroka-Beartooth Wilderness or write to:

Rocky Mountain Survey
P.O. Box 21558
Billings, MT 59104

For More Information

The best sources for more information on the Beartooths are the Forest Service ranger district offices. Unfortunately, three national forests and four different ranger districts manage parts of this wilderness; and the exact areas of management are confusing. Also, some trails go from one ranger district to another. The best approach is to contact the ranger district closest to the trailhead you intend to use.

Call or write the ranger districts at the following addresses:

Beartooth Ranger District
Custer National Forest
HC49, Box 3420
Red Lodge, MT 59068
(406) 446-2103

Big Timber Ranger District
Gallatin National Forest
P.O. Box 196
Big Timber, MT 59011
(406) 932-5155
Gardiner Ranger District

Gallatin National Forest
P.O. Box 5
Gardiner, MT 59030
(406) 848-7375

Clarks Fork Ranger District
Shoshone National Forest
808 Meadow Lane
Cody, WY 82414
(307) 527-6921

Vacation Planner

Adventures, 3–5 Nights

Base camps:
Lake Plateau North
Lake Plateau East
Martin Lake
Aero Lakes

Loops:
Three Passes
Columbine Pass
Lake Plateau West
Green Lake
Copeland Lake
Horseshoe Lake

Shuttles:
Slough Creek Divide
Stillwater to Stillwater
The Beaten Path
Jorden Lake
The Complete Stillwater

Moderate Backpacking Trips, 1–2 Nights

Base camps:
Island Lake
Quinnebaugh Meadows
Native Lake

Loops:
Beartooth Recreation Loop
Claw Lake
The Hellroaring

Out & back:
West Boulder River
Great Falls Creek Lakes
Silver Lake
Bridge Lake
Breakneck Park Meadows
Lake Wilderness
Granite Peak
Timberline Lake

Quinnebaugh Meadows
Lake Mary
Crow Lake
Upper Granite Lake
Lower Granite Lake
Ivy Lake
Curl Lake
Rock Island Lake
Fox Lake
Goose Lake
Elbow Lake
Thompson Lake
Pine Creek Lake

Shuttles:
Sundance Pass
Beartooth High Lakes
Crazy Lakes

Easy Backbacking Trips, Overnighters

Out & back:
- Sioux Charley Lake
- Elk Lake
- Hellroaring Lakes
- Hauser Lake
- Becker Lake
- Beauty Lake
- Native Lake
- Lady of the Lake

Serious Day Trips for Well-Conditioned Hikers

Loops:
- Claw Lake
- Curl Lake
- Elbow Lake
- Pine Creek Lake

Out & back:
- Great Falls Creek Lakes
- Silver Lake
- Bridge Lake
- Sylvan Lake
- Lake Mary
- Crow Lake

Shuttles:
- Rosebud to Rosebud
- Silver Run Plateau

Moderate Day Hikes

Out & back:
- Breakneck Park Meadows
- Quinnebaugh Meadows
- Upper Granite Lake
- Lower Granite Lake
- Ivy Lake
- Rock Island Lake
- Fox Lake
- Thompson Lake
- Pine Creek Lake

Easy Day Hikes

Out & back:
- West Boulder River
- East Fork Boulder River
- Sioux Charley Lake
- Mystic Lake
- Elk Lake
- Slough Lake
- Basin Creek Lakes
- Timberline Lake
- Broadwater Lake
- Hellroaring Lakes
- Glacier Lake
- Gardner Lake
- Hauser Lake
- Becker Lake
- Beartooth High Lakes
- Beauty Lake
- Native Lake
- Lake Vernon
- Lady of the Lake
- Passage Falls

The Author's Favorites

For That First Night in the Wilderness

West Boulder River
Timberline Lake
Hellroaring Lakes
Beartooth Recreation Loop
Hauser Lake

Becker Lake
Beauty Lake
Claw Lake
Lady of the Lake

For Anglers

West Boulder River
East Fork Boulder River
Columbine Pass
Slough Creek Divide
Stillwater to Stillwater
The Beaten Path
Hellroaring Lakes

Glacier Lake
Native Lake
Green Lake
Copeland Lake
Aero Lakes
Goose Lake

For Photographers

Columbine Pass
Rosebud to Rosebud
The Beaten Path
Silver Run Plateau

Sundance Pass
Glacier Lake
Beartooth High Lakes

For Climbers

Lake Wilderness
Granite Peak
The Beaten Path

Aero Lakes
Elbow Lake

For People Who Don't Want to See a Grizzly Bear

Rosebud to Rosebud
Sylvan Lake
Slough Lake
Sundance Pass
Hellroaring Lakes

Glacier Lake
Becker Lake
Beartooth High Lakes
Claw Lake
Native Lake

For People Who Wouldn't Mind Seeing a Grizzly Bear

Slough Creek Divide
Crazy Lakes

Horseshoe Lake
The Hellroaring

Clarks Fork Trailhead, one of the many scenic and well-maintained trailheads in the Beartooths.

For Parents with Small Children Who Want a Really Easy Day Hike

Sioux Charley Lake

Broadwater Lake

Hauser Lake

Lady of the Lake

Passage Falls

For People Who Like Long, Hard Day Hikes So They Can Eat Anything They Want for Dinner

Rosebud to Rosebud

Silver Run Plateau

Claw Lake

Elbow Lake

Pine Creek Lake

For People Who Just Can't Get Enough Adventure, Who Are Wilderness-wise, Who Like a Variety of Off-trail Side Trips

Three Passes

Columbine Pass

Stillwater to Stillwater

The Beaten Path

Martin Lake

Green Lake

Aero Lakes

For Trail Runners

Breakneck Park Meadows

Rosebud to Rosebud

Sylvan Lake

Quinnebaugh Meadows

Lake Mary

Sundance Pass

Beartooth High Lakes

Claw Lake

Pine Creek Lake

For Backcountry Horsemen

Slough Creek Divide

Jorden Lake

Copeland Lake

Crazy Lakes

The Complete Stillwater

The Hellroaring

For People Who Like Four-Wheel-Drive Access Roads

Lake Wilderness

Hellroaring Lakes

Goose Lake

Horseshoe Lake

Zero Impact

Going into a national park or wilderness area is like visiting a famous museum. You obviously do not want to leave your mark on an art treasure in the museum. If everybody going through the museum left one little mark, the piece of art would be quickly destroyed—and of what value is a big building full of trashed art? The same goes for a pristine wilderness, which is as magnificent as any masterpiece by any artist. If we all left just one little mark on the landscape, the wilderness would soon be despoiled.

A wilderness can accommodate human use as long as everybody behaves. But a few thoughtless or uninformed visitors can ruin it for everybody who follows. All wilderness users have a responsibility to know and follow the rules of zero-impact camping.

Nowadays most wilderness users want to walk softly, but some aren't aware that they have poor manners. Often their actions are dictated by the outdated habits of a past generation of campers who cut green boughs for evening shelters, built camp-fires with fire rings, and dug trenches around tents. In the 1950s, these "camping rules" may have been acceptable. But they leave long-lasting scars, and today such behavior is absolutely unacceptable. The wilderness is shrinking, and the number of users is mushrooming. More and more camping areas show unsightly signs of heavy use.

Consequently, a new code of ethics is growing out of the necessity of coping with the unending waves of people who want a perfect wilderness experience. Today, we all must leave no clues that we have gone before. Canoeists can look behind the canoe and see no sign of their passing. Hikers, mountain bikers, and four-wheelers should have the same goal. Enjoy the wildness, but make it a zero-impact visit.

FALCON'S ZERO-IMPACT PRINCIPLES

- Leave with everything you brought in.
- Leave no sign of your visit.
- Leave the landscape where you found it.

Most of us know better than to litter—in or out of the wilderness. Be sure you leave nothing, regardless of how small it is, along the trail or at the campsite. This means you should pack out everything, including orange peels, flip tops, cigarette butts, and gum wrappers. Also, pick up any trash that others leave behind. In addition, please follow this zero-impact advice.

- Follow the main trail. Avoid cutting switchbacks and walking on vegetation beside the trail.
- Don't pick up "souvenirs," such as rocks, antlers, or wildflowers. The next person wants to see them, too, and collecting such souvenirs violates national park regulations.
- Avoid making loud noises that may disturb others. Remember, sound travels easily to the other side of the lake. Be courteous.
- Carry a lightweight trowel to bury human waste 6 to 8 inches deep and pack out used toilet paper. Keep human waste at least 300 feet from any water source.
- Finally, and perhaps most importantly, strictly follow the pack-in/pack-out rule. If you carry something into the backcountry, consume it or carry it out.

Leave zero impact of your passing—and put your ear to the ground in the wilderness and listen carefully. Thousands of people coming behind you are thanking you for your courtesy and good sense.

Have a Safe Trip

Scouts have been guided for decades by what is perhaps the best single piece of safety advice—Be Prepared! For starters, this means carrying survival and first-aid materials, proper clothing, compass, and topographic map—and knowing how to use them.

Perhaps the second-best piece of safety advice is to tell somebody where you're going and when you plan to return. Pilots file flight plans before every trip, and anybody venturing into a blank spot on the map should do the same. File your "flight plan" with a friend or relative before taking off.

Close behind your flight plan and being prepared with proper equipment is physical conditioning. Being fit not only makes wilderness travel more fun, it makes it safer. To whet your appetite for more knowledge of wilderness safety and preparedness, here are a few more tips.

- Check the weather forecast. Be careful not to get caught at high altitude by a bad storm or along a stream in a flash flood. Watch cloud formations closely, so you don't get stranded on a ridgeline during a lightning storm. Avoid traveling during prolonged periods of cold weather.
- Avoid traveling alone in the wilderness.
- Keep your party together.
- Study basic survival and first aid before leaving home.
- Don't eat wild plants unless you have positively identified them and know they are safe to eat.
- Before you leave for the trailhead, find out as much as you can about the route, especially the potential hazards.
- Don't exhaust yourself or other members of your party by traveling too far or too fast. Let the slowest person set the pace.
- Don't wait until you're confused to look at your maps. Follow them as you go along from the moment you start moving up the trail, so you have a continual fix on your location.
- If you get lost, don't panic. Sit down and relax for a few minutes while you carefully check your topo map and take a reading with your compass. Confidently plan your next move. It's often smart to retrace your steps until you find familiar ground, even if you think it might lengthen your trip. Lots of people get temporarily lost in the wilderness and survive usually by calmly and rationally dealing with the situation.
- Stay clear of all wild animals.
- Take a first-aid kit that includes, at a minimum, the following items: sewing needle, snake-bite kit, aspirin, antibacterial ointment, two antiseptic swabs, two butterfly bandages, adhesive tape, four adhesive strips, four gauze pads, two triangular bandages, codeine tablets, two inflatable splints, Moleskin or Second Skin for blisters, one roll 3-inch gauze, CPR shield, rubber gloves, and lightweight first-aid instructions.
- Take a survival kit that includes, at a minimum, the following items: compass, whistle, matches in a waterproof container, cigarette lighter, candle, signal mirror, flashlight, fire starter, aluminum foil, water purification tablets, space blanket, and flare.

Last but not least, don't forget that the best defense against unexpected hazards is knowledge. Read up on the latest in wilderness safety information.

You Might Never Know What Hit You

The high altitude topography of the Absaroka-Beartooth is prone to sudden thunderstorms, especially in July and August. If you get caught by a lightning storm, take special precautions. Remember:

- Lightning can travel far ahead of the storm, so be sure to take cover before the storm hits.
- Don't try to make it back to your vehicle. It isn't worth the risk. Instead, seek shelter even if it's only a short way back to the trailhead. Lightning storms usually don't last long, and from a safe vantage point, you might enjoy the sights and sounds.
- Be especially careful not to get caught on a mountaintop or exposed ridge, under large solitary trees, in the open, or near standing water.
- Seek shelter in a low-lying area, ideally in a dense stand of small, uniformly sized trees.
- Stay away from anything that might attract lightning, such as metal tent poles, graphite fishing rods, or pack frames.
- Get in a crouch position and place both feet firmly on the ground.
- If you have a pack (without a metal frame) or a sleeping pad with you, put your feet on it for extra insulation against shock.
- Don't walk or huddle together. Instead, stay 50 feet or more from each other, so if somebody gets hit by lightning, others in your party can give first aid.
- If you're in a tent, stay there, in your sleeping bag with your feet on your sleeping pad.

The Silent Killer

Be aware of the danger of hypothermia—a condition in which the body's internal temperature drops below normal. It can lead to mental and physical collapse and death. This is a special item of concern when hiking in the Absaroka-Beartooth, particularly on the Beartooth Plateau, where you can get nailed with 6 inches of snow any day of the year.

Hypothermia is caused by exposure to cold and is aggravated by wetness, wind, and exhaustion. The moment you begin to lose heat faster than your body produces it, you're suffering from exposure. Your body starts involuntary exercise, such as shivering, to stay warm and makes involuntary adjustments to preserve normal temperature in vital organs, restricting blood flow in the extremities. Both responses drain your energy reserves. The only way to stop the drain is to reduce the degree of exposure.

With full-blown hypothermia, as energy reserves are exhausted, cold reaches the brain, depriving you of good judgment and reasoning power. You won't be aware that this is happening. You lose control of your hands. Your internal temperature slides downward. Without treatment, this slide leads to stupor, collapse, and death.

To defend against hypothermia, stay dry. When clothes get wet, they lose about 90 percent of their insulating value. Wool loses relatively less heat; cotton, down, and some synthetics lose more. Choose rain clothes that cover the head, neck, body, and legs and provide good protection against wind-driven rain. Most hypothermia cases develop in air temperatures between 30° and 50° F, but hypothermia can develop in warmer temperatures.

If your party is exposed to wind, cold, and wet, think hypothermia. Watch yourself and others for these symptoms: uncontrollable fits of shivering; vague, slow, slurred speech; memory lapses; incoherence; immobile, fumbling hands; frequent stumbling or a lurching gait; drowsiness (to sleep is to die); apparent exhaustion; and inability to get up after a rest. When a member of your party has hypothermia, he or she may deny any problem. Believe the symptoms, not the victim. Even mild symptoms demand treatment, as follows:

- Get the victim out of the wind and rain.
- Strip off all wet clothes.
- If the victim is only mildly impaired, give him or her warm drinks. Then get the victim into warm clothes and a warm sleeping bag. Place well-wrapped water bottles filled with heated water close to the victim.

If the victim is badly impaired, attempt to keep him or her awake. Put the victim in a sleeping bag with another person—both naked. If you have a double bag, put two warm people in with the victim.

Be Bear Aware

The first step of any hike in bear country is an attitude adjustment. Nothing guarantees total safety. Hiking in bear country adds a small additional risk to your trip. However, that risk can be greatly minimized by adhering to this age-old piece of advice: Be prepared. And being prepared doesn't only mean having the right equipment. It also means having the right information. Knowledge is your best defense.

You can—and should—thoroughly enjoy your trip to bear country. Don't let the fear of bears ruin your vacation. This fear can accompany you every step of the way. It can be constantly lurking in the back of your mind, preventing you from enjoying the wildest and most beautiful places left on Earth. And even worse, some bear experts think bears might actually be able to sense your fear.

Being prepared and knowledgeable gives you confidence. It allows you to fight back the fear that can burden you throughout your stay in bear country. You won't—nor should you—forget about bears and the basic rules of safety, but proper preparation allows you to keep the fear of bears at bay and let enjoyment rule the day.

And on top of that, do we really want to be totally safe? If we did, we probably would never go hiking in the wilderness—bears or no bears. We certainly wouldn't, at much greater risk, drive hundreds of miles to get to the trailhead. Perhaps a tinge of danger adds a desired element to our wilderness trip.

Hiking in Bear Country

Nobody likes surprises, and bears dislike them, too. The majority of bear maulings occur when a hiker surprises a bear. Therefore, it's vital to do everything possible to avoid these surprise meetings. Perhaps the best way is to know the five-part system. If you follow the following five rules, the chance of encountering a bear on the trail sinks to the slimmest possible margin.

- Be alert.
- Go with a group and stay together.
- Stay on the trail.
- Hike in the middle of the day.
- Make noise.

No substitute for alertness: As you hike, watch ahead and to the sides. Don't fall into the all-too-common and particularly nasty habit of fixating on the trail 10 feet ahead. It's especially easy to do this when dragging a heavy pack up a long hill or when carefully watching your step on a heavily eroded trail.

Using your knowledge of bear habitat and habits, be especially alert in areas most likely to be frequented by bears such as avalanche chutes, berry patches, streams, stands of whitebark pine, and so forth.

Watch carefully for bear signs, and be especially watchful (and noisy) if you see any. If you see a track or a scat, but it doesn't look fresh, pretend it's fresh. This area is obviously frequented by bears.

Watch the wind: The wind can be a friend or foe. The strength and direction of the wind can make a significant difference in your chances of an encounter with a bear. When the wind is blowing at your back, your smell travels ahead of you alerting any bear that might be on or near the trail ahead. Conversely, when the wind blows in your face, your chances of a surprise meeting with a bear increase, so make more noise and be more alert.

A strong wind can also be noisy and limit a bear's ability to hear you coming. If a bear can't smell or hear you coming, the chances of an encounter greatly increase, so watch the wind.

Safety in numbers: There have been very few instances where a large group has had an encounter with a bear. On the other hand, a large percentage of hikers mauled by bears were hiking alone. Large groups naturally make more noise and put out more smell and probably appear more threatening to bears. In addition, if you're hiking alone and get injured, there is nobody to go for help. For these reasons, rangers often recommend parties of four or more hikers when going into bear country.

If the large party splits up, the advantage is lost, so stay together. If you're on a family hike, keep the kids from running ahead. If you're in a large group, keep the stronger members from going ahead or weaker members from lagging behind. The best way to prevent this natural separation is to ask one of the slowest members of the group to lead. This keeps everybody together.

Stay on the trail: Although bears use trails, they don't often use them during midday when hikers commonly use them. Through generations of associating trails with people, bears probably expect to find hikers on trails, especially during midday.

Contrarily, bears probably don't expect to find hikers off trails. Bears rarely settle down in a daybed right along a heavily used trail. However, if you wander around in thickets off the trail, you are more likely to stumble into an occupied daybed or cross paths with a traveling bear.

Sleeping late: Bears—and most other wildlife—usually aren't active during the middle of a day, especially on a hot summer day. Wild animals are most active around dawn and dusk. Therefore, hiking early in the morning or late afternoon increases your chances of seeing wildlife, including bears. Likewise, hiking during midday on a hot August day greatly reduces the chance of an encounter.

Sounds: Perhaps the best way to avoid a surprise meeting with a bear is to make sure the bear knows you're coming, so make lots of noise. Some experts think metallic noise is superior to human voices, which can be muffled by natural conditions, but the important issue is making lots of noise, regardless of what kind of noise.

Running: Many avid runners like to get off paved roads and running tracks and onto backcountry trails. But running on trails in bear country can be seriously hazardous to your health. Bears can't hear you coming and you approach them faster than expected, and of course, it's nearly impossible to keep alert while running when you have to watch the trail closely to keep from falling.

Leave the night to the bears: Like running on trails, hiking at night can be very risky. Bears are more active after dark, and you can't see them until it's too late. If you get caught at night, be sure to make lots of noise, and remember that bears commonly travel on hiking trails at night.

You can be dead meat, too: If you see or smell a carcass of a dead animal when hiking, immediately vacate the area. Don't let your curiosity keep you near the carcass a second longer than necessary. Bears commonly hang around a carcass, guarding it and feeding on it for days until it's completely consumed. Your presence could easily be interpreted as a threat to the bear's food supply, and a vicious attack could be imminent.

If you see a carcass ahead of you on the trail, don't go any closer. Instead, abandon your hike and return to the trailhead. If the carcass is between you and the trailhead, take a very long detour around it, upwind from the carcass, making lots of noise along the way. Be sure to report the carcass to the local ranger. This might prompt a temporary trail closure or special warnings and prevent injury to other hikers. Rangers will, in some cases, go in and drag the carcass away from the trail.

Cute, cuddly, and lethal: If you see a bear cub, don't go one inch closer to it. It might seem abandoned, but it most likely is not. Mother bear is probably very close, and female bears fiercely defend their young.

It doesn't do you any good in your pack: If you brought a repellent such as pepper spray, don't bury it in your pack. Keep it as accessible as possible. Most pepper spray comes in a holster or somehow conveniently attaches to your belt or pack. Such protection won't do you any good if you can't have it ready to fire in one or two seconds. Before hitting the trail, read the directions carefully and test fire the spray.

Regulations: Nobody likes rules and regulations. However, national parks have a few that you must follow. These rules aren't meant to take the freedom out of your trip. They are meant to help bring you back safely.

But I didn't see any bears: Now, you know how to be safe. Walk up the trail constantly clanging two metal pans together. It works every time. You won't see a bear, but you'll hate your "wilderness experience." You left the city to get away from loud noise.

Yes, you can be very safe, but how safe do you want to be and still be able to enjoy your trip? It's a balancing act. First, be knowledgeable and then decide how far you want to go. Everybody has to make his or her own personal choice.

Here's another conflict. If you do everything listed here, you most likely will not see any bears—or any deer or moose or eagles or any other wildlife. Again, you make the choice. If you want to be as safe as possible, follow these rules religiously. If you want to see wildlife, including bears, do all of this in reverse, but then, you are increasing your chance of an encounter instead of decreasing it.

Camping In Bear Country

Staying overnight in bear country is not dangerous, but it adds a slight additional risk to your trip. The main difference is the presence of more food, cooking, and garbage. Plus, you are in bear country at night when bears are usually most active. Once again, however, following a few basic rules greatly minimizes this risk.

Storing food and garbage: If the campsite doesn't have a bear-proof storage box or bear pole, be sure to set one up or at least locate one before it gets dark. It's not only difficult to store food after darkness falls, but it's easier to forget some juicy morsel on the ground. Also, be sure to store food in airtight, waterproof bags to prevent food odors from circulating throughout the forest. For double protection, put food and garbage in zip-locked bags and seal them tightly in a larger plastic bag.

The accompanying illustrations depict three popular methods for hanging food bags. In any case, try to get food and garbage at least 10 feet off the ground.

Special equipment: It's not really that special, but one piece of equipment you definitely need is a good supply of zip-locked bags. This handy invention is perfect for keeping food smell to a minimum and helps keep food from spilling on your pack, clothing, or other gear.

Take a special bag for storing food. The bag must be sturdy and waterproof. You can get dry bags at most outdoor specialty stores, but you can get by with a trash compactor bag. Regular garbage bags can break and leave your food spread on the ground.

You also need 100 feet of nylon cord. You don't need a heavy climbing rope to store food. Go light instead. Parachute cord will usually suffice unless you plan to hang large quantities of food and gear (which might be the case on a long backpacking excursion with a large group).

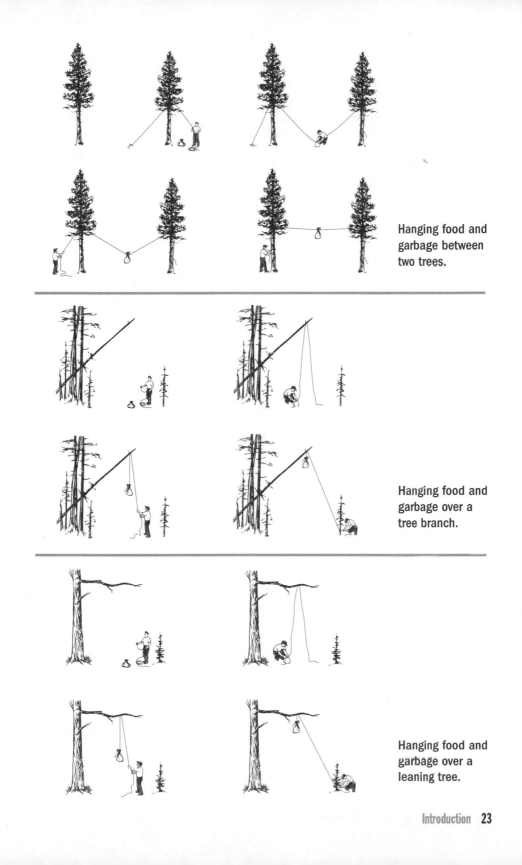

Hanging food and garbage between two trees.

Hanging food and garbage over a tree branch.

Hanging food and garbage over a leaning tree.

You can also buy a small pulley system to make hoisting a heavy load easier. Again, you can usually get by without this extra weight in your pack unless you have a massive load to hang.

What to hang: To be as safe as possible, store everything that has any food smell. This includes cooking gear, eating utensils, bags used to keep food in your pack, all garbage, and even clothes with food smells on them. If you spilled something on your clothes, change into other clothes for sleeping and hang clothes with food smells with the food and garbage. If you take them into the tent, you aren't separating your sleeping area from food smells. Try to keep food odors off your pack, but if you failed, put the food bag inside and hang the pack.

What to keep in your tent: You can't be too careful in keeping food smells out of the tent. Just in case a bear has become accustomed to coming into that campsite looking for food, it's vital to keep all food smells out of the tent. This often includes your pack, which is hard to keep odor-free. In general, take only valuables (like cameras and binoculars), clothing, and sleeping gear into the tent.

If you brought a bear repellent, such as pepper spray, sleep with it. Also, keep a flashlight in the tent. If an animal comes into camp and wakes you up, you need the flashlight to identify it.

The campfire: Regulations prohibit campfires in most campsites in many areas, but if you're in an area where fires are allowed, treat yourself. Besides adding the nightly entertainment, the fire might make your camp safer from bears.

The campfire provides the best possible way to get rid of food smells. Build a small but hot fire and thoroughly burn everything that smells of food—garbage, leftovers, fish entrails, everything. If you brought food in cans or other incombustible containers, burn them, too. You can even dump extra water from cooking or dishwater on the edge of the fire to erase the smell.

Be very sure you have the fire hot enough to completely burn everything. If you leave partially burned food scraps in the fire, you are setting up a dangerous situation for the next camper to use this site.

Before leaving camp the next morning, dig out the fire pit and pack out anything that has not completely burned, even if you believe it no longer carries food smells. For example, many foods like dried soup or hot chocolate come in foil packages that might seem like they burn, but they really don't. Pack out the scorched foil and cans (now with very minor food smells). Also, pack out foil and cans left by other campers.

Types of food: Don't get paranoid about the types of food you bring. All food has some smell, and you can make your trip much less enjoyable by fretting too much over food.

Perhaps the safest option is freeze-dried food. It carries very little smell, and it comes in convenient envelopes that allow you to "cook it" by merely adding boiling water. This means you don't have cooking pans to wash or store. However, freeze-dried food is very expensive, and many backpackers don't use it—and still safely enjoy bear country.

Dry, prepacked meals (often pasta- or rice-based) offer an affordable compromise to freeze-dried foods. Also, take your favorite high-energy snack and don't worry about it. Avoid fresh fruit and canned meats and fish.

The key point is this. *What* food you have along is much less critical than *how* you handle it, cook it, and store it. A can of tuna fish might put out a smell, but if you eat all of it in one meal, don't spill it on the ground or on your clothes, and burn the can later, it can be quite safe.

Hanging food at night is not the only storage issue. Also, make sure you place food correctly in your pack. Use airtight packages as much as possible. Store food in the containers it came in or, when opened, in zip-locked bags. This keeps food smells out of your pack and off your other camping gear and clothes.

How to cook: The overriding philosophy of cooking in bear country is to create as little odor as possible. Keep it simple. Use as few pans and dishes as possible.

Unless it's a weather emergency, don't cook in the tent. If you like winter backpacking, you probably cook in the tent, but you should have a different tent for summer backpacking.

If you can have a campfire and decide to cook fish, try cooking them in aluminum foil envelopes instead of frying them. Then, after removing the cooked fish, quickly and completely burn the fish scraps off the foil. Using foil also means you don't have to wash the pan you used to cook the fish.

Be careful not to spill on yourself while cooking. If you do, change clothes and hang the clothes with food odor with the food and garbage. Wash your hands thoroughly before retiring to the tent.

Don't cook too much food, so you don't have to deal with leftovers. If you do end up with extra food, however, you have only two choices: Carry it out or burn it. Don't bury it or throw it in a lake or leave it anywhere in bear country. A bear will most likely find and dig up any food or garbage buried in the backcountry.

Taking out the garbage: In bear country, you have only two choices: Burn garbage or carry it out. Prepare for garbage problems before you leave home. Bring along airtight zip-locked bags to store garbage. Be sure to hang your garbage at night along with your food. Also, carry in as little garbage as possible by discarding excess packaging while packing.

Washing dishes: This is a sticky problem, but there is one easy solution. If you don't dirty dishes, you don't have to wash them. So try to minimize food smell by using as few dishes and pans as possible. If you use the principles of zero-impact camping, you are probably doing as much as you can to reduce food smell from dishes.

If you brought paper towels, use one to carefully remove food scraps from pans and dishes before washing them. Then, when you wash dishes, you have much less food smell. Burn the dirty towels or store them in zip-locked bags with other garbage. Put pans and dishes in zip locked bags before putting them back in your pack.

If you end up with lots of food scraps in the dishwater, drain out the scraps and store them in zip-locked bags with other garbage or burn them. You can bring a lightweight screen to filter out food scraps from dishwater, but be sure to store the screen with the food and garbage. If you have a campfire, pour the dishwater around the edge of the fire. If you don't have a fire, take the dishwater at least 200 feet downwind and downhill from camp and pour it on the ground or in a small hole. Don't put dishwater or food scraps in a lake or stream.

Although possibly counter to accepted rules of cleanliness for many people, you can skip washing dishes altogether on the last night of your trip. Instead, simply use the paper towels to clean the dirty dishes as much as possible. You can wash them when you get home. Pack dirty dishes in zip-locked bags before putting them back in your pack.

Finally, don't put it off. Do dishes immediately after eating, so a minimum of food smell lingers in the area.

Choosing a tent site: Try to keep your tent site at least 100 feet from your cooking area. Unfortunately, some campsites do not adequately separate the cooking area from the tent site. Store food at least 100 yards from the tent. You can store it near the cooking area to further concentrate food smells.

Not under the stars: Some people prefer to sleep out under the stars instead of using a tent. This might be okay in areas not frequented by bears, but it's not a good idea in bear country. The thin fabric of a tent certainly isn't any real physical protection from a bear, but it does present a psychological barrier to a bear that wants to come even closer.

Do somebody a big favor: Report all bear sightings to the ranger after your trip. This might not help you, but it could save another camper's life. If rangers get enough reports to spot a pattern, they manage the area to prevent potentially hazardous situations.

The Bear Essentials of Hiking in Bear Country
- Knowledge is the best defense.
- There is no substitute for alertness.
- Hike with a large group and stay together.
- Don't hike alone in bear country.
- Stay on the trail.
- Hike in the middle of the day.
- Make lots of noise while hiking.
- Never approach a bear.
- Females with cubs are very dangerous.
- Stay away from carcasses.
- Defensive hiking works. Try it.
- Choose a safe campsite.
- Camp below timberline.

- Separate sleeping and cooking areas.
- Sleep in a tent.
- Cook just the right amount of food and eat it all.
- Store food and garbage out of reach of bears.
- Never feed bears.
- Keep food odors out of the tent.
- Leave the campsite cleaner than you found it.
- Leave no food rewards for bears.

Be Mountain Lion Aware, Too

The most important safety element for recreation in mountain lion country is simply recognizing their habitat. Mountain lions primarily feed on deer, so these common ungulates are a key element in cougar habitat. Fish and wildlife agencies usually have good information about deer distribution from population surveys and hunting results.

Basically, where you have a high deer population, you can expect to find mountain lions. If you are not familiar with identifying deer tracks, seek the advice of someone knowledgeable, or refer to a book on animal tracks such as the FalconGuide *Scats and Tracks* series.

Safety Guidelines for Traveling In Mountain Lion Country

To stay as safe as possible when hiking in mountain lion country, follow this advice.

- Travel with a friend or group. There's safety in numbers, so stay together.
- Don't let small children wander away by themselves.
- Don't let pets run unleashed.
- Avoid hiking at dawn and dusk—the times mountain lions are most active.
- Watch for warning signs of mountain lion activity such as cougar tracks or high deer numbers.
- Know how to behave if you encounter a mountain lion.

What to Do If You Encounter a Mountain Lion

In the vast majority of mountain lion encounters, the animals exhibit avoidance, indifference, or curiosity that does not result in human injury. But it is natural to be alarmed if you have an encounter of any kind. Try to keep your cool and consider the following:

Recognize threatening mountain lion behavior: There are a few cues that may help you gauge the risk of attack. If a mountain lion is more than 50 yards away, and it directs its attention to you, it may be only curious. This situation represents only a slight risk for adults, but a more serious risk to unaccompanied children. At this point, you should move away, while keeping the animal in your peripheral vision. Also, look for rocks, sticks, or something else to use as a weapon, just in case. If you have pepper spray, get it ready to discharge. If a mountain lion is crouched and staring intensely at you less than 50 yards away, it may be assessing the chances of a successful attack. If this behavior continues, the risk of attack may be high.

Do not approach a mountain lion: Instead, give the animal the opportunity to move on. Slowly back away, but maintain eye contact if close. Mountain lions are not known to attack humans to defend young or a kill, but they have been reported to "charge" in rare instances and may want to stay in the area. It's best to choose another route or time to hike through the area.

Do not run from a mountain lion: Running may stimulate a predatory response.

Make noise: If you encounter a mountain lion, be vocal and talk or yell loudly and regularly. Try not to panic. Shout to make others in the area aware of the situation.

Maintain eye contact: Eye contact presents a challenge to the mountain lion, showing you are aware of its presence. Eye contact also helps you know where it is. However, if the behavior of the mountain lion is not threatening (if it is, for example, grooming or periodically looking away), maintain visual contact through your peripheral vision and move away.

Appear larger than you are: Raise your arms above your head and make steady waving motions. Raise your jacket or another object above your head. Do not bend over, as this will make you appear smaller and more "prey-like."

Grab the kids: If you are with small children, pick them up. First, bring children close to you, maintain eye contact with the mountain lion, and pull the children up without bending over. If you are with other children or adults, band together.

Defend yourself: If attacked, fight back. Try to remain standing. Do not feign death. Pick up a branch or rock; pull out a knife, pepper spray, or other deterrent device. Remember that everything is a potential weapon, and individuals have fended off mountain lions with blows from rocks, tree limbs, and even cameras.

Defend others: Also, defend your hiking partners, but don't defend your pet. In past attacks on children, adults have successfully stopped attacks. However, such cases are very dangerous and risky, and physically defending a pet is not recommended.

Respect any warning signs posted by agencies.

Spread the word: Before leaving on your hike, discuss lions and teach others in your group how to behave in case of a mountain lion encounter. For example, anyone who starts running could bring on an attack.

Report encounters: If you have an encounter with a mountain lion, record your location and the details of the encounter, and notify the nearest landowner or land-management agency. The agency (federal, state, or county) may want to visit the site and, if appropriate, post education/warning signs. Fish and wildlife agencies should also be notified because they record and track such encounters. If physical injury occurs, it is important to leave the area and not disturb the site of attack. Mountain lions that have attacked people must be killed, and an undisturbed site is critical for effectively locating the dangerous mountain lion.

See the FalconGuide *Mountain Lion Alert* for more details and tips for safe outdoor recreation in mountain lion country.

How to Get Really Bear and Mountain Lion Alert

Most of the information in this book comes from *Bear Aware* and *Mountain Lion Alert*, handy, inexpensive FalconGuides. These small, "packable" books contains the essential tips you need to reduce the risk of being injured by a bear or mountain lion to the slimmest possible margin, and they are written for both beginner and expert:

Day Hikers	Mountain Bikers
Backpackers	Anglers
Tent Campers	Trail Runners
Backcountry Horseman	Outfitters
Hunters	Photographers

In addition to covering the all-important subject of how to prevent an encounter, these books include advice on what to do if you are involved in an encounter.

You can get these books at local bookseller specializing in outdoor recreation and at national park visitor centers.

The Beartooth Fishery

By Richard K. Stiff
Former High Mountain Lakes Survey Coordinator, 1999–2001
Montana Department of Fish, Wildlife & Parks

The Absaroka-Beartooth Wilderness contains about 944 lakes, and of these, 328 support fisheries and 616 are barren. Only a few lakes in the entire wilderness (within the Slough Creek drainage) are thought to contain native fish, with surviving original Yellowstone cutthroat stock. All other fisheries within the wilderness were created when fish were introduced to lakes or streams. In some cases, introduced fish migrated and established populations in new locations. Lakes are currently managed by drainage due to the nature of the drainages and fish migration within each drainage, although this has not always been the case.

More than 60 percent of the lakes within the wilderness are barren of fish, their natural condition. These provide an opportunity for backcountry travelers to get away from anglers and find more solitude. While most anglers would probably enjoy seeing fish in many of these lakes, leaving them in their natural state is a tribute to the Absaroka-Beartooth as a true "wilderness." Current laws prohibit the stocking of fish, without an environmental review, in lakes that have no history of a fishery.

The distribution of lakes (with and without fish) by drainage is:

Boulder River	103
Clarks Fork	426
East Rosebud	76
Rock Creek	91
Slough Creek	10
Stillwater River	154
West Rosebud	84
TOTAL	**944**

The majority of the lakes are above 8,500 feet, with a number of these above 10,000 feet. Because of the high elevation, lakes often remain ice-covered until late June and have surface temperatures that seldom reach 60° F. The size of the fish in a lake is generally related to the size of the population. There are usually a few large fish, many medium-sized fish, or lots of smaller fish.

Lakes that harbor self-sustaining populations of fish often tend to become over-populated, resulting in slower growth rates. Since brook trout have the least restrictive spawning requirements, they are most often the victims of poor growth rates. Lakes with brook trout tend to have stunted populations, although there are exceptions such as Cairn and Lower Aero Lakes.

Many of the lakes managed within the wilderness do not have a suitable place for trout to spawn and must be stocked to maintain a fishery. Most stocked lakes are planted with fish on a rotating cycle of three, four, six, and eight years, depending on use and management goals. Knowing the year these lakes are stocked can increase an angler's chance of catching good fish. Three- to four-year-old fish provide the best fishing for nice-sized trout.

Three- and four-year stocking cycles are generally used on lakes that receive significant fishing pressure and where a persistent good catch is desired. A six-year cycle allows at least some of the fish to grow larger, while still maintaining a constant fishery. Stocking at eight-year intervals is based on the premise that fish will live for seven years, and there will be a fallow year to allow the food population to recover. The eight-year cycle is used in lakes where a trophy-type fishery is desired, as well as in remote, relatively unproductive lakes. More lakes are being considered for the eight-year cycle.

There are many different species of fish in the Beartooths, although the majority of the lakes support only one species of fish. Cutthroat trout are the principal fish stocked because the area is in their original geographic range, and the hatchery in Big Timber provides an economical source of cutthroat trout. But many lakes were planted with brook trout in the first half of this century, and these have established populations.

Analysis of the fisheries reveals the following distribution of fish species:
Arctic grayling   11 lakes

Superb trout fishing complements the spectacular scenery of the Beartooths.

Cutthroat trout	117 lakes
Eastern brook trout	85 lakes
Golden trout	25 lakes
Rainbow trout	22 lakes
Mixed fishery	56 lakes
Undecided	12 lakes
TOTAL	**328 lakes**

Lake trout and brown trout are found in several mixed fisheries, mostly outside the wilderness boundaries.

Stream fisheries are different than lake fisheries. Since the Montana Department of Fish, Wildlife & Parks no longer plants fish in streams, the fish found there are self-supporting populations. Alpine streams, like alpine lakes, have a limited food supply. But in a stream the trout not only have to find food, they must also fight the current of the stream.

Trout rely on the current of the stream to bring food to them, while hiding from the current themselves. Places that do both of these things are at a premium, and the largest fish get the best spots. The number of good feeding spots and the amount of food available limit the number of fish that can be present in a given reach of stream. Streams tend to support fewer fish than lakes, but fish in streams are easier to locate. Anglers should note that stream and lake fishing regulations differ.

Trout can usually find suitable places to spawn in a stream, so reproduction is not a problem. The type of fish present usually reflects a combination of what was originally found in the stream, the fish that were planted, and the fish that have migrated down from lakes above.

One final note. The southeastern arm of the Beartooths straddles the border between Montana and Wyoming. Anglers in this area must be careful to fish only in the state for which they hold a valid fishing license. In some places, particularly where lakes actually straddle the border (as does Granite Lake, for example), it might be wise to carry licenses for both states. Also know and heed the appropriate regulations.

Boulder River Road

Most locals consider the Boulder River to be the dividing line between the Beartooths to the east and the Absaroka Range to the west. The Boulder River Road ends nearly 50 miles south of Big Timber, Montana, at Box Canyon Campground. In the 1970s there was a proposal to punch the road all the way through to Cooke City, Montana, splitting the wilderness into two smaller wild areas. Look at a topo map and the feasibility of such a road becomes obvious. After a hard fight by wilderness advocates, the two spectacular mountain ranges were permanently joined into one wilderness, the controversial road proposal was dropped, and the Absaroka-Beartooth became one spectacular unified wilderness.

The Boulder River is a popular place. The road is lined with vehicle campgrounds, dude ranches, and church camps in addition to numerous summer homes. During the early hunting season in September, fifty or more horse trailers crowd into the Box Canyon Trailhead parking lot.

The Lake Plateau region of the Beartooths is as popular as any spot in the entire wilderness. Two Lake Plateau trailheads (Box Canyon and Upsidedown Creek) attract many backpackers. Few backcountry horsemen use the Upsidedown Creek trail, but in September, many use Box Canyon, mostly hunters and outfitters going south toward Slough Creek. The Lake Plateau is a unique and spectacular part of the Beartooths. Trails into the Lake Plateau start at three trailheads—Box Canyon, West Fork Stillwater River, and Stillwater River.

On the west side of the road, the situation is quite different. The trailheads heading west into the Absaroka Mountains (West Boulder River, Great Falls Creek, Fourmile Creek, Speculator Creek, and Bridge Creek) receive little use during the summer and moderate use, again mostly by hunters and outfitters, during September and October.

To find Boulder River Road trailheads, take County Road 298 (locally referred to as Boulder River Road) south from Big Timber. The road doesn't take off from either of the two exits off Interstate 90. Instead, go into Big Timber and watch for signs for CR 298, which heads south and passes over the freeway from the middle of town between the two exits.

It's 48 miles from Big Timber to the Box Canyon Trailhead, so make sure to top off the gas tank. At 16 miles you'll pass the small community of McLeod, and at 24 miles the pavement ends, which, of course, means 24 more miles of bumpy, dusty gravel road to Box Canyon, but it's passable with any vehicle.

From Big Timber, mileage to the trailheads is as follows:

West Boulder River turnoff—17 miles
Great Falls Creek—30 miles
Speculator Creek—38 miles
Fourmile Creek—42 miles
Upsidedown Creek—46.5 miles
Bridge Creek—47 miles
Box Canyon—48 miles

A jeep road continues on from Box Canyon to the Independence Pass area, where signs of early 1900s mining operations still remain. But almost all of the trails in this region can be accessed without bumping and grinding up this four-wheel-drive road.

1 West Boulder River

General description: An easy route suitable for a moderate day hike or overnighter

Special attractions: The scenic, fish-filled river along the entire route

Type of trip: Out-and-back

Total distance: Up to 16 miles

Difficulty: Easy

Traffic: Light

Maps: USGS—Mount Rae and Mt. Cowen; RMS—Mt. Cowen Area

Starting point: West Boulder River Trailhead

Finding the trailhead: After driving 16.5 miles south of Big Timber, Montana, on Boulder River Road, 0.5 mile past McLeod, you cross the West Boulder River and then 0.5 mile later, 17 miles from Big Timber, turn right (west) on West Boulder Road, which starts out as pavement but quickly turns to gravel. After 7 miles, turn left (south) at a well-signed junction, continuing on West Boulder Road. Don't go straight here—it's private land. West Boulder Road also goes over private land, but it's a public road. Go 7 more miles until you see West Boulder Campground on your right. Park at the trailhead, a parking area left of the campground.

Parking and trailhead facilities: Ample parking; vehicle campground with toilet.

Key Points

0.25 Trail turns off private road; turn left.

1.00 Bridge over West Boulder River and wilderness boundary.

3.00 West Boulder Meadows.

8.00 Junction with Falls Creek Trail 18.

The Hike

One of the highlights of this hike is the drive to the trailhead. West Boulder Road winds through a scenic slice of the "real Montana"—wide-open spaces, snow-capped mountains, big valleys with rustic cattle ranches, aspens coloring the transitions between grassland and forest, and, of course, a beautiful stream all the way. We drove to the trailhead at dawn, and it was like a video game trying to dodge all the deer on the road.

You can make this trip any length that suits you. It's 8 miles to the junction with the Falls Creek Trail, but there is no need to hike that far. The West Boulder is a great day hike, but it also makes an easy overnighter for beginning backpackers or families.

From the campground, hike up a dirt road, through an open gate, for about 100 yards. Then, watch for a sign on the left and a trail heading left to the sign. Turn left here. Don't continue on the road, which goes to a private residence. This is all private land, but the landowner has been cooperative. Please show your appreciation by respecting the landowner's private property rights.

The first part of the trail is very well constructed—raised, drained, graveled, lined with logs, a regular highway. After the bridge over the West Boulder River about a mile down the trail, you enter the Absaroka-Beartooth Wilderness, where it becomes a normal trail.

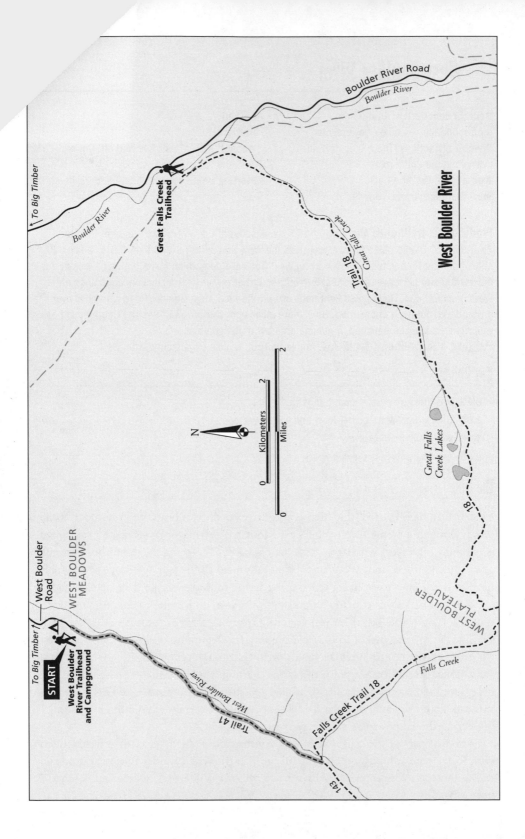

West Boulder River

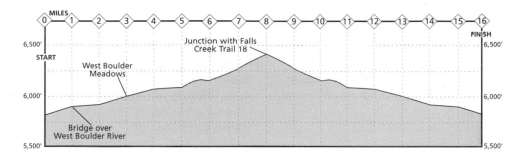

The first mile is flat, but then you climb two switchbacks and get a good view of the river. From here the trail goes through a pleasant, unburned forest, interspersed with gorgeous mountain meadows—and large, too, especially West Boulder Meadows. Several of the meadows have excellent campsites, and the river offers good fishing all the way. After West Boulder Meadows, you can see a beautiful waterfall.

This hike provides a reminder that wilderness is multiple-use management with livestock grazing allowed. A local rancher holds a grazing allotment in West Boulder Meadows. You'll see an unsightly steel-post fence at the west end of the meadows, very out of character for the surroundings. About 5 miles uptrail, you go through another barbwire fence with a gate over the trail. And, of course, expect to see a few cows and cow pies.

The entire trail is in great shape with a gradual stream-grade incline all the way. Unlike many trails, this one stays by the stream throughout its length.

Options

This trip provides the option of going as far as you choose, instead of targeting a specific destination.

Side Trips

An ambitious and experienced hiker staying two nights and planning a long side trip could try Kaufman Lake, which is partly off-trail hiking, or a long trek up the trail to Mill Creek Pass.

Camping

No designated campsites, but there are but many opportunities to set up a zero-impact camp in meadows along the route.

Fishing

In the lower stretches of the river, you can catch cutthroats, rainbows, or browns, but as you proceed upstream and get close to the Falls Creek junction, it's mostly cutts.

2 Great Falls Creek Lakes

General description: A long walk in the woods best suited for one or two nights out

Special attractions: Three beautiful mountain lakes

Type of trip: Out-and-back

Total distance: 16 miles

Difficulty: Difficult

Traffic: Light

Maps: USGS—Chrome Mountain and West Boulder Plateau; RMS—Mt. Cowen Area

Starting point: Great Falls Creek Trailhead

Finding the trailhead: On the Boulder River Road south from Big Timber, Montana, drive 30 miles and park in the small trailhead on the right (west) side of the road.

Parking and trailhead facilities: Limited parking; no toilet; Falls Creek Campground, a full-service vehicle campground, is about 2 miles north of the trailhead.

Key Points

1.5 Spur trail to falls.

5.0 First stream crossing.

7.0 Leave trail for Lower Great Falls Creek Lake.

8.0 Upper Great Falls Creek Lake.

The Hike

It's a tough 8 miles to reach Upper Great Falls Lake, but it's worth the effort. And you'll probably have the entire lake basin to yourself.

Great Falls Creek is different than trails up Bridge Creek and Fourmile Creek, which climb at the beginning and then level out. With a few minor flat sections, this trail climbs the entire way, not a steep grade but steadily uphill. The steepest section is a short stretch at the beginning of the trail, unless you hike the extra mile from the upper lake to the pass, which is called West Boulder Plateau.

The beginning of the trail could be slightly confusing. You walk along the Boulder River for about 100 yards before taking a sharp right then a sharp left. These two junctions were well signed when I hiked this route, but if the signs disappeared, you could get on the wrong trail at either of these junctions.

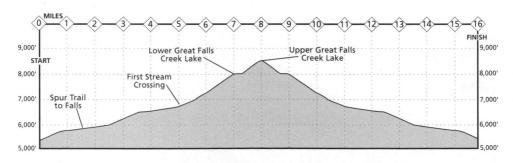

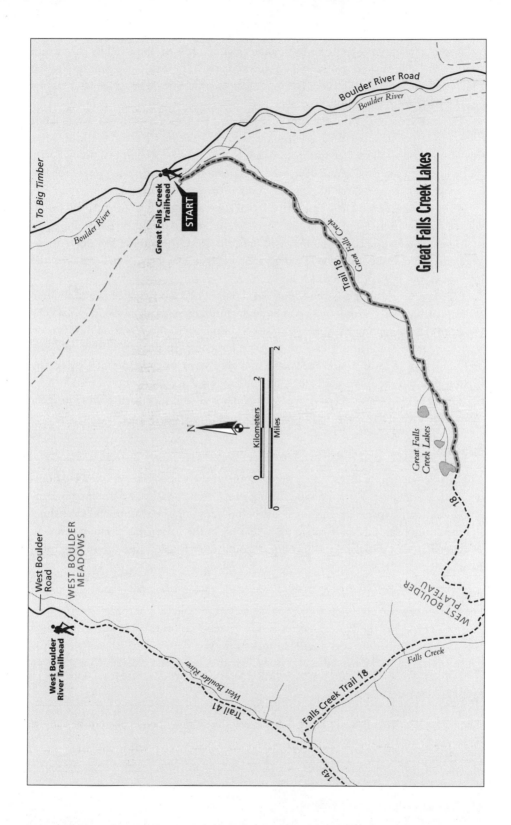

Great Falls Creek Lakes

About a mile up the trail, you get a nice view of a falls on the Boulder River, and about a half mile farther, you can take a short (about 100 yards), steep spur trail to see a waterfall on Great Falls Creek. This is a nice place for your first break, after finishing the first, steep section of the trail.

The trail stays away from the stream for the first 5 miles. This means no water, not even any feeder streams, so carry an extra bottle for the first part of the hike. After this, you'll have all the water you need because you cross the stream five times. Sorry, no bridges, but the fords aren't dangerous. Between crossings, the trail closely follows the creek. You can see some old mining ruins at the second crossing.

About a mile after the last crossing, the trail takes a sharp left (south). At this point, you can bushwhack about a half mile over to the lower lake. Use your compass to make sure you hit the lake, which can be difficult to find because of the thick forest. You can't see the lake until you're almost in it. I found a faint social trail going to the lower lake, but it was difficult to follow.

The first two lakes are in the forest, but the upper lake is barely above timberline at about 9,400 feet. If you haven't had enough climbing, you can tackle a few switchbacks on the way up the fairly easy, Category 3 climb up to the West Boulder Plateau. The view from the lake is great, but it's even better up on the 10,000-foot plateau, including a good look at all three lakes and a glimpse of mighty Mount Cowen, the highest point in the Absaroka Range, off to the west.

The trail is in good shape and easy to follow all the way to the West Boulder Plateau. It stays in the forest until just before the upper lake.

Side Trips

The major side trip is the 2-mile round-trip from the upper lake to the West Boulder Plateau, definitely worth taking. In big snow years, a large and potentially dangerous snowbank forms over the trail just before reaching the plateau and sometimes holds out until late July, so if you're up here early in the season, be careful crossing it. Also, regardless of which lake you camp at, you'll want to take time to visit the other two.

Camping

The upper lake has the best campsites and best view, but no fish. However, the upper lake is above timberline and fragile, so make sure you have a zero-impact camp. You can camp at the other two lakes, of course, but they are more difficult to reach.

Fishing

The lower lake has a few rainbows that can require some patience but can be caught. The other two lakes are fishless.

3 Silver Lake

General description: A long day hike or overnighter to the heart of the Absaroka

Special attractions: The super-scenic cirque containing Silver Lake

Type of trip: Out-and-back

Total distance: 17 miles

Difficulty: Difficult

Traffic: Light

Maps: USGS—Mount Douglas and The Needles; RMS—Mt. Cowen Area

Starting point: Fourmile Creek Trailhead

Finding the trailhead: On Boulder River Road south from Big Timber, Montana, drive 42 miles to the Fourmile Creek Trailhead on your right (west).

Parking and trailhead facilities: Minimal parking; no toilet.

Key Points

1.0 Junction with Meatrack Creek Trail 23; turn right.

3.5 Junction with Trail Creek Trail 231; turn right.

6.0 Junction with Silver Lake Trail 149; turn right.

8.5 Silver Lake.

The Hike

Silver Lake probably gets more use than most places in the Absaroka Range, but traffic is still light, mainly because it's an 8.5-mile hike through a mostly lodgepole forest to reach the lake, making it a tough day hike. If you're backpacking, the 8.5 miles may be more than you want on your first day, especially since it's all uphill, which is why backpackers commonly stay more than one night once they have made the effort to get to the lake.

The first 2 miles are quite steep, but then the trail becomes a gradual grade. The mature lodgepole forest lining the trail most of the way is broken here and there by big grassy meadows. Watch for big game in the meadows. Water sources are scarce, so plan on taking an extra bottle.

Silver Lake is, of course, the highlight of the trip. After you get there, you'll definitely believe it was worth the trip.

Side Trips

If you set up a base camp at Silver Lake and have an extra day, you can spend part of it going to Silver Pass and back. Another possibility for more experienced hikers is the off-trail scramble to two unnamed lakes above Silver Lake, perhaps as far as West Boulder Lake.

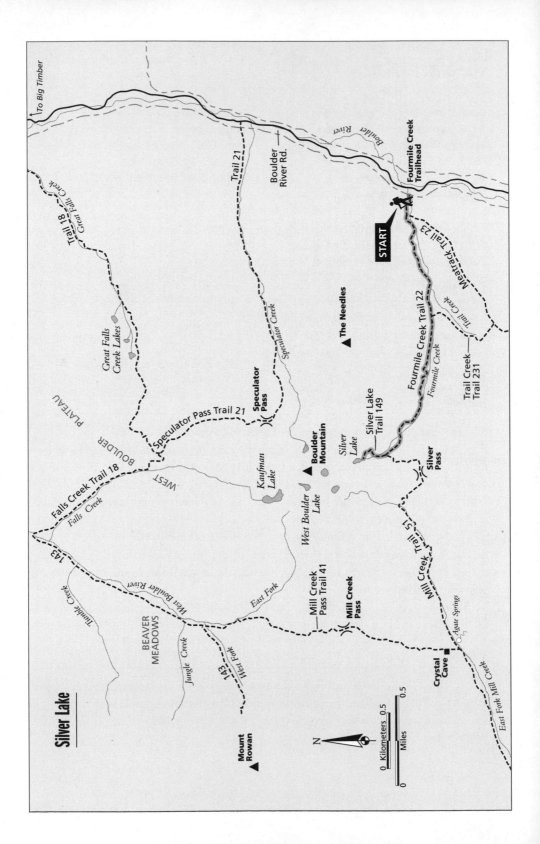

Silver Lake

To Big Timber

Trail 21

Boulder River Rd.

Boulder River

Fourmile Creek Trailhead

START

Neatrack Trail 23

Trail Creek

Fourmile Creek Trail 22

Trail Creek Trail 231

Fourmile Creek

Silver Lake Trail 149

Silver Pass

▲ The Needles

Silver Lake

Speculator Creek

Speculator Pass

Speculator Pass Trail 21

Great Falls Creek

Trail 18

Great Falls Creek Lakes

BOULDER PLATEAU

Falls Creek Trail 18

WEST

Falls Creek

Kaufman Lake

▲ Boulder Mountain

West Boulder Lake

East Fork

Mill Creek Pass Trail 41

Mill Creek Pass

Mill Creek Trail 51

Agate Springs

Crystal Cave

East Fork Mill Creek

143

West Boulder River

BEAVER MEADOWS

Jungle Creek

Tumble Creek

West Fork

143

▲ Mount Rowan

N

0 Kilometers 0.5

0 Miles 0.5

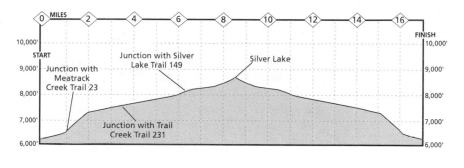

Camping

You can find five-star campsites at both the upper and lower ends of Silver Lake, but both sites show the wear and tear of past use, so be sure to set up a zero-impact camp in this fragile environment.

Fishing

Silver Lake has a good population of ultra-smart rainbow trout. They tend to rush to the other side of the lake at the first sign of a fly line on the water.

4 Three Passes

General description: A demanding route through the remote and uncrowded heart of the Absaroka Mountains

Special attractions: Three major passes in one trip and the chance to be alone in the wilderness

Type of trip: Loop

Total distance: 42.5 miles

Difficulty: Difficult and quite strenuous, especially Speculator Pass

Traffic: Light

Maps: USGS—Chrome Mountain, Mount Douglas, The Needles, The Pyramid, Mt. Cowen, and West Boulder Plateau; RMS—Mt. Cowen Area

Starting point: Fourmile Creek Trailhead

Finding the trailhead: On Boulder River Road south from Big Timber, Montana, drive 38 miles to the Speculator Creek Trailhead and 4 more miles to the Fourmile Creek Trailhead, both on your right (west).

Parking and trailhead facilities: Minimal parking at both trailheads; no toilet.

Key Points

1.0 Junction with Meatrack Creek Trail 23; turn right.

3.5 Junction with Trail Creek Trail 231; turn right.

6.0 Junction with Silver Lake Trail 149; turn right.

8.5 Silver Lake.

11.5 Back to Fourmile Creek Trail 22; turn right to Silver Pass.

14.0 Silver Pass and start of East Fork Mill Creek Trail 51.

18.0 Agate Springs and junction with Mill Creek Pass Trail 41; turn right.

18.3 Crystal Cave.

22.0 Mill Creek Pass.

24.5 Junction with West Boulder Trail 143; turn right.

25.5 Jungle Creek and start of Beaver Meadows.

28.0 Falls Creek and junction with Falls Creek Trail 18; turn right.

31.5 Junction with Speculator Creek Trail 21; turn right.

33.5 Speculator Pass.

42.5 Speculator Creek Trailhead and Boulder River Road.

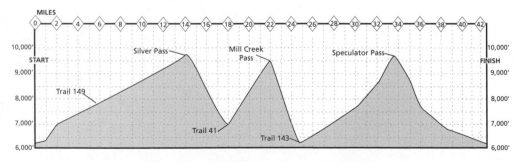

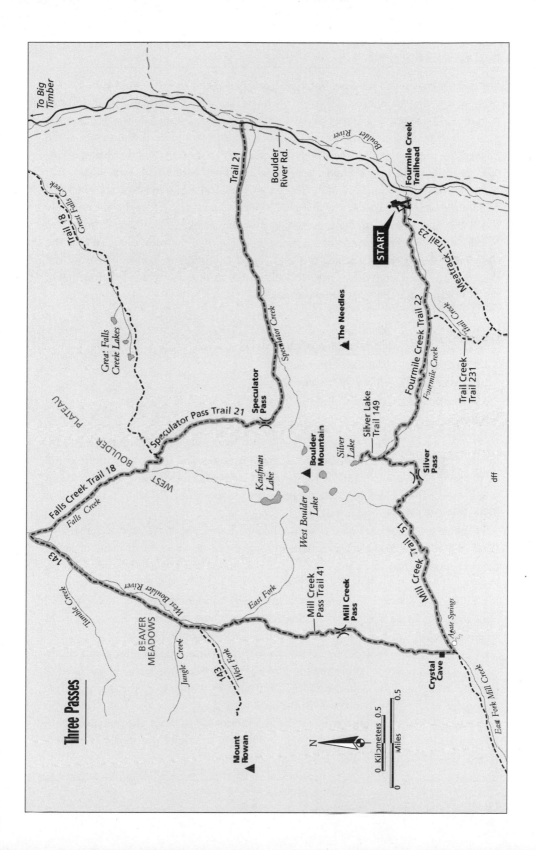

Three Passes

To Big Timber

Trail 21

Boulder River Rd.

Boulder River

Fourmile Creek Trailhead

START

Meattrack Trail 23

Trail 18

Great Falls Creek

Great Falls Creek Lakes

PLATEAU

BOULDER

WEST

Falls Creek Trail 18

Falls Creek

143

Tumble Creek

West Boulder River

BEAVER MEADOWS

Jungle Creek

143

West Fork

▲ Mount Rowan

Speculator Pass Trail 21

Speculator Creek

Speculator Pass

Kaufman Lake

Boulder Mountain ▲

West Boulder Lake

East Fork

Mill Creek Pass Trail 41

Mill Creek Pass

The Needles ▲

Silver Lake

Silver Lake Trail 149

Silver Pass

Fourmile Creek Trail 22

Fourmile Creek

Trail Creek

Trail Creek Trail 231

Mill Creek Trail 51

Agate Springs

Crystal Cave

East Fork Mill Creek

N

0 Kilometers 0.5

0 Miles 0.5

dff

Recommended Itinerary

We did this route in four days, but I wish we had taken five. It would have been a more enjoyable (though still difficult) trip. Even though it's 8.5 miles uphill (most of it gradual), I suggest trying to make it to Silver Lake, a delightful place, for the first night out. The next best option for the first campsite would be the junction of the Silver Lake and Fourmile Creek Trails, which means a shorter day but a less spectacular campsite. Spend the second night along East Fork Mill Creek somewhere near the junction of the East Fork Mill Creek Pass Trail and Agate Springs, and the third night along the West Boulder or first part of Falls Creek. The last night out probably won't be your best, with the best choice probably being somewhere in the open meadows just over Speculator Pass. Once you get out of the meadows and into the thick lodgepole forest of Speculator Creek, good campsites are scarce. When we did this trip, we hiked from Silver Lake to Falls Creek in one day, which was too much, but we didn't have the extra day we needed.

First night:	Silver Lake
Second night:	Agate Springs
Third night:	Falls Creek junction
Fourth night:	Upper Speculator Creek

The Hike

As you do for many long backpacking trips, you have to get away from the trailheads for the best hiking. In this case, both the first few miles and the last few miles could be described as slightly boring as you hike through mature lodgepole forests without much topography. However, after breaking out of the lower elevation timberland, it doesn't get much better than this.

One note of caution: This is not a national park or a popular wilderness area. One disadvantage (or advantage?) of this is getting exact distances from maps or signs. Consequently, I had to estimate mileage more than I did for any other trip in this book.

This trip is for well-conditioned backpackers. After getting to the top of Speculator Pass, you won't need to hit the StairMaster machine for a while. But if you want to get ready for this trip, you should spend many hours on it.

Fourmile Creek Trail 22 starts right at the Forest Service guard station and climbs steeply for about a mile before settling into a gradual ascent through lodgepole all of the way to the junction with the Silver Lake Trail 149, 6 miles from the trailhead. Two trails veer off to the left (south)—Meatrack Creek 23 (1 mile) and Trail Creek 231 (3.5 miles). You stay right (west) at both junctions. Just after the junction with Meatrack Creek Trail, a major social trail goes off to the right. You stay left on Fourmile Creek Trail.

Silver Lake.

Along the way to the Silver Lake Trail junction, you pass through two large meadows. Finding water is not a problem as several small feeder streams come in from the north on their way to Fourmile Creek. The trail is in great shape all the way to the Silver Lake Trail junction, kept that way by horse traffic, primarily during the fall hunting season. There definitely is not enough backpacker traffic to keep the trail distinct through the meadows. We did not, however, see a single stock party during our August trip.

At the Silver Lake Trail junction, you have a decision. You've hiked 6 miles and might be ready to pitch the tent. There are some campsites in this area, but you probably will enjoy staying at Silver Lake much more than along Fourmile Creek. Plan to start early in the day to leave enough time and energy for the climb up to Silver Lake. You follow Fourmile Creek to its source, Silver Lake, and the last mile to the lake is quite steep. You'll be ready to stop when you get there.

Silver Lake is a truly beautiful place. Boulder Mountain and an awesome, serrated ridge extending from it provide a gorgeous backdrop. The horseshoe of mountain ridges rising up from three sides of the lake keeps the sun out of camp in early morning and evening. There are three or four good campsites, but this is a most fragile place, so please use the strictest zero-impact camping techniques. The lake has a healthy population of rainbows, but they are smart and skittish. One fly line on the water sends them to the other end of the lake.

After a wonderful night in the five-star hotel called Silver Lake, retrace your steps back to the Silver Lake Trail junction and turn right. You might get your feet wet, depending on how high the water is, when you cross Fourmile Creek.

The upgrade is about 1,700 feet in about 2.5 miles to 9,673-foot Silver Pass, a demanding Category 1 climb. However, the trail has a nice grade with well-designed switchbacks that make it seem moderately easy. The steepest parts are right after Fourmile Creek and the last quarter mile to the pass.

Unfortunately, we did this section in a pouring rain and fog, so I didn't see what was surely some spectacular scenery. The trail is well defined up to about a half mile from the pass where it can get confusing. In fact, there is one place where it is easy to get off the main trail and onto a major social trail veering to the right (north). If you start going downhill on a trail marked with cairns, hit the brakes and backtrack to the main trail.

Silver Pass is an austere, knife-edged ridge. You can see an old "silvery" sign marking the pass from a half mile below. When we hiked, it was so wet that we couldn't keep our footing and had to virtually crawl up the last hundred yards, which is very steep. Once on top, though, we experienced the exhilaration of unbridled remoteness. I loved the old, weathered sign on Silver Pass—oh, the stories it could tell!

But keep in mind that this is only the first of three major passes on this trip—and definitely not the most difficult.

Silver Pass is part of the major east-west divide that forms the backbone of the Absaroka Range. On the pass, Fourmile Creek Trail 22 becomes East Fork Mill Creek Trail 51. After enjoying Silver Pass, head down toward East Fork Mill Creek on switchbacks for about a mile before the trail enters a fairly open forest. On the way to Agate Springs, you cross East Fork Mill Creek two more times than those crossings shown on the topo maps for the area. Sorry, no bridges. This is the wilderness, not a national park. When we hiked Upper Mill Creek, heavy rain had turned East Fork Mill Creek into a brown, silt-laden torrent, and we actually had a hard time finding clean water to drink. There were, however, lots of huckleberries to eat.

After spending a night along East Fork Mill Creek somewhere near the junction (no trail sign when I was there), go right (north) on East Fork Mill Creek Pass Trail 41, heading toward Mill Creek Pass. About a quarter mile up the trail from East Fork Mill Creek, stop briefly to see Crystal Cave. As you'll note, this isn't much of a cavern, but there are several major caves in this area. Local cavers spend lots of time around here exploring and mapping the caves, but their locations are carefully concealed to preserve the caves from overuse and notoriety.

The trail climbs steeply for the first 1.5 miles, but switchbacks make the climb easier. Then, the switchbacks end, the trail straightens out, and the grade gets gradual for about a mile before heading up another series of switchbacks all the way to the pass. The well-defined trail stays in the timber until just before the pass and gains 2,400 feet in 4 miles from Mill Creek, another Category 1 climb (but easier than Silver Pass) to another spot on the Absaroka Divide.

From Mill Creek Pass you get a spectacular view to the north down the West Boulder River valley, to the south of The Pyramid and Crow Mountain, and in all directions a sweeping panorama of wild country.

As the trail descends into the West Boulder from the pass, it fades away twice. You can stay on track, however, by following a series of well-placed cairns. After a short, steep section on top, the well-defined trail gradually descends all the way to Falls Creek. The West Boulder valley is more open with lots of beautiful meadows and is arguably more scenic than Fourmile Creek or East Fork Mill Creek. The West Boulder River is also a much larger stream especially after Tumble Creek and Falls Creek join in.

You can go all the way to Falls Creek to camp, or you can pick one of many campsites along the way. It would be challenging to find a bad campsite in this scenic valley. If you have any extra time, you can exercise members of the abundant cutthroat population in the river.

So far on this trip, you have had many stream crossings, but crossing the West Boulder at Falls Creek might qualify as a ford, so be careful, especially early in July when the river will be close to maximum levels. When you get across Falls Creek and start heading toward Speculator Pass, you are entering one of the wildest drainages in the Absaroka Range. The trail is less defined and brushy, as it follows cascading (and well-named) Falls Creek. The scenery is amazing in this, the fourth of five mountain valleys you hike through on this trip. As you hike up Falls Creek, you are treated with views of Boulder Mountain, The Needles, and, in the distance, The Pyramid.

About 3.5 miles up from the West Boulder, you see the junction with Speculator Trail 21. Trail 18 goes left (east) to Great Falls Creek Lakes and out to the Boulder River Road. You can take this route, but you'll be a long way from your vehicle, and you'll miss Speculator Pass, so go right (south) toward the pass.

At this point the trail significantly worsens and becomes difficult to follow. This is not a popular route, so you might have to use some route-finding skills and even get the compass out here and there. However, the route to the pass is still fairly obvious even if you get off the trail momentarily.

The scenery is incredible and rugged as you climb 3,300 feet in 5.5 miles from the West Boulder River. Actually, the last 2 miles up to Speculator Pass, a rare Category H hill, is the steepest designated trail I have ever hiked. Your lungs will feel it, and your calves will get stretched out.

Photo op on Speculator Pass.

On top of the pass, we had fun speculating on why it was named Speculator Pass. One theory was that there was speculation whether you could make it at all or have a heart attack trying to get up there. Another theory was that some mountain man couldn't spell "spectacular," so he jotted down "speculator." In any regard, you won't forget Speculator Pass.

On the south side of Speculator Pass, the trail goes through open Upper Speculator Creek and disappears in several places. This section will test your route-finding skills. While trying to stay on the trail, keep your eye open for a good campsite.

After spending your last night in the extreme wildness of Upper Speculator Creek, you hike through a lodgepole forest similar to Fourmile Creek all the way to the Boulder River Road. This stretch of trail seems to go on forever. We were wasted after climbing three passes, and I couldn't stop thinking about that big steak I planned to attack aggressively as soon as I could find a restaurant.

At the Speculator Creek Trailhead, you need to hang your packs and take an easy 4-mile stroll to the Fourmile Creek Trailhead where you left your vehicle. When we did this trip, I stashed an old bicycle at the Speculator Creek Trailhead and rode back to my vehicle.

Options

If you aren't quite ready for the wildness of the Speculator Pass area, you can hike out from Falls Creek to the Boulder River Road by going out Great Falls Creek, which is, oddly, only 1–2 miles shorter than going out Speculator Creek. You need two vehicles to do this route because it's 11 miles up the Boulder River Road to get back to the Fourmile Creek Trailhead.

You could also skip Falls Creek and keep going out the West Boulder for 8 gradually descending miles to the West Boulder Road Trailhead and a vehicle campground. This is a nice hike with a long shuttle.

And for a really, really long shuttle, you could keep going down East Fork Mill Creek and come out at the Mill Creek Trailhead in Paradise Valley near Pray, Montana. It's an easy 7 miles from Agate Springs to the Mill Creek Trailhead.

Side Trips

Silver Lake could be a side trip instead of the first campsite. Depending on how early you hit the trail, you can pitch your tent somewhere around the junction with Silver Lake Trail and day hike up to the lake. Great Falls Creek Lakes might look like a nice side trip, but make sure you have plenty of daylight left to get over the intensely demanding Speculator Pass.

From Silver Lake, try an off-trail trek to two unnamed lakes at the head of the cirque. From the Falls Creek Trail, try the climb up to the divide above Great Falls Creek or Kaufman Lake.

Camping

Regulations allow you to set up a zero-impact campsite anywhere along this route. Be especially careful not to leave your mark in the nearly untouched meadows at the head of Upper Speculator Creek.

Fishing

Silver Lake has some nice rainbows, but they've seen a few flies, so be stealthy. East Fork Mill Creek has some nice cutthroats, as well as a few rainbows and browns, but fishing is fairly lean at the upper stretches of the creek along the route of this hike. The upper stretches of the West Boulder are great fishing for small cutthroat, and as you get farther downstream, you might snag a brown or rainbow.

5 Bridge Lake

General description: A very long day hike or overnighter
Special attractions: A remote, uncrowded mountain lake, one of the nicest places in the entire Wilderness Preservation System that nobody goes to
Type of trip: Out-and-back

Total distance: 20 miles
Difficulty: Difficult
Traffic: Light
Maps: USGS—Mount Douglas and The Needles; RMS—Mt. Cowen Area
Starting point: Bridge Lake Trailhead

Finding the trailhead: On the Boulder River Road south from Big Timber, Montana, drive 47 miles to the Bridge Lake Trailhead on your right (west), less than a mile past the Upsidedown Creek Trailhead.
Parking and trailhead facilities: Minimal parking at trailhead; no toilet; Hicks Park Campground, a full-service vehicle campground, is right at the trailhead.

Key Points

0.5 Bridge over Bridge Creek.

2.5 Wilderness cabin.

4.0 Junction with Trail 24; turn left.

9.0 End of trail.

10.0 Bridge Lake.

The Hike

Like trails to Silver Lake and Great Falls Creek Lakes, this route is long for a day hike or an overnighter. Only well-conditioned backpackers could make it into Bridge Lake in one day; on the other hand, it's a tad short for two days.

The trail starts out with a serious upgrade for about 2.5 miles. Then, it levels out for about 5 miles until you start the last pitch up to the lake. At 2.5 miles, you'll see one of the few private cabins still remaining in the wilderness. This cabin is on public land, and the Forest Service has decided to let nature gradually reclaim it instead of destroying it.

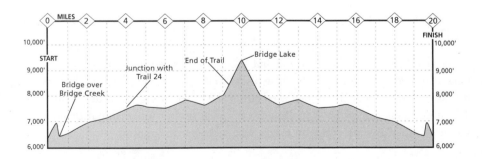

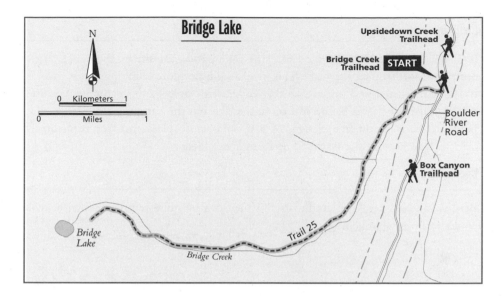

After you cross Bridge Creek on a bridge shortly after leaving the trailhead, you stay on the north side of the stream until about 2 miles before the lake. You cross several feeder streams with no bridges. After about 4 miles from the trailhead, the trail leaves the thick forest and winds through a series of scenic meadows before breaking out above timberline.

The trail is in great shape over the entire route. I especially liked the "no nonsense" switchbacks on the first climb and on the last pitch up to the lake. These switchbacks are generous curves in the trail as opposed to the near-level switchbacks that double the length of the trail. If the switchbacks on this route were like those on the Upsidedown Creek Trail, it would add 2 or 3 miles to the route.

You might think the map is wrong because the trail doesn't go all the way to the lake, but the map is correct. The trail ends about a mile before the lake, and you go off-trail the rest of the way. This is well above timberline, though, and easy hiking, with the exception of one 50-foot stretch along the creek just before the lake. Stay on the left (south) side of Bridge Creek even though it looks easier on the other side. It isn't. Keep your topo map out so you can see where the lake is.

Options

You could camp along Bridge Creek about 6 or 7 miles up the trail and day hike to Bridge Lake. This will spare you the pain of lugging your overnight pack up the last off-trail pitch to the lake. It wouldn't be hard to find a good campsite, but it's probably not as nice as staying at the lake.

Camping

If you decide to camp at Bridge Lake, look for a good campsite on the bench above the right (north) side of the lake. This involves a little more climbing, but it's worth it. If you're wasted and can't make that last quarter mile to this campsite, you can camp on the bench just before you get to the lake, but this camping area isn't as nice. Bridge Lake is almost free of signs of past campers, so please practice zero-impact principles to keep it that way. And no campfires, please.

Fishing

Bridge Lake has nice-size cutthroats, but they can be quite temperamental, so you could go home skunked.

6 East Fork Boulder River

General description: An easy day hike or overnighter

Special attractions: A beautiful stream with good fishing

Type of trip: Out-and-back

Total distance: 7 miles

Difficulty: Easy

Traffic: Moderate

Maps: USGS—Mount Douglas and Haystack Peak; RMS—Mount Douglas-Mount Wood and Cooke City-Cutoff Mountain

Starting point: Box Canyon Trailhead

Finding the trailhead: On the Boulder River Road south of Big Timber, Montana, drive 48 miles to the end of the improved road and the Box Canyon Trailhead.

Parking and trailhead facilities: A large trailhead with toilets and plenty of parking most of the year, but crowded in September and October.

The Hike

This trail is actually the "approach" to the popular routes into Lake Plateau and Slough Creek. Consequently, even though many people use this area, most of them hurry right through the East Fork Boulder River on their way to somewhere else. This makes it a pleasant day hike or an easy overnighter for beginning backpackers.

From the Box Canyon Trailhead, Trail 27 climbs gradually along the East Fork. The trail stays a fair distance from the river for about 3 miles. The first part of this trail was once a wagon road, and it still looks like one. Fortunately, this isn't because of heavy traffic, although the area receives moderate use during July and August and heavy use from stock parties in September during the early hunting season.

The trail leads to a great camping area about 3.5 miles from the trailhead and then crosses the East Fork on a well-constructed bridge. The large camping area just before the bridge can handle a large party or several parties. However, stock users should check the Forest Service regulations for the area (including group size limits) when planning to stay here.

Day hikers can easily spend a few hours fishing or lounging around this area, and even those bound for higher regions might want to linger. The stream is as charming as they get, and the fishing is great. The bridge marks a good turnaround point for day hikers. Those with more time and energy can continue east to where the trail forks, leading to extended trips up to Lake Plateau or south along Slough Creek.

Camping

If you're staying overnight, set up a zero-impact camp at the large camping area just before the bridge over the East Fork

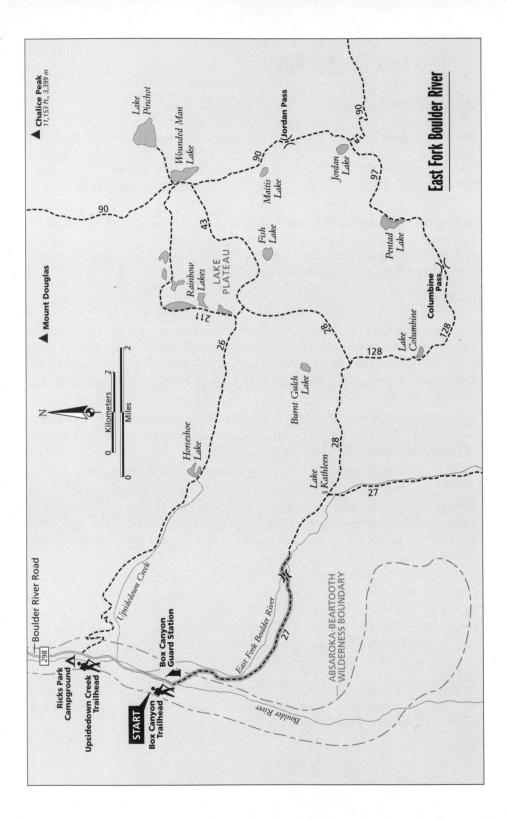

East Fork Boulder River

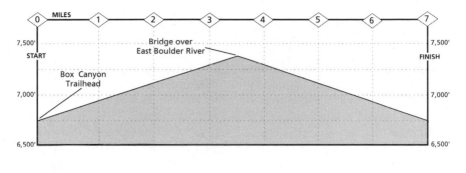

Fishing

Above Box Canyon the East Fork Boulder River contains mostly cutthroat trout, although rainbows dominate the fishery below. Some of these cutthroats may be descendants of native stocks. A smattering of rainbows (immigrants from Rainbow Lakes above) can be found near where Rainbow Creek enters the East Fork Boulder River.

Cutthroat trout are aggressive and often easy to catch. As a result, where cutthroats dominate the fishery, fishing tends to be great. While this has been the fish's downfall in lower streams, most anglers in the Beartooths only keep enough for dinner, and populations seem to be stable.

None of the lakes near this route supports a fishery. Lake Kathleen provides an opportunity to observe a lake in its natural, untarnished state.

7 Columbine Pass

General description: A weeklong backpacking vacation into a popular hiking area with a myriad of side trip opportunities; nicely suited to backpackers who like to set up a base camp
Special attractions: A gorgeous, lake-dotted, high-altitude plateau, plus the equally spectacular Columbine Pass
Type of trip: Loop, but can be a shuttle or out-and-back base camp

Total distance: 34.3 miles, without side trips
Difficulty: Moderate
Traffic: Moderate to heavy; plan on seeing a few stock parties
Maps: USGS—Mount Douglas, Tumble Mountain, Pinnacle Mountain, and Haystack Peak; RMS—Mount Douglas-Mount Wood and Cooke City-Cutoff Mountain
Starting point: Box Canyon Trailhead

Finding the trailhead: Refer to East Fork Boulder River, Hike 6.
Parking and trailhead facilities: Refer to East Fork Boulder River, Hike 6.

Key Points

3.5 East Fork Boulder River (follow Trail 27).

5.2 Junction with Trail 28; turn left.

5.4 Lake Kathleen.

7.9 Junction with Trail 128; turn right.

9.3 Lake Columbine.

11.1 Columbine Pass.

12.5 Pentad Lake.

14.5 Jordan Lake and junction with Trail 90; turn left.

15.9 Jordan Pass.

18.7 Wounded Man Lake and junction with Trail 43; turn left.

18.9 Junction with Trail 211; turn left.

21.0 Rainbow Lakes.

22.5 Junction with Trail 26; turn right.

25.9 Horseshoe Lake.

34.3 Upsidedown Creek Trailhead.

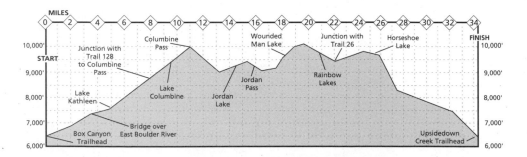

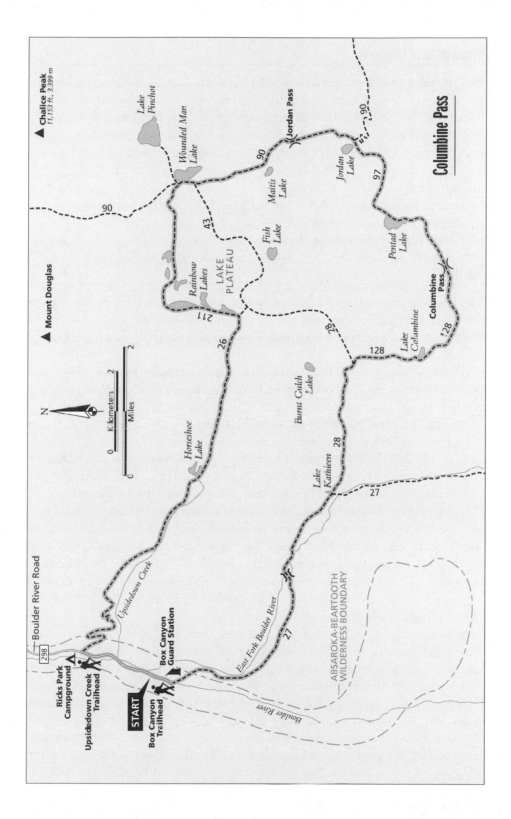

▲ **Chalice Peak**
11,153 ft, 3,399 m

▲ Mount Douglas

Boulder River Road

298

Ricks Park
Campground

Upsidedown Creek
Trailhead

START

Box Canyon
Trailhead

Box Canyon
Guard Station

Upsidedown Creek

N

Kilometers

Miles

0   1   2

Horseshoe
Lake

Lake Pinchot

Wounded Man
Lake

90

43

Rainbow
Lakes

LAKE
PLATEAU

Fish
Lake

Mattis
Lake

Jordan Pass

90

Jordan
Lake

97

Pentad
Lake

Columbine Pass

Lake
Columbine

128

211

26

28

128

Burnt Gulch
Lake

Lake
Kathleen

28

27

East Fork Boulder River

27

Boulder River

ABSAROKA-BEARTOOTH
WILDERNESS BOUNDARY

90

90

Columbine Pass

Recommended Itinerary

This trip works best if you get an early start from Box Canyon, but since the drive to the trailhead is long, it might be difficult to hit the trail early. If you start later in the day, try East Fork Boulder River for the first night out. This may lengthen the trip by one day—not a bad price to pay for sleeping late. The following recommended itinerary lays out a five-day trip, but you could easily spend more time on Lake Plateau.

First night: Lake Columbine
Second night: Lake Pinchot, Wounded Man, Owl, or other nearby lake
Third night: Same campsite
Fourth night: Diamond or Horseshoe Lake

The Hike

The hiker can choose from a variety of options for hiking into the Lake Plateau, but this route is special because there aren't many opportunities like this one to see so much wild country without working out a burdensome shuttle or retracing your steps for half of the trip.

From the Box Canyon Trailhead, Trail 27 climbs gradually through timber and open parks along the East Fork Boulder River for about 3.5 miles before crossing a sturdy bridge. If you started late, you may wish to stay the first night in one of several excellent campsites located just before the bridge.

It would be wise to get up early on the first day, drive to Box Canyon Trailhead, and cover at least the first 3.5 miles to a series of excellent campsites just before the bridge over the East Fork Boulder River. This area can accommodate a large party or several parties, as long as Forest Service limits for group size aren't exceeded.

After crossing the East Fork, the trail follows the river for a half mile before climbing away through heavy timber. Several trout-filled pools beckon along the riverside stretch, so be prepared to fight off temptations to stop and rig up the fly-casting gear.

In less than 2 miles you reach the junction with Trail 28. Trail 27 goes straight and eventually ends up in Yellowstone National Park. Turn left here onto Trail 28. In about a quarter mile, watch for tranquil little Lake Kathleen off to the left. This is also a possible first-night campsite.

About 2 miles from Lake Kathleen, the trail joins Trail 128 to Columbine Pass. Turn right onto this trail, which climbs a big hill and breaks out of the forest into a subalpine panorama. From the junction it's about 1.5 miles to Lake Columbine. With an early start on the first day, this would also make a good first campsite. If it's your second day out, consider pushing on to Pentad or Jordan Lake for the second night's camp.

From Lake Columbine continue another scenic 2 miles up to 9,850-foot Columbine Pass. In a good snow year, snowbanks cover the trail on Columbine Pass well

Lake Columbine from Columbine Pass.

into July. The trail fades away twice between Lake Columbine and the pass, so watch the topo map carefully to stay on track. A few well-placed cairns make navigation here easier.

After the Category 2 climb to Columbine Pass, take a break and enjoy a snack and the vistas, including 10,685-foot Pinnacle Mountain to the south. From here the trail leaves the Boulder River drainage behind and heads into the Stillwater River drainage. Hereafter, the trip leapfrogs from one lake to another for the next 14 miles.

Those who camped at Lake Columbine can make it all the way into the Lake Plateau for the next night's campsite. Otherwise, plan to pitch a tent at Pentad or Jordan Lake. Pentad is more scenic, but Jordan offers better fishing (and suffers more from overuse). There are also several smaller lakes near Pentad—Mouse, Favonius, Sundown, and several unnamed lakes. Many great campsites can be found in the area, and they won't be as crowded as Jordan Lake probably will be. Don't rush to take the first campsite. Look around for a while and you'll find a better one. It might be wise to stop at the south end of Pentad anyway, as the trail is difficult to follow because of all the tangent trails created by backcountry horsemen to various campsites. To untangle the maze check the topo map. The trail skirts the east shore of Pentad Lake heading north.

Jordan Lake, another 2 miles down the trail from Pentad, has limited camping with one campsite at the foot of the lake. The campsite is, however, large enough to serve a large party or several parties—although it may be too heavily impacted to be used by parties with stock animals.

At Jordan Lake the trail meets Trail 90, coming out of Lake Plateau and dropping east down into the Middle Fork of Wounded Man Creek. Turn left (north) here onto Trail 90, which climbs gradually 1.5 miles over Jordan Pass and drops into the Lake Plateau. This isn't much of a pass, but it's a great spot to take fifteen minutes to marvel at the mountainous horizons in every direction.

If you camped last at Jordan or Pentad Lake, you have lots of options for the next night out or for a base camp. The closest site is at Wounded Man Lake, but this is a busy place. The best campsite is along the North Fork of Wounded Man Creek just southwest of the lake. But consider hiking the short mile northeast from Wounded Man Lake to Lake Pinchot to stay at the crown jewel of the Lake Plateau. The third option is to turn left onto Trail 211 at the junction on the west side of Wounded Man Lake and stay at Owl Lake or one of the Rainbow Lakes that follow shortly thereafter. These offer some of the best base camps in the area because there are innumerable sights to see all within a short walk.

After a night or two on the plateau, follow Trail 211 along the west shore of Rainbow Lakes down to the junction with Trail 26 at the south end of Lower Rainbow Lake. Turn right (west) here, and spend the last night out at Diamond or Horseshoe Lake (sometimes called Upper and Lower Horseshoe Lakes). Horseshoe Lake is probably better because it has more campsites and it leaves the shortest possible distance along Upsidedown Creek the last day. And that's still about 8.5 miles, plus the 1.5 miles some lucky volunteer has to walk or try to catch a ride up to the Box Canyon Trailhead to get the vehicle. Sorry—there are no real campsites anywhere from Horseshoe Lake to the Boulder River Road.

Options

If you can arrange transportation for a shuttle, you can hike out the West Stillwater River or the main Stillwater River. You might need a four-wheel-drive vehicle to get to the West Stillwater River Trailhead. You can also make this an out-and-back trip from either the Box Canyon or Upsidedown Creek Trailhead.

Side Trips

Refer to Exploring the Lake Plateau on page 68.

Camping

The Lake Plateau has hundreds of terrific campsites, all undesignated. Find one for your base camp, and please make it a zero-impact camp.

Fishing

Refer to Fishing the Lake Plateau on page 69.

8 Lake Plateau West

General description: A weeklong backpacking vacation that can be done as a loop or an out-and-back
Special attractions: A gorgeous, lake-dotted, high-altitude plateau
Type of trip: Loop with out-and-back option
Total distance: 25.5 miles, not counting side trips

Difficulty: Moderate
Traffic: Moderate
Maps: USGS—Mount Douglas, Tumble Mountain, and Haystack Peak; RMS—Mount Douglas-Mount Wood and Cooke City-Cutoff Mountain
Starting point: Box Canyon Trailhead

Finding the trailhead: Refer to East Fork Boulder River, Hike 6.
Parking and trailhead facilities: Refer to East Fork Boulder River, Hike 6.

Key Points

These key points follow the main route, not including side trips such as Lake Pinchot.

- **3.5** East Fork Boulder River.
- **5.2** Junction with Trail 28; turn left.
- **5.4** Lake Kathleen.
- **7.9** Junction with Trail 128; turn left.
- **10.5** Junction with Trail 211; turn left.
- **11.4** Junction with Trail 26; turn right.
- **12.3** Rainbow Lakes.
- **13.2** Wounded Man Lake and junction with Trail 90; turn right.
- **13.5** Junction with Trail 43; turn right.
- **15.0** Junction with Trail 28; turn right.
- **15.9** Junction with Trail 26; turn left.
- **17.2** Horseshoe Lake.
- **25.5** Upsidedown Creek Trailhead.

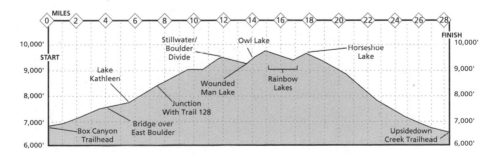

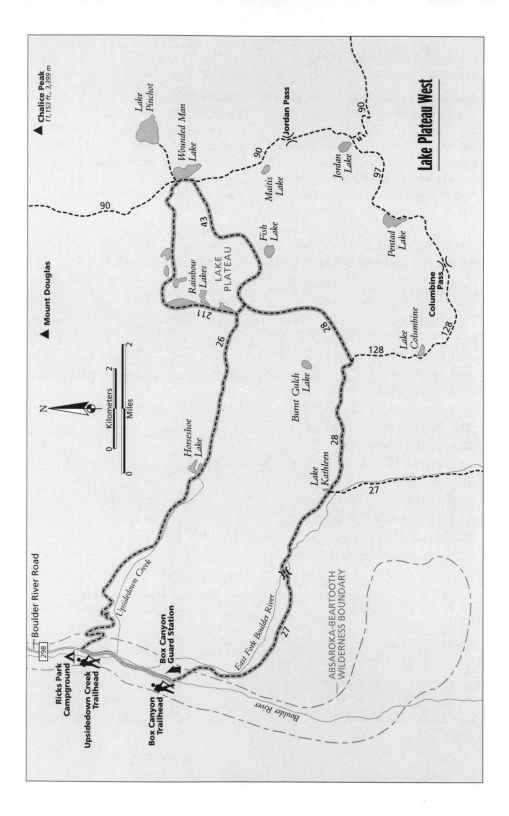

Lake Plateau West

Recommended Itinerary

Since it's such a long drive to Box Canyon Trailhead from just about anywhere, most hikers don't hit the trail until afternoon. This actually works well for this route because there aren't many good camping areas between the East Fork Boulder River and Rainbow Lakes, which is more than 12 miles down the trail, too far for a single day for many backpackers. If you stay at East Fork Boulder River, though, you only have 8.8 miles to the Rainbow Lakes for the second night out. You could also set up a base camp at Rainbow Lakes or hike 2 to 3 miles farther the second day to set up the base camp.

First night: East Fork Boulder River
Second night: Along Rainbow Creek or at Rainbow Lakes
Third night: Set up base camp somewhere on the Lake Plateau
Fourth night: Same campsite
Fifth night: Same campsite
Sixth night: Horseshoe or Diamond Lake

The Hike

From the Box Canyon Trailhead, Trail 27 climbs gradually through timber and open parks along the East Fork Boulder River for about 3.5 miles before crossing a sturdy bridge. If you started late, you may wish to stay the first night at the excellent camping area just before the bridge.

Camping here is not a bad idea. Otherwise, it's a tough 12- to 14-mile day to get onto the Lake Plateau, depending on where you decide to set up base camp. And there really aren't any decent campsites at the convenient 5- to 7-mile range to split up the distance. So either plan to camp at the 3.5-mile mark or aim for the valley just below the Lake Plateau, about 10 miles in, where several great campsites are nestled along Rainbow Creek.

After crossing the East Fork, the trail follows the river for about a half mile before climbing away through heavy timber. Several trout-filled pools beckon along the riverside stretch, so be prepared to fight off temptations to stop and rig up the fly-casting gear.

After 2 miles Trail 27 heads south toward Slough Creek Divide. Turn left here on Trail 28.

In a couple hundred yards, the trail passes little Lake Kathleen on the left. Then, 2 miles farther, Trail 128 breaks off to the right and heads for Columbine Pass. Stay left on Trail 28.

After another 3 miles, the trail meets Trail 211. At this point you need to decide where you intend to base camp. Here are a few options: (1) Head left up the steep switchbacks 0.75 mile to the junction with Trail 26 and turn right to any of six Rainbow Lakes to the northwest; (2) go right less than 1 mile up Trail 211 to Fish Lake,

Base camp on the Lake Plateau.

reached after a short, steep climb; or (3) continue past Fish Lake another 3 to 4 miles on Trail 211 to Lake Pinchot. All three options have plenty of great campsites.

On the way to Lake Pinchot, Wounded Man Lake might look like a good place to base camp, but it has limited camping. Lake Pinchot adds an extra mile when you really don't want it, but this beautiful lake is the heart of the Lake Plateau. If you don't base camp here, be sure to visit on a day trip.

If you can't make up your mind on where to base camp, set up a temporary camp for one night and then spend the next day trekking around, enjoying the scenery, fishing, and searching for that five-star campsite. Then return to the temporary camp early enough to move everything to the base camp.

Once the base camp is established, start taking advantage of the numerous adventures waiting in all directions. For anglers, there are two dozen lakes within the reach of an easy day hike. For peak-baggers, there are 11,298-foot Mount Douglas, 11,153-foot Chalice Peak, and other summits to reach.

To return to the Box Canyon Trailhead, follow whichever leg of the Lake Plateau loop trail (211 or 43) you didn't take on the way in. This way you will have covered the entire Lake Plateau circle (about a 6-mile loop).

You can drop back to the junction with Trail 28 and retrace the route down Rainbow Creek. To avoid backtracking on Trail 28, however, take Upsidedown Creek Trail 26, which heads west from the foot of Lower Rainbow Lake. Plan on two days to get out, camping at Horseshoe or Diamond Lake (sometimes called Upper and Lower Horseshoe Lakes) before heading out Upsidedown Creek. This route may be slightly shorter, but it involves a steep downhill after a 600-foot climb. The trail hits Boulder River Road about 1.5 miles north of the Box Canyon Trailhead. Here, pick the most energetic member of your party to jog up to Box Canyon to get your vehicle.

The Lake Plateau gets more use than most areas in the Beartooths, but a large number of destinations and campsites dilute the crowd to a tolerable level. A week in this wonderland will undoubtedly be a memorable vacation. So expect a few remorseful moments when you realize that you must return to your hectic lifestyle back home. Be forewarned: The first days back at work may seem quite unpleasant.

Options

It seems slightly easier to do this trip as noted above, but the route could be reversed: going in Upsidedown Creek and out along the East Fork. This option, however, involves a steady, dry, 8.3-mile climb to Horseshoe Lake. If you take this option, take extra water. You can also retrace your steps down Rainbow Creek to Box Canyon and skip the Upsidedown Creek Trail.

Side Trips

You could spend weeks exploring the Lake Plateau. Check out the list of possible side trips in Exploring the Lake Plateau on page 68.

Camping

The Lake Plateau has hundreds of terrific campsites, all undesignated. Find one for your base camp, and please make it a zero-impact camp.

Fishing

Refer to Fishing the Lake Plateau on page 69.

EXPLORING THE LAKE PLATEAU
Any trip to the Lake Plateau should include some extra time for exploring the many hidden treasures in the area. Here's a list of suggestions rated for difficulty as follows: Human (easy for almost everyone, including children), Semi-human (moderately difficult), or Animal (don't try it unless you're very fit and wilderness-wise). Also refer to more detailed rating information in the chapter Using this Guidebook.

Destination	Difficulty
Lake Pinchot	Human
Flood Creek lakes	Semi-human
Asteroid Lake Basin	Animal
Chalice Peak	Animal
Lightning Lake	Animal
Lake Diaphanous	Human
Fish Lake	Human
Barrier Lake	Animal
Mirror Lake	Semi-human
Chickadee Lake	Animal
Squeeze Lake	Animal
Mount Douglas	Animal
Lake Plateau Loop	Human
Martes Lake	Semi-human
Columbine Pass	Human
Jordan Lake	Human
Sundown Lake	Semi-human
Pentad and Favonius Lakes	Human
Burnt Gulch Lake	Animal

FISHING THE LAKE PLATEAU

Anglers who want to fish the first day of the trip should camp near the East Fork Boulder River or Rainbow Creek. Above Box Canyon the East Fork Boulder River contains mostly cutthroat trout, although rainbows dominate the fishery below. Some of these cutthroats may be descendants of native stocks. A smattering of rainbows (immigrants from Rainbow Lakes above) can be found near where Rainbow Creek enters the East Fork Boulder River.

The Lake Plateau offers a variety of fishing opportunities, consisting mostly of rainbow and cutthroat trout. Cutthroats are frequently found along rocky shorelines on the downwind sides of lakes. Anglers often fish "past the fish" by casting out into the lake.

Cutthroat trout are aggressive and often easy to catch. As a result, where cutthroats dominate the fishery, the fishing tends to be great. This has been the cutthroat's downfall in lower streams, so take only enough for dinner to help keep populations stable.

The lakes of the Lake Plateau are located in both the Stillwater and Boulder River drainages and offer cutthroat, rainbow, and some golden trout fishing. Keep in mind that not all lakes contain fish, but most of the lakes along the trails have self-sustaining populations and contain plenty of fish. Golden trout were once planted on the plateau, but only a few remain. Flood Creek, including Lake Pinchot, has beautiful mixed species of fish (golden, cutthroat, rainbow), due to migrations of planted fish. A small drainage south of Flood Creek (Asteroid Lake) contains pure goldens.

Wounded Man Creek supports a mainly cutthroat trout fishery, although rainbows share Pentad and Favonius Lakes with cutts. Jordan Lake holds nice cutthroats that can be counted on to provide dinner.

For solitude, lakes off the trail such as Burnt Gulch, Barrier, and Martes Lakes also provide good fishing. Aufwuchs Lake is a tough cross-country hike but has good cutthroat fishing. Beautiful hybrids live in Lake Pinchot and along Flood Creek.

Many high mountain streams are too steep to harbor large populations of trout, so look for the slow spots.

9 Slough Creek Divide

General description: A long trip unlike any other trail in the Beartooths, with no lakes but a beautiful stream all the way

Special attractions: Excessive remoteness and excellent chance to see wildlife, including bears

Type of trip: Shuttle

Total distance: 39.4 miles

Difficulty: Difficult

Traffic: Light on most of trip, heavy on lower stretches of Slough Creek

Maps: USGS—Mount Douglas, Haystack Peak, Roundhead Butte, and Mount Hornaday; RMS—Mount Douglas-Mount Wood and Cooke City-Cutoff Mountain; Trails Illustrated—Tower/Canyon Yellowstone National Park Map

Starting point: Box Canyon Trailhead

Finding the trailhead: Refer to East Fork Boulder River, Hike 6.

Parking and trailhead facilities: Refer to East Fork Boulder River, Hike 6.

Key Points

3.5 East Fork Boulder River.

5.2 Junction with Trail 28; turn right.

8.2 Junction with unnumbered trail to Wool Lake; turn left.

9.5 Junction with Trail 104 to Independence Peak; turn left.

10.0 Slough Creek Divide.

11.8 Slough Creek.

15.7 Junction with Trail 309 up Wounded Man Creek; turn right.

17.0 Junction with Trail 9 to Horseshoe Basin; turn right.

21.1 Junction with Trail 84 up Lake Abundance Creek; turn right.

22.2 Junction with Trail 84 up Bull Creek; turn left.

24.9 Junction with Trail 193 up Wolverine Creek; turn right.

25.2 Slough Creek Guard Station.

26.2 Junction with Trail 102 up Tucker Creek; turn left.

28.0 Silver Tip Ranch.

28.4 Yellowstone National Park boundary.

31.4 Junction with trail up to Bliss Pass; turn right.

39.4 Slough Creek Campground.

Recommended Itinerary

A three-night itinerary means approximately 10 miles per day. If this is too ambitious for you, make this a four-night trip by spending the first night along the East Fork Boulder River.

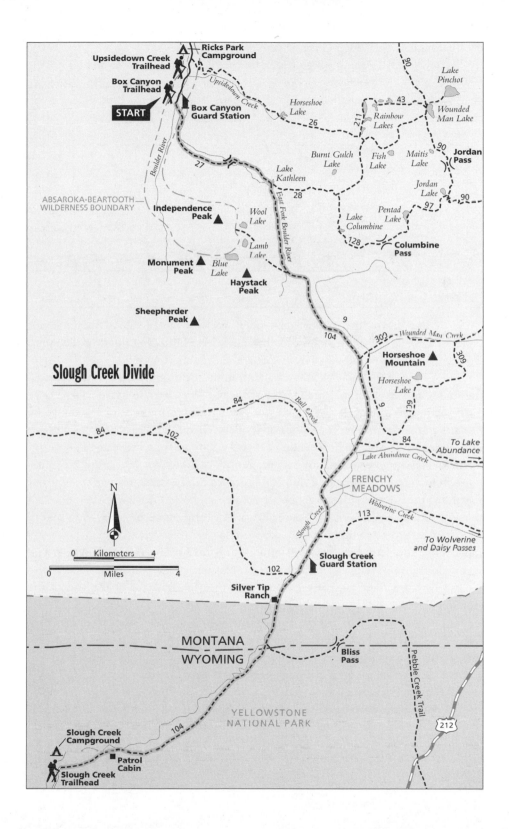

Ricks Park
Campground

Upsidedown Creek
Trailhead

Box Canyon
Trailhead

START

Box Canyon
Guard Station

Upsidedown Creek

Horseshoe
Lake

26

Lake
Pinchot

90

43

211

Rainbow
Lakes

Wounded
Man Lake

Boulder River

27

Lake
Kathleen

Burnt Gulch
Lake

Fish
Lake

Maitis
Lake

90

Jordan
Pass

ABSAROKA-BEARTOOTH
WILDERNESS BOUNDARY

Independence
Peak

Wool
Lake

East Fork Boulder River

28

Jordan
Lake

97

90

Monument
Peak

Blue
Lake

Lamb
Lake

Haystack
Peak

Lake
Columbine

Pentad
Lake

Lake
Columbine

128

Columbine
Pass

Sheepherder
Peak

Slough Creek Divide

9

104

300

Wounded Man Creek

309

Horseshoe
Mountain

Horseshoe
Lake

6

6

84

Bull Creek

84

102

84

To Lake
Abundance

Lake Abundance Creek

N

FRENCHY
MEADOWS

Wolverine Creek

Slough Creek

113

To Wolverine
and Daisy Passes

0   Kilometers   4

0   Miles   4

102

Slough Creek
Guard Station

Silver Tip
Ranch

MONTANA

WYOMING

Bliss
Pass

Pebble Creek Trail

YELLOWSTONE
NATIONAL PARK

212

104

Slough Creek
Campground

Patrol
Cabin

Slough Creek
Trailhead

First night: Slough Creek Divide area
Second night: Along Slough Creek halfway between the divide and the park
                     boundary
Third night: Along Slough Creek in Yellowstone National Park

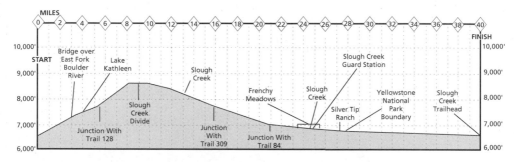

The Hike

Most of the Beartooths is subalpine—open, rocky country full of mountainous panoramas—but not this trail. Instead, this trail starts in the deep forest of the upper Boulder River valley and stays below timberline for almost 40 miles.

This is one of the most phenomenal trails in the Beartooths. Yet during the summer it doesn't get much use, mainly because the trail doesn't go to a lake or the top of a mountain, and it requires a very time-consuming shuttle. In the fall, however, many hunters and outfitters use the area in search of elk, deer, and other big game common in Boulder River/Slough Creek country. If you're looking for solitude and remoteness and the chance to see all kinds of wildlife, put this trail high on your list of priorities.

The first step is to arrange a shuttle. This route can be done from either end, but starting at the north end is slightly better because it allows a net loss in elevation and the trip ends up in Yellowstone National Park. If your group is big enough to split in two, start at opposite ends and trade keys when you meet each other. This greatly reduces the trouble in arranging the shuttle. If not, leave a vehicle at the Slough Creek Campground and Trailhead in Yellowstone National Park and drive all the way around (about a four-hour drive) to the Box Canyon Trailhead at the end of the Boulder River Road.

The second step is to call the backcountry office at Yellowstone National Park (307–344–7381) and ask about camping in Slough Creek. The park has a policy of not giving out backcountry camping permits more than forty-eight hours in advance. If you plan to camp in Slough Creek in the park on the way out, you'll need one of these permits. You'll also need an exception to the forty-eight-hour policy. Be sure to contact the park far enough in advance to get the permit before you leave. If you don't get a permit for one of the park's designated campsites in Slough Creek, you won't be able to camp in the park and you'll have at least 11 miles to cover on the last day of the trip. If you plan carefully, you might be able to pick up the permit and arrange shuttle transportation at the same time.

It's best to do the shuttle early in the day and start in the afternoon so you can spend the first night at the East Fork Boulder River. Either stay where the trail first crosses the river about 3.5 miles up the trail or at the second crossing 2 miles later just after the junction with Trail 28, which goes north into the Lake Plateau. At this junction, go straight, staying on Trail 27. In about a quarter mile, the trail turns south and crosses the East Fork. There are also good campsites here, but no bridge.

After crossing the East Fork a second time, the trail narrows down to the normal size from the broad "two-lane." It then heads gradually uphill for about 5 miles to the Slough Creek Divide.

The Slough Creek Divide is a wonderful place. It's well signed and is, surprisingly, the highest point of the trip: a mere 8,576 feet, significantly below timberline and unusually low for the Beartooths.

On the way up to the divide, be wary that you don't accidentally get on the side trail heading up to Wool Lake (not named on USGS topo map). When the trail meets the stream coming down from Lamb (not named on USGS topo map) and Blue Lakes, it's all too easy to follow the trail up the right side of the stream. Instead, stay on Trail 27, which crosses the stream at that point.

An excellent choice for a second campsite would be the huge open park at the headwaters of the East Fork about a quarter mile before the divide. This differs from most campsites in the Beartooths, but it's no disappointment. Campers can spend lots of time marveling at the view across the lush meadow at Monument Peak and Haystack Peak. About halfway through the big meadow, the trail comes to a junction with Trail 104 to the ghost town of Independence. This trail leads back to the end of the jeep road that continues on past the Box Canyon Trailhead. Bear left here, crossing the East Fork for the third and last time, and go straight (southeast) on Trail 104.

The next 10-mile section is not a good place for people deathly afraid of bears. When I hiked this route, I observed tracks, scat, and other bear signs everywhere, and I saw one grizzly at an uncomfortably close distance. This area obviously supports a healthy population of both grizzly and black bears.

You can also find another great campsite when the trail first hits Slough Creek. Keep in mind that this is bear country, so be extra careful with food and garbage, including fish entrails.

From this point on, the trail follows Slough Creek all the way to Slough Creek Campground in Yellowstone Park. After dropping off the divide, there's an unmarked trail junction with a fairly good trail going off to the right (southwest). Bear left (southeast) here; going right ends up on the west side of the stream on a trail that the Forest Service is in the process of abandoning. Some maps also show parallel trails going down both sides of Slough Creek, but stay on the east side of the creek.

Good campsites are common in the frequent meadows at least until the junction with Trail 309 that goes up Wounded Man Creek. Incidentally, this is not any relation to the Wounded Man Creek leaving the Lake Plateau and rushing down into the Stillwater River, the next major drainage east of Slough Creek. It would be interesting to know why we have two streams with the same name in the same area, but nobody seems to know. The dramatic fires of 1988 scorched the Slough Creek drainage all the way up to Wounded Man Creek.

The side trails up Wounded Man Creek, Horseshoe Basin, and Lake Abundance are not regularly maintained. Explorers who want to take a side trip up any of these drainages should allow plenty of time for finding the trail and climbing over deadfall from the 1988 burn. Expect to find quiet and utter solitude. The Forest Service attempts to clear these trails once every four years, but they may be in poor shape.

For the third night out, push on to excellent campsites at Lake Abundance Creek and Bull Creek. Or camp anywhere along upper Slough Creek. Those looking for solitude might want to avoid camping right at Bull Creek, the site of a large outfitter camp.

Just after Bull Creek, the trail breaks out into oversized Frenchy Meadow, an inholding (privately owned land) within the boundaries of the Absaroka-Beartooth Wilderness that has been cultivated in the past, as witnessed by some old farm equipment rusting away here and there. At the south end of the meadow stands the Slough Creek Guard Station and accompanying corrals, managed by the Forest Service.

About 3 miles farther is the Silver Tip Ranch, another inholding, this one precisely on the northern boundary of Yellowstone Park. Remember that this is private land, so hurry through. There's a gate at each end; be sure to leave the gate the way you found it. Rest assured, however, that you aren't trespassing. The Forest Service has a conservation easement that allows the public to cross both Frenchy Meadows and the Silver Tip Ranch. In the past the trail followed an old wagon road through the middle of the Silver Tip Ranch, but the Forest Service has rerouted the trail. When you reach the Silver Tip Ranch, the trail goes left (east) and skirts the fence line on the edge of the meadow before rejoining the wagon road. Part of the trail still crosses private land, so please be respectful of private property rights.

The park boundary is right at the south end of the ranch. The trail from the park boundary to the Slough Creek Trailhead is actually a two-lane road, and it would be physically possible to drive all the way up Slough Creek to the Silver Tip Ranch from the Slough Creek Campground in the park. This, however, is strictly prohibited. The only vehicle allowed on this trail is a horse-drawn wagon operated by the owners of the Silver Tip Ranch.

A good choice for the fourth night out would be one of the three designated campsites in Yellowstone Park—if you can get a permit. If you don't have a campsite reserved, then arrange your earlier campsites so you can camp somewhere between the Slough Creek Guard Station and the Silver Tip Ranch. Unfortunately, this leaves 11 miles or more out on the last day. This won't be that bad, as the last leg of the trip is an easy, stream-grade, downhill walk along lower Slough Creek, world famous for large cutthroat trout. Expect to see anglers fly casting the slow-moving waters of

Slough Creek as it meanders through an expansive meadow. In fact, the entire lower Slough Creek Valley is bordered by lush meadows.

Options

You can do this trip in reverse, but it involves slightly more elevation gain.

Side Trips

Take some time to explore the meadows around the Slough Creek Divide.

Camping

This route is lined with acceptable campsites, along the East Fork Boulder River near the beginning of the trip, in large meadows in the Slough Creek Divide area, and then all along Slough Creek to the vehicle campground in the park.

Fishing

Of all the 944 lakes in the Beartooths, a few lakes in the Slough Creek drainage may have been the only ones that originally contained fish. Both Heather and Peace Lakes, for example, contain indigenous Yellowstone cutthroat trout. There is no record of fish being planted in either lake, although there have been plants of Yellowstone cutthroats in Slough Creek.

This trail offers anglers a choice of cutthroat trout or cutthroat trout, with a possibility of an errant rainbow from the East Fork Boulder River side of the divide. Blue Lake is the only lake near the route, on the Boulder side, with fish—nice fat cutthroat trout.

Slough Creek is the premier cutthroat trout stream fishery in Montana, although a great deal of it is found in Yellowstone Park. Anglers need a special fishing permit from Yellowstone National Park to fish Slough Creek in the park. Current park regulations call for catch-and-release fishing. Be sure to check both Montana and Yellowstone regulations before wetting a line.

The Beartooth Front

T he Beartooth Front is a huge rock mastiff facing north. In the shadow of the front, you'll find traditional ranching operations and a scattering of small towns. Several large streams have sliced notches through the front and provide access to normal folks on foot or hoof. Eventually, the streams carry massive amounts of snowmelt into the mighty Yellowstone River.

The trailheads covered in this section include, from west to east, the West Fork Stillwater River, Stillwater River, West Rosebud, Lake Wilderness, and East Rosebud. You would be wise to use a high-clearance, four-wheel-drive vehicle to access the Lake Wilderness and West Fork Stillwater River Trailheads, but the other trailheads can be reached with any vehicle.

The West Fork Stillwater River Trailhead receives much less use than trailheads to the east (Stillwater River) or to the west (West Boulder Road), but not due to a shortage of scenic attributes or excellent trails. To the contrary, the trail up the West Fork Stillwater River is definitely worth seeing.

Perhaps one reason for the lower use is tougher access. Unlike the Boulder and the Stillwater (and most other major river drainages in Montana), the West Fork Stillwater River does not have an access road along its banks. Instead, travelers have to take a rough Forest Service gravel road over the ridge separating the West Fork Stillwater River and the Stillwater River drainages to get to the West Fork Stillwater River Trailhead. One interesting peculiarity of this trailhead is that the wilderness boundary has been extended downstream to the trailhead to include more of the river and its fragile habitat, mainly to protect this critical area from future mining development.

The Stillwater River Trailhead is one of the most accessible and heavily used access points to the Beartooths, and getting there is a treat. The route up the Stillwater River is one of the most scenic drives in Montana. The Stillwater River flows majestically through a landscape dominated by large ranches interspersed with small ranching communities like Fishtail, Nye, Beehive, Dean, and Moraine. Watch for bighorn sheep near the Stillwater Mine.

The Stillwater carries more water out of the Beartooths than any other stream, and it's certainly one of the most beautiful drainages. Nowadays, however, it is a little less wild than in the recent past. The north rim of the Beartooths, and especially the Stillwater River area, is highly mineralized. In recent years, several controversial mining developments have sprung up in this area, including some large operations. The rapid growth of mines and the associated residential development have brought many more people into this remote part of Montana.

The Lake Wilderness Trailhead involves a long, dusty drive on a gravel road, the last part of which requires a high-clearance, four-wheel-drive vehicle. Only one hike starts at this trailhead.

At the West Rosebud Trailhead, all hikes start on a trail in a power company work area and climb to a man-made dam on Mystic Lake. The dam raised the water level of the natural lake, making Mystic the deepest lake in the Beartooths (more than 200 feet). Plus, two delightful lakes—Emerald and West Rosebud—lie right at the trailhead.

Located about 80 miles southwest of Billings, the West Rosebud is similar to the East Rosebud and other trailheads on the northern face of the Beartooths. The gravel access road follows a beautiful stream (West Rosebud Creek) through traditional Montana ranching country, mostly undeveloped. The road may be rough in sections, but it's still suitable for two-wheel-drive vehicles. Besides, the scenery is well worth the bumps. Travelers can see the narrow valley opening up in the mountains long before they arrive.

This area also resembles East Rosebud because of the little community at the trailhead. Instead of summer cabins, however, the structures at this trailhead house workers employed by the owner of Mystic Dam Power Station, the Montana Power Company.

The West Rosebud is the only major drainage in the Beartooths that's closed to horse traffic during the summer. This is due to hazardous rock fields and snowdrifts common on a section of trail just before Mystic Lake early in the season. Horses are allowed into the area, however, during the fall big-game hunting seasons, usually starting in mid-September.

A short way up the trail, look for a plaque placed in a stone in memory of Mark E. Von Seggern, a Boy Scout from Columbus, Montana, who died in 1979 after a tragic slide down a snowbank near Mystic Lake. The plaque also offers that age-old (but never out-of-date) advice: "Be Prepared." This is especially true for weekend adventurers heading up to Froze-to-Death Plateau to climb Montana's highest mountain, Granite Peak. Actually, Granite isn't a difficult climb for experienced climbers, but many people going up the mountain aren't that experienced. Perhaps the plaque will remind them of that fact.

Many people who know the Beartooths say the East Rosebud is the most scenic valley of all. It's filled with lakes and waterfalls that would be major tourism attractions anywhere else. Here, there are so many, most don't even have names. The trout-filled lakes bring a smile to any angler's face, and climbers love the place because of the endless array of rock faces. Families and friends frequently choose The Beaten Path, Hike 20, for that long-planned wilderness adventure. Consequently, the East Rosebud Trailhead is probably the most heavily used trailhead in the Absaroka-Beartooth Wilderness.

Adding even more activity to the area is the small community of summer homes, called Alpine, right at the trailhead. The summer homes extend up both sides of the lower sections of East Rosebud Lake, closing off much of the lake to public use.

Actually, there are three trailheads at East Rosebud Lake. Phantom Creek Trail 17 (Slough Lake, Granite Peak, Rosebud to Rosebud) begins on the right (west) side of the road a quarter mile before the lake. This is a popular route to Froze-to-Death Plateau and Granite Peak. About a half mile farther, as the road swings by Alpine and around the east side of the lake, turn left into East Rosebud Campground to reach the trailhead for Trail 13 to Sylvan Lake. Finally, Trail 15 up the East Rosebud Creek (The Beaten Path and Elk Lake) begins at the end of the road about a quarter mile past the campground.

10 Breakneck Park Meadows

General description: An excellent overnight trip or long day trip

Special attractions: An unusually large, gorgeous mountain meadow

Type of trip: Out-and-back

Total distance: 16 miles

Difficulty: Moderate

Traffic: Light

Maps: USGS—Picket Pin Mountain and Tumble Mountain; RMS—Mount Douglas-Mount Wood

Starting point: West Fork Stillwater River Trailhead

Finding the trailhead: From Interstate 90 at Columbus, Montana, drive 15 miles south on Montana Highway 78 to Absarokee. Continue south from town about 2 miles and turn right on the Nye Road (County Road 419). Drive about 25 miles southwest, through Nye, to the Stillwater Mine (which is about 2 miles before the Stillwater River Trailhead and Woodbine Campground at road's end). Immediately after the mine, turn right (west) on Forest Road 846 at a well-marked intersection. From here it's a long 8 miles to the trailhead.

Parking and trailhead facilities: Ample parking, but large horse trailers might have some difficulty; no toilet; an undeveloped vehicle campground less than a mile before the trailhead.

Key Points

3.4	Crescent Creek.
7.8	Divide Creek.
8.0	Breakneck Park Meadows.

The Hike

Those who want to see a remote and beautiful mountain river drainage without making it a weeklong trip should try an overnighter into Breakneck Park Meadows. The hike in and out can be done in a day, but at 16 miles, it's a long haul.

The well-maintained trail closely follows the West Fork Stillwater River most of the way, hugging the north and west bank. But just before Breakneck Park Meadows, it gradually climbs out of sight of the stream through several smaller meadows. Some of these clearings seem big enough to be a worthy destination, but there's no mistaking the expansive Breakneck Park Meadows when you get there. The trail hits

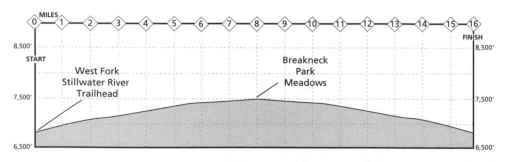

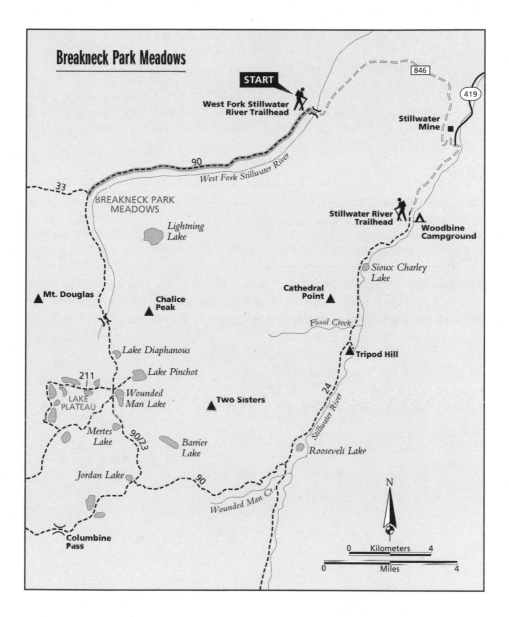

Breakneck Park Meadows

START

West Fork Stillwater
River Trailhead

846

419

Stillwater
Mine

90

West Fork Stillwater River

33

BREAKNECK PARK
MEADOWS

Lightning
Lake

Stillwater River
Trailhead

Woodbine
Campground

Sioux Charley
Lake

Mt. Douglas

Chalice
Peak

Cathedral
Point

Flood Creek

Lake Diaphanous

Tripod Hill

Lake Pinchot

211

LAKE
PLATEAU

Wounded
Man Lake

Two Sisters

Stillwater River

24

Mertes
Lake

90/23

Barrier
Lake

Roosevelt Lake

Jordan Lake

90

N

Wounded Man Cr.

Columbine
Pass

0   Kilometers   4

0   Miles   4

Breakneck Park Meadows about a quarter mile above the West Fork Stillwater River. Take a break here, and if you're staying overnight, look around for that ideal campsite. Campers who want a fire can usually find enough wood nearby, but try for a low-impact fire.

Once settled in, most visitors just want to relax, fish, or watch for deer, moose, or elk, all abundant in the area. Even though it's an 8-mile return trip to the trailhead, this stretch goes fast because of the gradual gradient and the excellent condition of the trail.

Side Trip

For an interesting side trip, take the trail leaving Breakneck Park Meadows about halfway through, and climb the 3 miles to Breakneck Plateau at the foot of 10,232-foot Breakneck Mountain.

Camping

The logical choice is Breakneck Park Meadows, but there are also numerous great camping areas along the stream on the way in.

Fishing

The West Fork of the Stillwater River harbors a mixed fishing opportunity. The lower reaches have brown trout, brook trout, and rainbow trout. The browns phase out upstream leaving rainbows and brookies, while cutthroats start to appear. The upper West Fork contains mostly cutthroats.

11 Lake Plateau North

General description: A long, base-camp trip into the Lake Plateau

Special attractions: A beautiful and natural mountain stream, the West Fork Stillwater River, along much of this route

Total distance: 34 miles

Type of trip: Out-and-back

Difficulty: Moderate, but long

Traffic: Light along West Fork, moderate on Lake Plateau

Maps: USGS—Pickett Pin Mountain and Tumble Mountain; RMS—Mount Douglas–Mount Wood

Starting point: West Fork Stillwater River Trailhead

Finding the trailhead: Refer to Breakneck Park Meadows, Hike 10.

Parking and trailhead facilities: Refer to Breakneck Park Meadows, Hike 10.

Key Points

8.0	Breakneck Park Meadows.
9.5	First bridge over the West Fork Stillwater River.
14.3	Lewis Creek Bridge over the West Fork Stillwater River.
16.2	Lake Diaphanous.
17.0	Wounded Man Lake.

Recommended Itinerary

You will want at least four nights for this trip, but planning for five nights gives you an extra day for exploring the Lake Plateau before heading back to your vehicle.

First night:	Breakneck Park Meadows
Second night:	Your base camp on the Lake Plateau
Third night:	Same campsite
Fourth night:	Same campsite
Fifth night:	Breakneck Park Meadows

The Hike

The West Fork Stillwater River provides the third major access route, along with the East Fork Boulder and Stillwater Rivers, into this popular, high plateau. It also provides the longest and most remote route, but it may be the easiest because of the absence of any steep climbs.

Even though this trail might not be as popular as others in the Beartooths, it's still in wonderful condition, well maintained, and easy to follow. It follows the West Fork Stillwater River for 17 miles to Lake Diaphanous, crossing two major bridges along the way, so don't fret about getting wet feet.

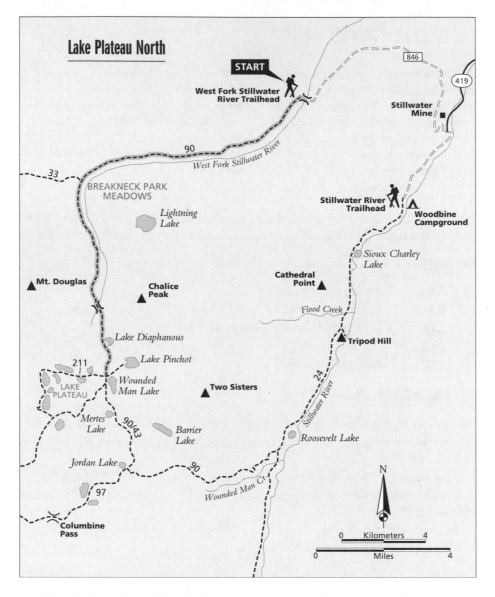

Lake Plateau North

START
West Fork Stillwater
River Trailhead

846
419

Stillwater
Mine

90

West Fork Stillwater River

33

BREAKNECK PARK
MEADOWS

Lightning
Lake

Stillwater River
Trailhead

Woodbine
Campground

Sioux Charley
Lake

Cathedral
Point

Mt. Douglas

Chalice
Peak

Flood Creek

Lake Diaphanous

Tripod Hill

Lake Pinchot

211

24

Stillwater River

LAKE
PLATEAU

Wounded
Man Lake

Two Sisters

Mertes
Lake

90/43

Barrier
Lake

Roosevelt Lake

Jordan Lake

90

N

97

Wounded Man Cr.

Columbine
Pass

0   Kilometers   4

0   Miles   4

Most backpackers will probably want to take two days to reach a base camp on Lake Plateau. Fortunately, the West Fork Stillwater River accommodates this schedule with a perfect camping area at the halfway point, Breakneck Park Meadows. Although the trail into Breakneck Park Meadows is interrupted by several beautiful smaller meadows, the expansive Breakneck Park Meadows is exceptional and much larger. Campers can choose from many grand campsites with plenty of wood for a campfire.

After leaving Breakneck Park Meadows, the trail worsens slightly but is still in good shape. The stream gradient increases slightly, but there are no big climbs, the

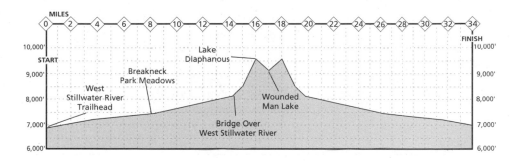

steepest grade being the mile after crossing the second bridge over the West Fork Stillwater River. Even this is much less of a climb than coming into the plateau from the east or west.

The trail continues along the east bank for just under 2 miles to the Lewis Creek Bridge, which crosses not Lewis Creek but a small branch of the West Fork Stillwater River. From here the trail climbs another 2 miles to the plateau and Lake Diaphanous. This small, high-altitude lake has one excellent campsite, so it might not be the best choice for your base camp. Lake Diaphanous lies above timberline, and the views are fantastic. Even though there are a few trees around the campsite, the wood supply is too scant for a campfire.

Most people prefer to go into the Lake Plateau for a base camp. Wounded Man Lake is another 0.8 mile down the trail, and there are many excellent campsites at nearby lakes. Take some extra time to find that five-star campsite. This means you should get an early start from your campsite at Breakneck Park Meadows, so you can reach the Lake Plateau early enough in the day to allow time to find your ideal base camp.

After spending a few enjoyable days on the Lake Plateau, return down the West Fork Stillwater River, an equally enjoyable, gradual downhill all the way.

Options

If you can arrange a shuttle or leave a vehicle at the Stillwater River Trailhead, you can make this a shuttle trip. Refer to Hike 12, Stillwater to Stillwater.

Side Trips

The side trip to Lightning Lake is enticing, but it isn't easy. There are two route options. Scramble up Lightning Creek, which joins the West Fork Stillwater River about 5 miles from the West Fork Stillwater River Trailhead. Or leapfrog over Chalice Peak from Lake Diaphanous. Be wary of the trip up Lightning Creek. It's shorter, but it's very steep and difficult, definitely a Category H hill. Although the cross-country trip over Chalice Peak looks long and difficult, it really isn't that difficult. If you visit Lightning Lake, you may experience one of your best days ever in the wilderness—

but make sure you are in good shape, have good weather, and leave camp at or before daybreak. Also, refer to Exploring the Lake Plateau on page 68.

Camping

Breakneck Park Meadows offers a variety of good campsites, and once on Lake Plateau, it's easy to find a good place for your tent near one of the many lakes.

Fishing

This trail follows the West Fork of the Stillwater (see the stream fishery description in Breakneck Park Meadows, Hike 10). Lake Diaphanous is in the main Stillwater River drainage and supports some nice rainbows. Expect company, as this is a logical place to stop coming and going. From here, it's straight downhill, southeast to Lake Pinchot for great camping and fishing for beautiful hybrids of golden, cutthroat, and rainbow descent. Flood Creek itself provides a pretty good alpine fishery and would be worth a try. There are pure golden trout in Asteroid and some of the surrounding lakes, but getting there isn't easy.

The Lake Plateau offers a variety of fishing opportunities, mostly for rainbow and cutthroat trout, and most of the lakes along trails harbor fish. For solitude, get off the trails, but ask beforehand to learn which lakes hold fish before counting on trout for dinner.

Refer to Fishing the Lake Plateau on page 69.

12 Stillwater to Stillwater

General description: A long, point-to-point route through the Lake Plateau
Special attractions: A rare chance to follow two splendid mountain rivers through the wilderness and, along the way, see the famous Lake Plateau
Total distance: 38.5 miles
Type of trip: Shuttle
Difficulty: Moderate, but long

Traffic: Light in West Fork, moderate on Lake Plateau, light over rest of route except around Sioux Charley Lake, which gets heavy use
Maps: USGS—Cathedral Point, Little Park Mountain, Pinnacle Mountain, Tumble Mountain, and Pickett Pin Mountain; RMS—Mount Douglas–Mount Wood and Cooke City–Cutoff Mountain.
Starting point: West Fork Stillwater River Trailhead

Finding the trailhead: Refer to Breakneck Park Meadows, Hike 10.
Parking and trailhead facilities: Refer to Breakneck Park Meadows, Hike 10.

Key Points

8.0	Breakneck Park Meadows.
9.5	First bridge over West Fork Stillwater River.
14.3	Lewis Creek Bridge over West Fork Stillwater River.
16.2	Lake Diaphanous.
17.0	Wounded Man Lake and junctions with Trail 211 and unofficial trail to Lake Pinchot; continue heading south on Trail 90 along the lakeshore.
17.3	Junction with Trail 43; turn left.
20.3	Jordan Pass.
21.5	Jordan Lake and junction with Trail 97; turn left.
28.5	Junction with Stillwater Trail 24; turn left.
32.3	Tripod Hill.
33.0	Flood Creek.
35.5	Sioux Charley Lake.
38.5	Stillwater River Trailhead.

Recommended Itinerary

The itinerary depends on how many nights you can spend in your base camp—ideally, at least two nights.

First night:	Breakneck Park Meadows
Second night:	Your base camp on the Lake Plateau
Third night:	Same campsite
Fourth night:	Same campsite or move to Jordan Lake
Fifth night:	Along the Stillwater River

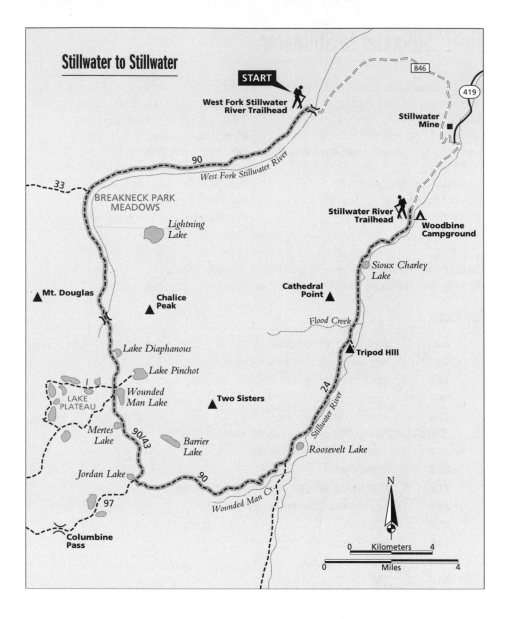

Stillwater to Stillwater

START
West Fork Stillwater
River Trailhead

846
419

Stillwater
Mine

90
West Fork Stillwater River

33

BREAKNECK PARK
MEADOWS

*Lightning
Lake*

Stillwater River
Trailhead

Woodbine
Campground

*Sioux Charley
Lake*

Mt. Douglas

Chalice
Peak

Cathedral
Point

Flood Creek

Lake Diaphanous

Lake Pinchot

Tripod Hill

LAKE
PLATEAU

*Wounded
Man Lake*

Two Sisters

24

Stillwater River

*Mertes
Lake*

90/43

*Barrier
Lake*

Roosevelt Lake

Jordan Lake

90

N

97

Wounded Man Cr.

Columbine
Pass

0   Kilometers   4

0   Miles   4

The Hike

If you can arrange a shuttle and want to see lots of wild country in one week, there's no use making the West Fork Stillwater River an out-and-back trip. Instead, just keep going through the Lake Plateau and out to civilization at the Stillwater River Trailhead and Woodbine Campground.

For the first part of the trail, refer to Breakneck Park Meadows, Hike 10, and Lake Plateau North, Hike 11. You can still set up a base camp for one or two days on the

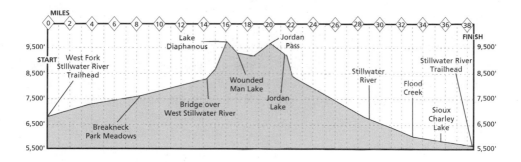

Lake Plateau, but then, instead of heading back down the West Fork, head south from Wounded Man Lake on Trail 90 over Jordan Pass to Jordan Lake. Consider staying at Jordan Lake before heading down Wounded Man Creek, still on Trail 90. Jordan Lake gets lots of use, so even though it's a forested lake, camp softly and resist the temptation to have a campfire.

A good choice for the last night out would be the confluence of Wounded Man Creek and the Stillwater River or at a huge open area along the river about a mile farther down the trail.

Be sure to read through the Lake Plateau North, Hike 11, and Lake Plateau East, Hike 14, descriptions before hitting the trail.

Options

This trip could be done in reverse, but the climb up Wounded Man Creek is tougher than the climb up the West Fork.

Side Trips

Refer to Exploring the Lake Plateau on page 68.

Fishing

Refer to page 69 for Fishing the Lake Plateau, and the fishing section of Breakneck Park Meadows, Hike 10, for fishing in the West Fork Stillwater River.

This route offers many opportunities to sample the lakes of the Lake Plateau. There are rainbows in Lake Diaphanous, rainbows and cutthroats in Wounded Man Lake, and the interesting fishery noted earlier in the Flood Creek drainage.

Heading out along the main Stillwater River can provide a lot of pan-sized trout for hungry hikers. There is a mixture of cutthroats, rainbows, and brookies to be had with minimal effort. Much of the slower water is dominated by brookies; please eat them—they taste great!

13 Sioux Charley Lake

General description: A short, easy day hike or first backpacking trip

Special attractions: A beautiful wilderness river

Type of trip: Out-and-back

Total distance: 6 miles

Difficulty: Easy

Traffic: Heavy

Maps: USGS—Cathedral Point; RMS—Mount Douglas-Mount Wood

Starting point: Stillwater River Trailhead

Finding the trailhead: This is also one of the easiest trailheads to find. In fact, you can't miss it. From Interstate 90 at Columbus, Montana, drive 15 miles south on Montana Highway 78 to Absarokee. Continue south 2 miles, turn west on the paved Nye Road (County Road 419), and go through Fishtail and Nye. Stay on this road, which eventually ends at the trailhead, about 2 miles past the Stillwater Mine. It's about 42 miles southwest of Columbus.

Parking and trailhead facilities: Plenty of parking and toilets at the Woodbine Campground at the trailhead.

The Hike

This easy day trip into Sioux Charley Lake is one of the most popular day hikes in the Beartooths, so don't be surprised to see lots of people on the trail. From the trailhead, it's 3 miles to the lake, all on an easy and gradual, consistently uphill grade.

Soon after leaving the trailhead, the trail enters a narrow canyon where, right next to the trail, the Stillwater River tumbles over a series of cascades and rapids. Many a hiker has paused here to wonder why this stream was ever named the "still water."

After passing through the narrow canyon, the trail winds its way through a heavy forest all the way to Sioux Charley Lake. Now the reason behind the river's name becomes clear. The lake is really just a large, slow-moving or "still" section of the river. Farther upstream, the river slows into several similar still-water stretches.

Look across the lake to the east to see the northernmost reaches of the dramatic forest fires of 1988. The Storm Creek Fire burned all the way down the Stillwater River drainage to Sioux Charley Lake, almost completely through the Beartooths.

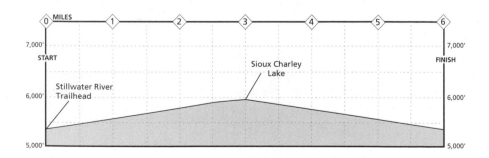

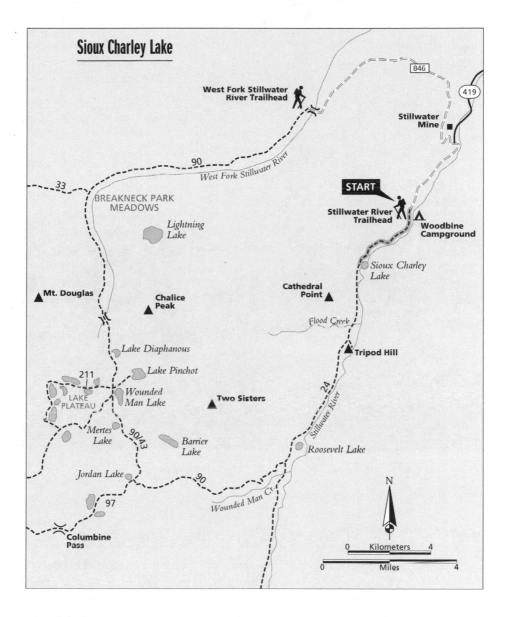

Sioux Charley Lake

West Fork Stillwater River Trailhead

846

419

Stillwater Mine

90

START

33

BREAKNECK PARK MEADOWS

Lightning Lake

West Fork Stillwater River

Stillwater River Trailhead

Woodbine Campground

Sioux Charley Lake

Mt. Douglas

Chalice Peak

Cathedral Point

Flood Creek

Lake Diaphanous

Tripod Hill

Lake Pinchot

211

LAKE PLATEAU

Wounded Man Lake

Two Sisters

24

Stillwater River

Mertes Lake

90/43

Barrier Lake

Roosevelt Lake

Jordan Lake

90

97

Wounded Man Cr.

Columbine Pass

N

0   Kilometers   4

0   Miles   4

Camping

Although this is most often considered a day trip, camping at Sioux Charley Lake is possible. The lake is heavily used, however, so be extra careful to leave zero impact while camping here. The area is already showing wear and tear, and all of us must do our part to help it reclaim its natural character.

The Stillwater River actually has some still water. Photo: Michael S. Sample

Fishing

The Stillwater River can yield a lot of pan-sized trout. There is a mixture of rainbows and brookies, with an occasional cutthroat to be found along this route. Much of the slower water is dominated by brookies. Since brook trout tend to overpopulate (to the detriment of other species), please eat them and help out the cutts and rainbows. Catch and release doesn't improve the brookies' size—it only limits the amount of food per fish. Besides, they taste great! Sioux Charley Lake is one of the best places to catch these tasty morsels, and the omnipresent brookies can provide dinner for many large parties.

14 Lake Plateau East

General description: A long, base-camp trip, the least used access route into the Lake Plateau

Special attractions: An untamed wilderness river and remoteness of Wounded Man Creek as well as a visit to the popular Lake Plateau

Type of trip: Out-and-back

Total distance: 45 miles

Difficulty: Moderate, but long

Traffic: Heavy to Sioux Charley Lake, light thereafter; moderate on Lake Plateau

Maps: USGS—Cathedral Point, Little Park Mountain, Pinnacle Mountain, and Tumble Mountain; RMS—Mount Douglas-Mount Wood and Cooke City-Cutoff Mountain

Starting point: Stillwater River Trailhead

Finding the trailhead: Refer to Sioux Charley Lake, Hike 13.
Parking and trailhead facilities: Plenty of parking and toilets at the Woodbine Campground at the trailhead.

Key Points

3.0	Sioux Charley Lake.
5.5	Flood Creek.
6.2	Tripod Hill.
11.0	Junction with Trail 90; turn right.
11.2	Wounded Man Creek.
18.0	Jordan Lake and junction with Trail 97; turn right.
19.2	Jordan Pass.
22.5	Wounded Man Lake.

Recommended Itinerary

Because of the terrain along this route, it's best to plan on two tough days to reach the plateau, even though this might be more mileage per day than you would prefer.

First night:	Along the Stillwater River, near junction with Trail 90
Second night:	Lake Plateau base camp
Third night:	Same campsite
Fourth night:	Same campsite
Fifth night:	Along the Stillwater River, near junction with Trail 24

The Hike

The first 11 miles of the trail follow the Stillwater River, a magnificent mountain stream, well-named for its frequent "still" sections. With the exception of the first 3 miles into Sioux Charley Lake, the Stillwater area was badly burned by the 1988 fires. But the forest is rapidly coming back, and the valley is lush and moist all the way.

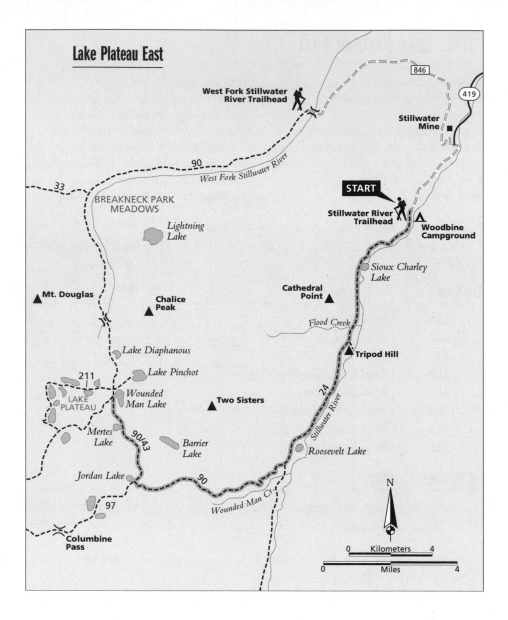

Lake Plateau East

West Fork Stillwater
River Trailhead

846

419

Stillwater
Mine

90

West Fork Stillwater River

33

BREAKNECK PARK
MEADOWS

START

Stillwater River
Trailhead

Woodbine
Campground

*Lightning
Lake*

*Sioux Charley
Lake*

Cathedral
Point

Mt. Douglas

Chalice
Peak

Flood Creek

Lake Diaphanous

Tripod Hill

211

Lake Pinchot

24

LAKE
PLATEAU

*Wounded
Man Lake*

Two Sisters

Stillwater River

*Mertes
Lake*

90/43

*Barrier
Lake*

Roosevelt Lake

Jordan Lake

90

N

Wounded Man Cr.

97

Columbine
Pass

0   Kilometers   4

0   Miles   4

Keep an eye open for the abundant white-tailed deer and moose, both common along the river.

From Sioux Charley Lake the trail runs south 2.5 miles to the base of well-named Cathedral Point and a bridge over Flood Creek. Just after the bridge a side trail heads off to the left (east) up to a scenic point, aptly named Tripod Point. The overlook affords a full perspective of the grandeur of the Stillwater River drainage, and it's definitely worth the extra stroll.

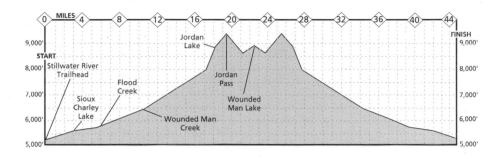

Those who make good mileage on the first day can make it to Jordan Lake for the second night out. Some backpackers might choose to spend two nights along the Stillwater before climbing the 7 miles up to Jordan Lake. Turn right onto Trail 90 going up Wounded Man Creek. It's a moderately steep climb for the first 6 miles, but the last mile is a lung-busting, Category 2 climb as the trail switchbacks 700 feet up to the lake.

To continue the main hike from Jordan Lake, head north, still on Trail 90, for almost 5 miles over Jordan Pass to Wounded Man Lake. Jordan Pass is a very easy climb from Jordan Lake, so don't fret over it. Actually, there's another climb just before Wounded Man Lake that's more difficult.

When you reach the vicinity of Wounded Man Lake, start looking for your base camp. When you find one that's just right for you, spend at least two more days enjoying and exploring the Lake Plateau before retracing your steps back down the Stillwater to the trailhead.

Options

Instead of retracing your steps down Wounded Man Creek and the Stillwater River, you could keep going and leave the Lake Plateau via the West Fork Stillwater River, Rainbow Creek, or Upsidedown Creek, but these would involve leaving a vehicle at another trailhead or arranging a pickup.

Side Trips

Really ambitious hikers can take a side trip up to Barrier Lake. Where the trail crosses the North Fork of Wounded Man Creek, scramble up the stream for about 1.25 miles. After about a quarter mile, the stream disappears, but you keep going. This is a very unusual lake. It looks like a reservoir that has been drawn down and has a flat bench around it. Even though the map shows a fairly large stream (the North Fork of Wounded Man Creek) leaving Barrier Lake, the lake actually has no outlet. Instead, the stream flows underground for about a mile before suddenly bursting out of the rocks as a giant spring, and the North Fork of Wounded Man Creek is reborn. Notice that the North Fork has very cold water, almost painful to drink. You can also hike to the Barrier Lake from the Lake Plateau.

For a great side trip from Jordan Lake, get up early the next morning and take Trail 97 from the south end of the lake over to Columbine Pass. Along the way the trail skirts Pentad and Favonius Lakes, and the scenery is magnificent, especially near the pass.

Refer to Exploring the Lake Plateau on page 68 for more side trips.

Camping

Camping is available anywhere along the Stillwater River. With an early start, travelers might make it to a great campsite on a smooth stretch of river about 1 mile before the junction with Trail 90 (and about 10 miles from the trailhead). This is a slightly better campsite than camping at Wounded Man Creek. Looking at the map, some people may want to head for Roosevelt Lake as a potential campsite. But this is really Roosevelt "marsh," and it doesn't have any good campsites. Wood is abundant throughout the Stillwater for evening campfires.

Jordan Lake is a delightful place with several campsites on the south end just east of where the trail hits the lake. Together, the sites make a camping area large enough to accommodate a large party or two or three small parties. The campsite is marginal for campfires, but if a fire is absolutely needed, there is an adequate supply of firewood in the area.

Once at Wounded Man Lake, spend some time selecting a good site for base camp. There are many options such as the Rainbow Lakes to the west or Lake Pinchot to the east. The best campsite at Wounded Man Lake is just southwest of the lake.

Fishing

This route offers less opportunity to sample lakes on the way to the Lake Plateau, but there's plenty of good fishing along the way. Heading up along the main Stillwater River can provide a lot of great fishing for lunch-sized trout. There is a mixture of cutthroats, rainbows, and brookies to be had without much effort. Much of the slower water is dominated by brookies, with cutthroats becoming more common as you get closer to the Wounded Man Creek drainage, which supports a mainly cutthroat trout fishery, although rainbows share Pentad and Favonius Lakes with cutts. Jordan Lake holds nice cutthroats that can be counted on to provide dinner. Also, refer to the fishing information for Sioux Charley Lake on page 92, and Fishing the Lake Plateau on page 69.

15 Lake Wilderness

General description: A little-used, off-trail overnighter
Special attractions: Extraordinary mountain scenery and solitude—a favorite of climbers
Total distance: 14 miles
Type of trip: Out-and-back

Difficulty: Mostly off-trail and difficult
Traffic: Light
Maps: USGS—Mount Wood; RMS—Mount Douglas-Mount Wood
Starting point: Lake Wilderness Trailhead

Finding the trailhead: The unofficial Lake Wilderness Trailhead is difficult to find, so allow for some extra time to get there. Drive 15 miles south from Columbus, Montana, on Montana Highway 78 through Absarokee. About 2 miles after Absarokee, turn right (west) onto County Road 419. On the west edge of the tiny community of Dean, turn southwest onto the Benbow Mine Road. Follow the road 12 miles to the mine. Go by the mine; after a half mile or so, the road turns west and switchbacks another half mile up to The Golf Course, a large, open meadow that long ago somebody thought looked like a golf course. The poorly marked trailhead is at the south end of The Golf Course, right by a lone fence post where the road gradually narrows to become a trail. You need a high-clearance, four-wheel-drive vehicle to reach this trailhead.
Parking and trailhead facilities: Limited parking; no toilet.

Key Points

2.0	Snow chute; end of established trail.
6.0	Edge of plateau; drop down to Lake Wilderness.

The Hike

To do this mostly off-trail, high-elevation trip, hikers must be proficient with compass and topo map—and be well conditioned. Also wait for good weather, but prepare for the worst in case a storm blows in.

The well-defined trail heads off in a southerly direction from The Golf Course above Benbow Mine. It immediately (but briefly) descends into a forested saddle and then climbs gradually up to the magnificent Stillwater Plateau. After a few short zigzags, the trail heads off to the west. The second mile of the trail is lined with cairns even though the tread is distinct.

After 2 miles, at 10,000 feet and at the head of a snow chute, the trail disappears. Get out the topo map and compass and keep them handy for the next 4 miles until Lake Wilderness is in sight.

Take off cross-country, bearing southwest for about a mile and then turn south for about another 2.5 miles. Be sure to continue climbing gradually, trying to stay on or slightly above the 10,500-foot contour instead of dropping elevation to where cliffs block the way. As soon as you get close to the steepening slopes of 12,661-foot Mount Wood, look off to the south to see Lake Wilderness.

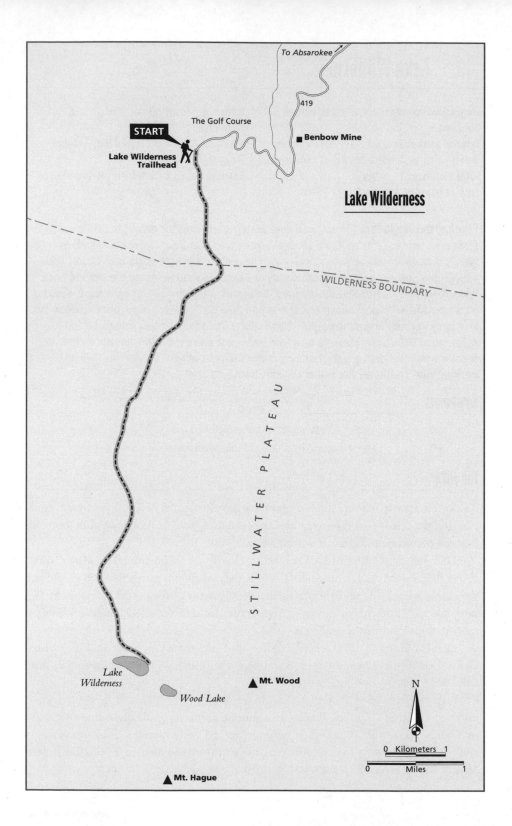

To Absarokee

419

The Golf Course

START

Lake Wilderness
Trailhead

■ Benbow Mine

Lake Wilderness

WILDERNESS BOUNDARY

S T I L L W A T E R   P L A T E A U

Lake
Wilderness

Wood Lake

▲ Mt. Wood

N

0   Kilometers   1

0   Miles   1

▲ Mt. Hague

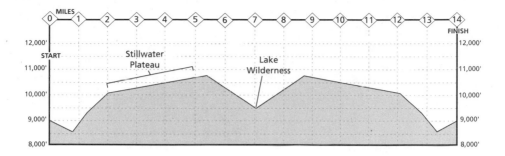

There's no graceful way to get down the 1,000-foot drop to the lake, but it's slightly better to head out across the talus slope to the left into the forest until you intersect the inlet stream and then follow the stream to the lake.

Side Trips

For a great side trip, take the half-mile scramble over to Wood Lake. It's a short but tough trip. Wood Lake has deep emerald green water and a fantastic backdrop of 12,661-foot Mount Wood and 12,328-foot Mount Hague. A fluted, cathedral-like wall extends across the saddle between the two peaks creating a gothic effect.

Camping

Lake Wilderness has a shortage of great campsites, but you can find a few good sites for small parties along the north shore and near the outlet. There's also a possible camp-site in a meadow about a quarter mile northwest of the lake. The outlet stream is deep and difficult to ford. Wood is plentiful, so enjoy a low-impact campfire. Campsites are even more limited at Wood Lake than Lake Wilderness, so it's better to visit this spot on a side trip and camp elsewhere.

Fishing

Lake Wilderness supports a nice population of cutthroat trout. Wood Lake is stocked with cutthroats, by helicopter, on an eight-year cycle (due again in 2005). Fly-fishing in both lakes is tough because of the forested shoreline. Any fish in nearby streams will be migrants from these lakes.

16 Mystic Lake

General description: An easy day trip
Special attractions: Mystic Lake, definitely worth the trip, and the Mystic Lake hydroelectric project
Type of trip: Out-and-back
Total distance: 7 miles

Difficulty: Moderate
Traffic: Heavy
Maps: USGS—Granite Peak and Alpine; RMS—Cooke City-Cutoff Mountain
Starting point: West Rosebud Trailhead

Finding the trailhead: Drive 15 miles south from Columbus, Montana, on Montana Highway 78 through Absarokee. About 2 miles past Absarokee, turn right (west) to Fishtail on County Road 419. Drive through Fishtail and go west and south about 1 mile. Turn left (south) along West Rosebud Road. About 6 miles later, take another left (southeast) at the sign for West Rosebud Lake. It's another 14 miles of bumpy gravel road from this point to the trailhead. In total, it's 27 miles from Absarokee and 42 miles from Columbus. The road ends and the trail begins right at the Mystic Dam Power Station.

It might not seem clear exactly where the trail begins. After parking your vehicle, walk up the road about 200 yards through the Montana Power Company compound to the actual trailhead.
Parking and trailhead facilities: Spacious parking lot with toilet.

The Hike

For those who aren't interested in strenuous mountain climbing or long arduous trips, the Mystic Lake trail offers an excellent choice for an unhurried day in the wilderness. It also offers some spectacular scenery with the unusual twist of being able to observe how the Mystic Lake Power Station was built.

Besides being a popular day trip, this is also the major launching point for the legions attempting to climb Granite Peak each year. Don't expect to have the trail to yourself.

From the trailhead follow West Rosebud Creek. After crossing an overpass and a bridge over the creek, the trail follows a power line for a short way. After leaving this "sign of civilization" behind, the trail switchbacks through open rock fields, offering a great view of the West Rosebud valley, including West Rosebud and Emerald Lakes.

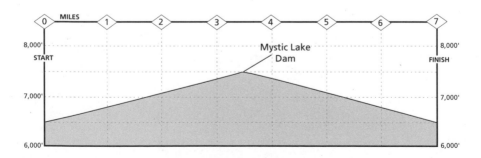

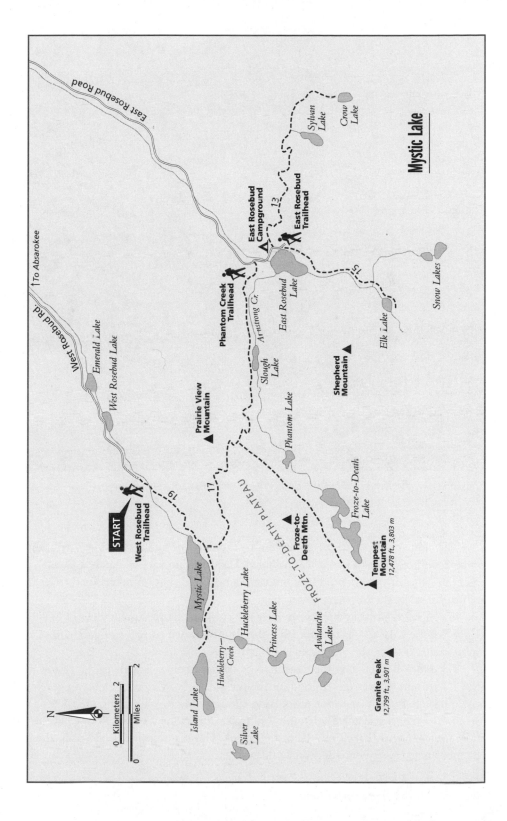

Mystic Lake

Mystic Lake, the deepest lake in the Beartooths.

The climb doesn't seem that steep, but by the time the trail reaches the dam at the eastern end of Mystic Lake, it has ascended 1,200 feet in 3 miles, barely a Category 3 climb. Normally, that would be considered a big climb, but for hikers who aren't in a hurry, it really doesn't seem like it.

When the trail finally breaks out over the ridge, it affords a great view of Mystic Dam. Mystic Lake is a natural lake, but the dam increased its size and depth, now, at more than 200 feet, the deepest in the Beartooths.

The sandy beach along the east shore of the lake below is perhaps the largest in the Beartooths. This makes a good lunch spot for those who plan to turn back for the trailhead. But it's far better to set aside enough time to walk along the lake for a while. The trail is very scenic, flat, and well maintained. Plus, it's difficult to realize the full scope of Mystic Lake from the first overlook. This is a huge lake, and a walk along its shore is the best way to appreciate this fact.

Some people might think that the presence of the dam detracts from the wildness of the place. But Montana Power Company has done as much as possible to keep the intrusion to a minimum, and after all, the dam was here long before the Absaroka-Beartooths was designated as wilderness. At any rate, most visitors have little difficulty enjoying the scenery and fresh air.

Side Trips

If you still have some energy left when you reach Mystic Lake, consider hiking along the shoreline for one or two miles before heading back. If you're very energetic, you could hike up to the top of Froze-to-Death Plateau from the lake.

Camping

You can find several camp spots along Mystic's east shore, but the shoreline is heavily used and seems more suited to leisurely day hiking than camping.

Fishing

There are a lot of fish willing to be caught north of the trailhead at Emerald and West Rosebud Lakes. Both lakes support hefty fish with brown trout, cutthroat trout, and whitefish all common. Rainbows are stocked in both lakes to provide some additional excitement.

Mystic Lake supports a rainbow trout fishery that is great when the fish are feeding and frustrating when they are not, although the fickle rainbows found there can usually be coaxed. The rainbows can be counted on for a good workout. The stream up to Mystic is very steep and doesn't provide great habitat for fish, so save your effort for the lake.

17 Granite Peak

General description: A long, steep backpack to a traditional launching point for ascents of Montana's highest mountain, Granite Peak; strictly for experienced, well-conditioned hikers

Special attractions: A chance to view or climb 12,799-foot Granite Peak.

Type of trip: Out-and-back

Total distance: 21 miles, plus the climb up Granite Peak

Difficulty: Difficult

Traffic: Moderate

Maps: USGS—Granite Peak and Alpine; RMS—Cooke City-Cutoff Mountain and Alpine-Mount Maurice

Starting point: West Rosebud Trailhead

Finding the trailhead: Refer to Mystic Lake, Hike 16.
Parking and trailhead facilities: Spacious parking lot with toilet.

Key Points

3.0	Mystic Lake Dam.
3.5	Junction with Phantom Creek Trail 17.
6.4	Froze-to-Death Divide.
10.5	Tempest Mountain.

The Hike

Of the two trailheads used for this hike (West Rosebud and East Rosebud), the West Rosebud is more popular, mainly because it's slightly shorter and cuts 400 feet of elevation gain off the approach to Granite Peak. Either trailhead leads to the same place—the saddle between Prairie View Mountain and Froze-to-Death Mountain. And whether coming from the east or west, the trails are for rugged individuals. Just reaching the saddle where the two trails meet is a climb of 3,500 feet from Mystic Lake or 3,900 from East Rosebud Lake.

Once at the saddle, turn southwest and follow a series of cairns around the north side of Froze-to-Death Mountain. The destination is an 11,600-foot plateau on the west edge of Tempest Mountain, 1.6 miles north of Granite Peak. You can camp here.

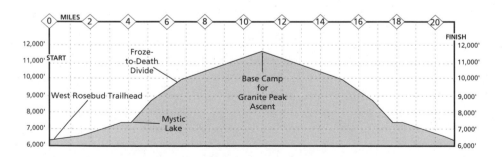

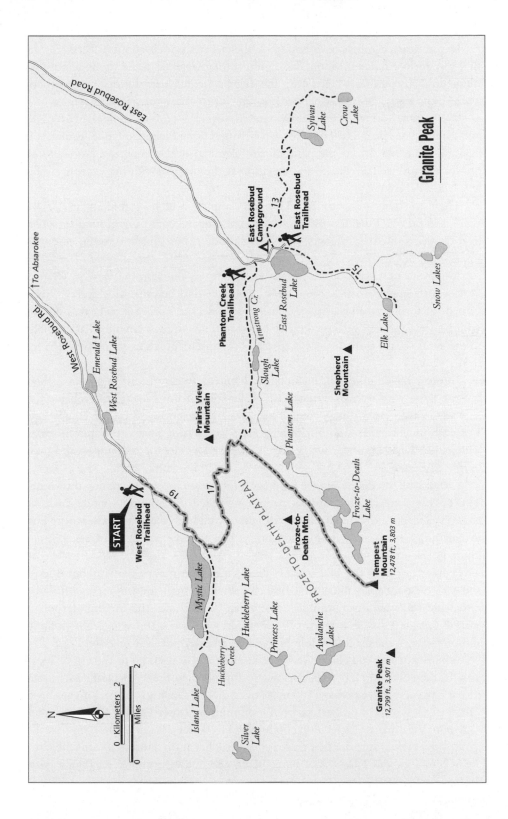

Granite Peak

N

0 Kilometers 2
0 Miles 2

To Absarokee

East Rosebud Road

West Rosebud Rd.

Emerald Lake

West Rosebud Lake

Island Lake

Silver Lake

Mystic Lake

Huckleberry Creek

Huckleberry Lake

Princess Lake

Avalanche Lake

FROZE-TO-DEATH PLATEAU

Froze-to-Death Mtn.

Tempest Mountain
12,478 ft, 3,803 m

Granite Peak
12,799 ft, 3,901 m

START
West Rosebud Trailhead

19

17

Prairie View Mountain

Phantom Creek Trailhead

Armstrong Cr.

Slough Lake

Phantom Lake

Froze-to-Death Lake

Shepherd Mountain

Elk Lake

East Rosebud Campground

East Rosebud Trailhead

East Rosebud Lake

13

15

Snow Lakes

Sylvan Lake

Crow Lake

In past years, climbers have built rock shelters (rock walls about 3 feet high) on the west edge of Tempest Mountain to protect themselves from the strong winds that frequently blast the area. However, the Forest Service may have removed them because the area is designated wilderness, which prohibits permanent structures.

By the time you reach Tempest Mountain, you have covered more than 10 miles and gained more than 5,000 feet. You have crossed timberline many miles earlier, and now, rock, ice, and sky are the predominant elements of the landscape. No plants or grasses can survive the climate and elevation at the plateau, with the exception of a few hardy lichens.

There are some advantages to hiking and camping in such a forbidding place. The wind is so prevalent that few mosquitoes ever attempt takeoffs from ground zero. The bear danger is nil. And, of course, the high altitude grants superb views in all directions.

Along the west edge of the plateau leading up to Tempest, the view of Granite Peak is awesome. Granite buttresses rise almost vertically from Huckleberry Creek Canyon to form a broad wall nearly a half mile wide. The north face is heavily etched with fissures running almost straight up between the buttresses. Granite Glacier clings to the center of the wall. At the top, a series of pinnacles builds from the west side up to the peak.

To those skilled in technical climbing, Granite is an easy ascent in good weather, but for those with little experience, it's challenging, if not dangerous. Probably the best advice is to go with someone who has the experience and proper equipment. Especially important is a good climbing rope for crossing several precipitous spots. The easiest approach is across the ridge that connects Granite to Tempest and then up the east side.

Check with the Forest Service for more information before attempting this climb. The FS has a special brochure for people interested in climbing Granite Peak. In recent years not one summer has passed without mishaps and close calls, mostly due to bad judgment. One sobering concern is the extreme difficulty of rescuing an injured person from Granite.

People have tried this hike and climb at almost all times of the year, but August and early September are the most logical choices. Even then, sudden storms with subzero wind chills are a real possibility. Snow can fall anytime. And the thunderstorms around Granite Peak are legendary. Be prepared with warm and windproof clothing and preferably a shelter that will hold together and stay put in strong wind.

Whether or not you climb Granite, take the time to walk up to the top of Tempest. To the north and 2,000 feet below are Turgulse and Froze-to-Death Lakes. On a clear day you can see perhaps 100 miles out onto the Great Plains. And if you move a little east toward Mount Peal, you can look southwest over Granite Peak's shoulder to Mount Villard and Glacier Peak, both over 12,000 feet.

It should be no surprise that there is little wildlife at this altitude. Nearer the saddle, where grass and other hardy alpine plants eke out an existence, mountain goats

Granite Peak, Montana's highest mountain and one of the most popular destinations in the Beartooths. Photo: Michael S. Sample

are commonly seen. An occasional golden eagle soars through this country looking for marmots and pikas. Down closer to the trailheads, a few mule deer and black bears make their summer homes.

Options

Those who come in from the East Rosebud Trailhead may wish to take an alternate way back. From the east edge of the plateau to the west-northwest of Turgulse Lake, it's possible to descend into the bowl that holds Turgulse and hike past Froze-to-Death Lake and Phantom Lake. Then cross the hill back to rejoin the trail above Slough Lake. There is no trail for most of this route, and some investigating between Froze-to-Death and Phantom Lakes may be necessary, but it is an interesting way out for the fit and adventurous. And high adventure is what this trip is all about in the first place. If you have arranged a shuttle or pickup, you can go out the East Rosebud instead of retracing your steps back to the West Rosebud.

Side Trips

Even if you elect to retrace your steps back to the West Rosebud, you might want to dip over to Turgulse and Froze-to-Death Lakes.

Camping

Camping on the Froze-to-Death Plateau or Tempest Mountain is for hardy, well-prepared backpackers only. There are plenty of places to camp. The trick is keeping your tent from blowing away. This entire area is way above timberline and gets heavy use, so please adhere strictly to zero-impact camping ethics.

Fishing

No fishing on this route with the exception of Mystic Lake. Refer to fishing information in Mystic Lake, Hike 16.

18 Rosebud to Rosebud

General description: A moderately long and difficult shuttle best suited for a long day trip

Special attractions: Outstanding scenery

Type of trip: Shuttle

Total distance: 13 miles

Difficulty: Difficult

Traffic: Moderate

Maps: USGS—Granite Peak and Alpine; RMS—Cooke City-Cutoff and Alpine-Mount Maurice

Starting point: West Rosebud Trailhead

Finding the trailhead: Refer to Mystic Lake, Hike 16.

Parking and trailhead facilities: Spacious parking lot with toilet.

Key Points

3.0	Mystic Lake Dam.
3.5	Junction with Phantom Creek Trail 17.
6.4	Froze-to-Death Plateau.
10.2	Slough Lake.
13.0	Phantom Creek Trailhead.

The Hike

If you're not a climber, but you're in good shape and want to see lots of sensational scenery in one long day, consider arranging a shuttle from West Rosebud Trailhead to East Rosebud Trailhead via the Phantom Creek Trail. Even better, talk some friends into a "trade keys" hike. This hike is a perfect choice for such a plan. One party starts at West Rosebud and the other at East Rosebud. Meet on top of Froze-to-Death Plateau for lunch, trade keys, and drive each other's vehicle home.

The trading keys plan can be risky on long trips where folks want to stop to fish, climb, or partake in other activities that might lead them off the trail. In this case, most of the trip is above timberline and on a well-maintained trail. It's almost impossible to miss each other. Whoever gets to the top of the plateau first should just relax and wait for the other party.

But be sure to pick a day with a good weather forecast. And roll out of bed early. This is a 13-mile day hike with lots of elevation gain—3,668 feet from West Rosebud and 3,932 feet from East Rosebud. Weather can be completely unpredictable at this elevation, but normally the morning is better weather for hiking. Thunderstorms commonly roll over the plateau in midafternoon.

It would be difficult to argue which approach to the plateau is more scenic—definitely a win-win situation. It's about the same distance to an ideal rendezvous site on the top of Froze-to-Death Plateau. The trail is in terrific shape the entire way.

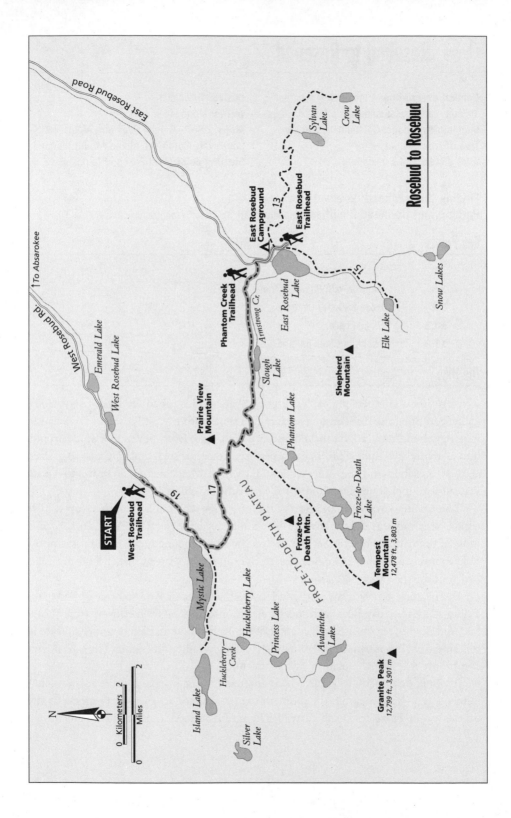

Rosebud to Rosebud

To Absarokee

West Rosebud Rd

East Rosebud Road

START — West Rosebud Trailhead

19

17

Emerald Lake

West Rosebud Lake

Mystic Lake

Island Lake

Silver Lake

Huckleberry Lake

Huckleberry Creek

Princess Lake

Avalanche Lake

Prairie View Mountain ▲

FROZE-TO-DEATH PLATEAU

Froze-to-Death Mtn. ▲

Granite Peak
12,799 ft., 3,901 m ▲

Tempest Mountain ▲
12,478 ft., 3,803 m

Froze-to-Death Lake

Shepherd Mountain ▲

Phantom Lake

Slough Lake

Armstrong Cr.

Phantom Creek Trailhead

East Rosebud Lake

East Rosebud Campground

East Rosebud Trailhead

13

15

Sylvan Lake

Crow Lake

Elk Lake

Snow Lakes

N

0   Kilometers   2

0   Miles   2

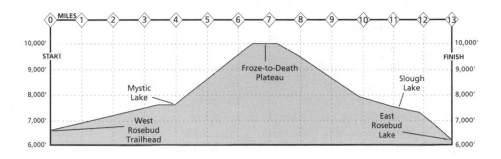

Options

This long day hike can be launched from either end with no real difference in difficulty.

Side Trips

Since this is a long, strenuous day hike, there probably won't be much time or energy for side trips, but a stroll along the shoreline of Mystic Lake is most pleasant. Ditto for a walk on Froze-to-Death Plateau, assuming, of course, that thunderheads are not descending upon you.

Camping

This trip really doesn't offer much for overnight campsites. But camping is available at the upper end of Slough Lake on the East Rosebud side and along the east shore of Mystic Lake on the West Rosebud side. Those who camp should practice strict zero-impact camping techniques, as this area receives heavy use (mainly because of the fanatical interest in climbing Granite Peak).

Fishing

If doing this as a day hike, there won't be much time to get in any relaxed fishing. The rainbows are generally willing in Mystic Lake, as are the brookies along the lower stretches of Phantom Creek.

19 Island Lake

General description: One of the easiest-to-reach base camps in the Beartooths, but still with numerous options for side trips
Special attractions: So much to see and do all within reach of base camp at Island Lake
Type of trip: Out-and-back
Total distance: 12 miles, plus side trips

Difficulty: Moderate, but with some difficult (optional) side trips
Traffic: Heavy around Mystic Lake, light at Island Lake
Maps: USGS—Granite Peak; RMS—Cooke City-Cutoff Mountain
Starting point: West Rosebud Trailhead

Finding the trailhead: Refer to Mystic Lake, Hike 16.
Parking and trailhead facilities: Spacious parking lot with toilet.

Key Points

3.0	Mystic Lake Dam.
3.5	Junction with Phantom Creek Trail 17.
5.7	Huckleberry Creek.
6.0	Island Lake.

The Hike

The West Rosebud Trailhead seems to have one disadvantage—or advantage, depending on your point of view. It's mostly suited for "just passing through."

The first three trips from this trailhead offer either day hikes or trips that pass through the West Rosebud for other destinations. Island Lake, however, affords a great chance to stay a few days and enjoy the many wonders of the Upper West Rosebud valley. It's especially suited for hikers who like to base camp.

The first 3 miles up to the Mystic Lake Dam are described in the Mystic Lake trip, Hike 16. From the junction of the Mystic Lake and Phantom Creek Trails, hike along the east shore of Mystic Lake on a well-maintained trail for 2.5 miles. Then it's another 0.5 mile to Island Lake. Just before the end of the lake, the trail crosses Huckleberry Creek, which tumbles down from several lakes in the west shadow of Gran-

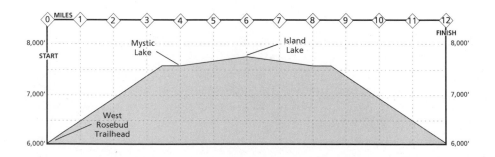

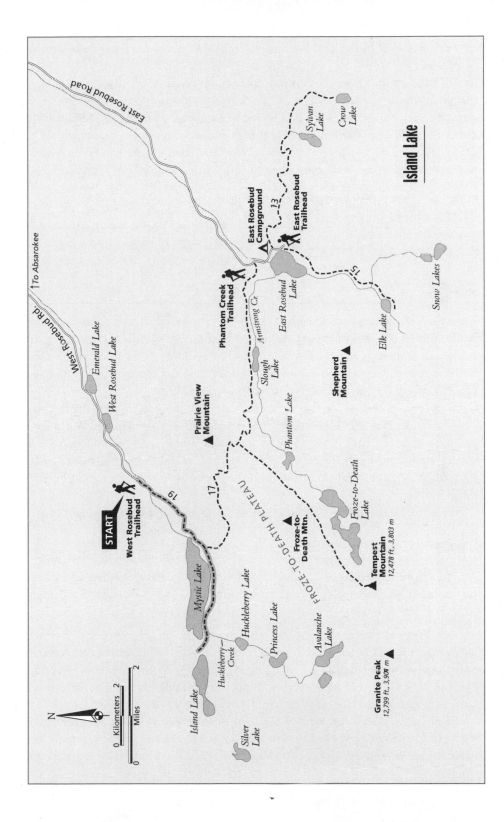

Island Lake

ite Peak. This is a big stream, but fortunately, the Forest Service has built a sturdy bridge over it.

If you're staying overnight at Island Lake, you must cross West Rosebud Creek to get to the choice campsites on the west side of the stream, and there's no bridge. In August or September, this won't be a problem. You can cross easily on a logjam at the outlet of Island Lake. Early in the year at high water, however, this crossing could be more difficult. Lots of water comes down West Rosebud Creek. The Forest Service does not maintain the trail beyond a point just before crossing West Rosebud Creek or above Island Lake.

Options

This route works well as a base camp, but you can also make this an enjoyable day hike.

Side Trips

The trail continues on beyond Island Lake to Silver Lake, which also offers base camp opportunities. The trail to Silver Lake is muddy and brushy, and the campsites aren't as pleasant as those at Island Lake. Instead, consider visiting Silver Lake on a day trip from base camp. Another good possibility is a hike up Huckleberry Creek to Princess Lake and, for the well conditioned, on to Avalanche Lake.

Two more potential side trips include a long trek to Grasshopper Glacier and a climb up to a series of lakes—Nugget, Beckworth, Frenco, Nemidji, and Weeluma— just west of Island Lake. Only those in good shape and savvy in wilderness skills should attempt these side trips. It's possible, of course, to just hang around and explore the Island Lake and Mystic Lake country for a day or two and not miss out on anything.

Refer to the list of side trips in Where to Go from Island Lake on page 115.

Camping

Just after crossing West Rosebud Creek, you'll find a huge flat area where many large parties could camp and still not bother each other.

Fishing

Starting at Island Lake anglers will begin to find an occasional cutthroat trout mixed in with the rainbow population. These have migrated down from Weeluma, Nemidji, Nugget, Beckworth, and Frenco Lakes, all pure cutthroat fisheries. Silver Lake sports some nice-size hybrid trout that are hard to catch, but worth the effort.

While many people use Trail 17 to access Granite Peak, a lesser-used alternative is up Huckleberry Creek. Huckleberry Lake supports a healthy rainbow population, while Avalanche and the Storm Lakes above are stocked with willing cutthroats that grow above average in size and weight. Mountain goats frequent this basin, and although this route is a steeper approach to Granite Peak, the added aspect of great fishing may make the climb worth it.

WHERE TO GO FROM ISLAND LAKE
After arriving at base camp at Island Lake, most people want to spend a day or two exploring. Here's a list of suggested day trips rated for difficulty as follows: Human (easy for almost everyone, including children), Semi-human (moderately difficult), or Animal (don't try it unless you're very fit and wilderness-wise). Also refer to more detailed rating information in the chapter Using this Guidebook.

Destination	Difficulty
Granite Peak	Animal
Froze-to-Death Plateau	Human
Silver Lake	Human
Princess Lake	Semi-human
Avalanche Lake	Animal
Weeluma and Nemidji Lakes	Animal
Frenco, Nugget, and Beckworth Lakes	Animal
Star Lake	Animal
Grasshopper Glacier	Animal

20 The Beaten Path

General description: The most popular trans-Beartooth route

Special attractions: Perhaps the best opportunity to really experience the breadth and diversity of the Beartooths

Type of trip: Shuttle

Total distance: 26 miles, not counting side trips

Difficulty: Long and strenuous, but not technically difficult or dangerous

Traffic: Heavy

Maps: USGS—Alpine, Castle Mountain, and Fossil Lake; RMS—Alpine-Mount Maurice and Cooke City-Cutoff Mountain

Starting point: East Rosebud Trailhead

Finding the trailhead: From Interstate 90 at Columbus, Montana, drive south 29 miles on Montana Highway 78 to Roscoe. Drive through this small ranching community, being careful not to stop at the Grizzly Bar—until the return trip, of course, when you'll be really ready for the famous Grizzly Burger. At the north end of Roscoe, the road turns to gravel and goes about 14.5 miles to the East Rosebud Trailhead. About 7 miles from Roscoe, the road crosses East Rosebud Creek and forks. Take a sharp right and continue south along the creek. The road is mostly gravel, except for a 4-mile paved section near the end.

Parking and trailhead facilities: A huge parking lot at the trailhead with room for large horse trailers; toilet; also has a campground nearby.

Key Points

3.0	Elk Lake.
6.0	Rimrock Lake.
7.0	Rainbow Lake.
9.0	Lake at Falls.
9.9	Big Park Lake.
10.2	Junction with trail to Echo Lake; turn left.
11.8	Duggan Lake.
12.0	Impasse Falls.
12.8	Twin Outlets Lake.
14.0	Dewey Lake.
16.0	Fossil Lake.
16.8	East Rosebud/Clarks Fork Divide.
16.8	Gallatin/Custer National Forest boundary.
17.1	Windy Lake.
17.8	Skull Lake.
18.4	Bald Knob Lake.
18.8	Ouzel Lake.
20.0	Russell Lake.

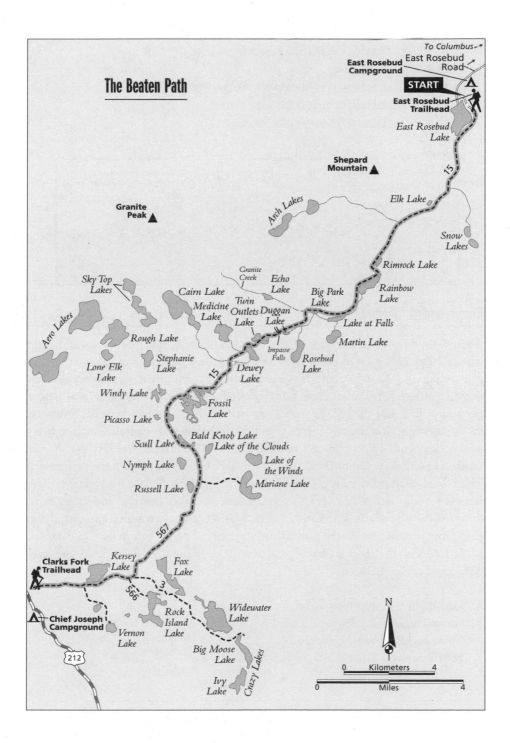

The Beaten Path

To Columbus

East Rosebud Campground

East Rosebud Road

START

East Rosebud Trailhead

East Rosebud Lake

Shepard Mountain ▲

Arch Lakes

Elk Lake

15

Snow Lakes

Granite Peak ▲

Rimrock Lake

Sky Top Lakes

Granite Creek

Echo Lake

Big Park Lake

Rainbow Lake

Cairn Lake

Twin Outlets Lake

Medicine Lake

Duggan Lake

Lake at Falls

Aero Lakes

Rough Lake

Impasse Falls

Martin Lake

Stephanie Lake

Rosebud Lake

Lone Elk Lake

15

Dewey Lake

Windy Lake

Fossil Lake

Picasso Lake

Bald Knob Lake

Scull Lake

Lake of the Clouds

Nymph Lake

Lake of the Winds

Russell Lake

Mariane Lake

567

Clarks Fork Trailhead

Kersey Lake

Fox Lake

3

566

Chief Joseph Campground

Rock Island Lake

Widewater Lake

Vernon Lake

Big Moose Lake

Crazy Lakes

212

Ivy Lake

N

0 Kilometers 4

0 Miles 4

22.0	Junction with trail to Fox Lake; turn right.
22.2	Junction with Crazy Lakes Trail No. 3; turn right.
23.0	Junction with Trail 566 to Rock Island Lake; turn right.
24.5	Kersey Lake.
24.7	Junction with trail to Vernon Lake; turn right.
25.2	Junction with trail to Curl Lake; turn left.
26.0	Clarks Fork Trailhead, U.S. Highway 212.

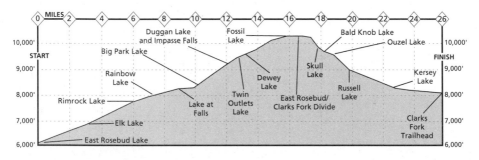

Recommended Itinerary

Twenty-six miles is not a bragging distance, and a strong hiker could do the entire trip in a day. However, to really make this a best backpacking vacation, you should plan on taking at least four days. If you get a late start, you might want to stay the first night at little Elk Lake, but most hikers go at least as far as Rainbow Lake before pitching a tent. For the second night, you have a choice of hundreds of campsites. Pick a good one and stay two nights, spending the second day experiencing the heart of the Beartooth Plateau around Fossil Lake. You can hike all the way out to the Clarks Fork Trailhead from Fossil Lake in one day, but if you prefer a less demanding schedule, there are also many campsites along the way. Russell Lake is a logical choice, but everybody else has that idea, too, so this lake is always crowded and shows signs of overuse. Strive for an alternate campsite. Many backpackers search for that idyllic base camp somewhere on the plateau and stay several nights before leaving paradise. Be sure to read the most current Forest Service camping regulations at an information board at the trailhead.

First night: Rainbow Lake
Second night: Somewhere around Fossil Lake
Third night: Same campsite
Fourth night: Russell, Fox, or Rock Island Lake

The Hike

Many people who know the Beartooths say the East Rosebud is the most scenic valley of all. It's filled with lakes and waterfalls that would be major tourism attractions anywhere else. Here, there are so many, most don't even have names. The cutthroat-filled lakes bring a smile to any angler's face, and climbers love the place because of the endless array of rock faces. Families and friends frequently choose The Beaten Path for that long-planned wilderness adventure. Consequently, the East Rosebud Trailhead is probably the most heavily used in the Beartooths. Adding even more use to the area is the small community of summer homes called Alpine right at the trailhead. The summer homes extend up both sides of the lower sections of East Rosebud Lake, closing off much of the lake to public use.

This backpacking trip showcases all the beauty, austerity, emptiness, and majesty of the Beartooths. It's a great introduction to the region's richness, diversity, and starkness, traveling through the lowest bottomlands and the highest plateaus. Along the way the route skirts dozens of trout-filled lakes and stunning waterfalls. It penetrates rich forests and wanders the treeless, lichen-covered Beartooth Plateau. This trail touches the true essence of the Beartooths.

This is the land of rushing water. Waterfalls and frothy, cascading streams are everywhere. There's no such scenery in Yellowstone National Park. Nonetheless, we should all be elated to have the park so near, because it sucks up most of the visitors and leaves places like the East Rosebud for us.

Still, this trail receives relatively heavy use compared to other routes in the Beartooths. Amazingly, however, The Beaten Path does not seem crowded. Even though hundreds of people may be somewhere along the 26-mile trail at any given time, most hikers would never know it. It's always a surprise to meet another party on the trail, and quiet spots to camp abound.

For uninterrupted solitude, and to really enjoy and experience the Beartooths, do make an effort to get off The Beaten Path. This trail has dozens of options for off-trail adventures—which is one reason the Beartooths can swallow up hundreds of people and leave the trail seemingly abandoned.

Don't take this trip lightly. It requires a minimum of four nights out, but avid explorers could stay two weeks and not see anything twice. This trail description assumes a minimum of four nights out.

It's also hard to make good time on this trail. There are simply too many distractions—too many scenic vistas, too many hungry trout, too many fields of juicy berries. Plan on traveling about a mile per hour slower than normal.

Also, be sure to plan this trip carefully. The first big issue is transportation. The best option is to arrange with another group of hikers to do the trip at the same time. Each party starts at opposite ends of the trail, meeting at a campsite midway along the trail. Spend a day or two together, then head out and drive each other's vehicle home. Or leave a vehicle at one end of the trip and drive around to the other trailhead, or arrange to be picked up.

The entire 26 miles of trail is well maintained and easy to follow, so even a beginning backpacker can master it with ease. However, getting off The Beaten Path requires advanced wilderness skills.

The first 3 miles into Elk Lake are well-traveled and go by quickly. Expect to see lots of people on this popular stretch of trail. But every step of the way beyond Elk Lake is a step deeper and deeper into the wilderness, and it really seems like it. Elk Lake has a few campsites, but Rainbow Lake (7 miles in) is a better choice for the first night out if there's enough daylight left to get there.

Just after Elk Lake, the trail passes through an area where wild berries are as abundant as anywhere in the Beartooths, so browsers beware. Progress can slow to glacial speed. For about a mile a kaleidoscope of berries beckons from trailside, with huge crops of most species found in the Beartooths in abundance, especially huckleberries, thimbleberries, and wild raspberries, all nicely ripe in mid-August.

From berry heaven the trail breaks out of the forest and climbs about 800 feet through a monstrous rock field to Rimrock Lake. For a mile or so below the lake, East Rosebud Creek is little more than a long set of rapids. Apparently a big rockslide formed a natural dam and backed up Rimrock Lake. Take a rest on the rock field and look around at the trail to marvel at how it was constructed. Building a trail here was no small feat, especially negotiating the steep slopes around Rimrock Lake.

The trail crosses East Rosebud Creek on a sturdy wooden bridge at the outlet. Then it skirts above the west side of the lake, the tread expertly etched out of the rock face. After the climb to get here, camping at Rimrock Lake might seem like a good idea. But campsites are limited here, so it's better to drag on for another mile to Rainbow Lake for the first night out.

Both Rimrock and Rainbow Lakes display a beautiful blue-green color (often called "glacier milk") indicative of a glacier-fed lake. Camping at Rainbow Lake affords a great view of Whirlpool Creek as it falls into the lake after tumbling down from Sundance Glacier on 12,408-foot Castle Rock Mountain.

The terrain at the upper end of Rainbow Lake flattens out and offers plenty of good campsites. Other parties probably will be camped here, but the area is big enough to provide ample solitude for all campers. Horse campers use this place heavily, but the Forest Service has required horses to stay above the trail, leaving several excellent campsites below the trail for backpackers only.

After the great scenery at Rimrock and Rainbow Lakes, you might think that it can't get much better. Guess again. Plan on lots of camera stops on the trip from Rainbow Lake to Fossil Lake. Also watch for the mountain goats that inhabit this section of the East Rosebud drainage.

If the falls on Whirlpool Creek was impressive, the two falls from Martin Lake that drop into well-named Lake at Falls are awe inspiring. Yet another mile or so up the trail, be prepared for perhaps the most astounding sight of the trip, massive Impasse Falls, which plunges about 100 feet into Duggan Lake. Travelers get great views of the torrent from both below and above as the trail switchbacks beside the falls.

From Impasse Falls, the trail goes by two more large, unnamed waterfalls before arriving at Twin Outlets Lake. And the short stretch between Twin Outlets Lake and Dewey Lake features another series of waterfalls.

Dewey Lake.

With all this scenery (and all the film you'll put through your camera) on the second day of this trip, it's hard to hold a steady pace. Each person's mileage and time on the trail will vary widely. It's 9 miles from Rainbow Lake to Fossil Lake. Figuring four nights from trailhead to trailhead, there are two options for the second night's camp. Either camp somewhere along the trail or push on to Fossil Lake and stay two nights there.

From the standpoint of available campsites, it's slightly better to forge on to Fossil Lake. Even though the scenery is great along this stretch, it lacks a good selection of campsites. The most serviceable sites are at Big Park Lake, Twin Outlets Lake, or Dewey Lake and along the stream above Big Park Lake. Lake at Falls and Duggan Lake offer virtually no campsites.

Twin Outlets Lake is just below timberline, and it's the last place along this trail where the Forest Service allows campfires. Campfires are prohibited in the Fossil Lake area too, which is at about 10,000 feet in elevation, but this should take nothing away from the grand experience of spending a few nights in the absolute core of the Beartooths.

One more choice for the second campsite is Echo Lake, which entails a 1-mile side trip. The trail breaks off to the west from the main trail above Big Park Lake and just before the bridge across Granite Creek. This isn't an official trail, but it's easy to follow. Watch for mountain goats on the slopes on the south side of Echo Lake.

Count on spending at least one night in the Fossil Lake area. Arriving fairly early on the third day allows extra time to search for that flawless, dream campsite. If you can't find that ideal campsite at Fossil, try nearby Windy, Bald Knob, or Mermaid Lake.

The Fossil Lake area is the beating heart of a great wilderness, and much of the spirit of this top-of-the-world environment seems to flow from it, just as East Rosebud Creek does. You'll really be missing something if you just pass through it.

From a five-star base camp here, a multitude of remarkable day trips await. Always keep a close eye on the weather, and head back to camp if a storm rolls in—as they often do in this high-elevation paradise. Try to rise early and cruise around in the mornings instead of the afternoons, which is when thunderstorms rip through the Beartooths on an almost daily basis. Figure on spending a full day just to walk the perimeter of Fossil Lake.

About halfway along the trail around octopus-like Fossil Lake, a huge cairn marks the divide between two drainages (East Rosebud Creek and the Clarks Fork of the Yellowstone River) and the boundary between Custer and Gallatin National Forests. Fossil Lake drains into the East Rosebud, and Windy Lake empties into the Clarks Fork. On the Forest Service maps, the trail numbers change from Trail 15 to Trail 567. This is also the place for cross-country hikers to break off the main trail and head over to Windy Lake, which can be seen off to the west. Windy Lake might be called Fizzle Lake on some maps, just as several other lakes in this area have different names on different maps. That's reason enough to bring along a complete selection of maps.

A scenic but unusually named area, Lake at Falls.

Leaving Fossil Lake, the trail goes by Skull, Bald Knob, and Ouzel Lakes before dipping below timberline on the way to Russell Lake. Russell is nicely located for the last night out. Camp at either the upper or lower end of Russell Lake. To reach the campsite at the lower end, ford the stream, which gets seriously large as it slowly leaves the lake. Unfortunately, Russell Lake receives heavy use and shows it, so you might want to camp elsewhere. Other choices for the last night out would be Fox or Rock Island Lake. The trail to Fox isn't an official trail, but it's well marked.

The trail from Russell Lake is probably the least attractive stretch of the trip, but most people would still rate it quite highly. For 6 miles, it passes through a dense lodge-pole forest. The 1988 fires burned the section around Kersey Lake.

With luck you'll come out on a hot day. Besides being the most scenic trailhead in the Beartooths, the Clarks Fork Trailhead offers the best swimming hole. Wearing a five-day accumulation of sweat and grime, most hikers feel an overpowering temptation to jump in. Don't fight it; just do it.

Options

Less elevation is gained by starting this trip at the south end at the Clarks Fork Trailhead, at 8,036 feet. However, since the north end is more accessible and scenic, hikes usually start from the East Rosebud Trailhead at 6,208 feet. Either way, the uphill climb isn't really severe; it's more of a gradual ascent most of the way. Perhaps the steepest section is between Elk Lake and Rimrock Lake. Many backpackers choose the base camp option and stay several nights on the plateau around Fossil Lake, sometimes called the "top of the world," before leaving the area.

Side Trips

Refer to Getting Off The Beaten Path, following this hike.

Camping

Choosing a campsite is a big issue on this trail, mainly because of the heavy use this route receives. Several camping areas such as Elk and Russell Lakes show signs of serious overuse. Other lakes, such as Rimrock Lake and Lake at Falls, may look like logical camping areas on the map but offer few if any good campsites. On the other side of the coin, if you get off the trail a mile or so, you can frequently find a good campsite that looks as though it has never been used. If you take this option, please make sure it looks as if nobody has ever camped there when you leave in the morning. Also, be sure to check current regulations for camping and campfires at the information board at the trailhead.

Fishing

The Montana Department of Fish, Wildlife & Parks (DFWP) knows this is the most popular trail in the Beartooths and tries hard to complement this popularity with a great fishery.

East Rosebud Lake houses a mixed bag of brown trout, brookies, rainbows, and cutthroat trout. The steep terrain keeps the browns from moving far upstream, but brookies, rainbows, cutthroats, and even a few goldens survive in various places upstream in East Rosebud Creek. Goldens were stocked in several lakes along this trail in the 1950s, but they have readily crossbred with both rainbows and cutthroats. Unless you really know trout, the golden trout characteristics are difficult to see.

With the exception of Cairn and Billy Lakes, there are no brook trout above Elk Lake in this drainage. Rainbows dominate in Rimrock and Rainbow Lakes, and cutthroat trout dominate in the lakes above Rainbow Lake. Because of its popularity, Fossil Lake is stocked frequently with cutts to keep the fishing hot, although they can be hard to find because they tend to school.

If you camp at Elk Lake, you might have time for a side trip up to Snow Lakes. These lakes hold some nice rainbows, but the tough climb up the east side of Snow Creek keeps all but the most determined anglers away.

Anglers who camp near Big Park Lake might want to reserve an entire day for climbing (and it truly is a climb) into and out of Scat and Martin Lakes. DFWP is trying to establish a pure golden trout fishery there, and it may be worth the climb.

Cairn Lake would also provide a worthwhile side trip for those camping near Dewey Lake. Cairn and Billy Lakes both have brook trout well above average in size. The trout don't reproduce well here, allowing those remaining to grow larger. DFWP closely monitors these lakes—a downstream migration of brook trout would seriously harm the cutthroat/rainbow fishery down below. If you catch brookies below Billy Lake, notify DFWP.

Entering the Clarks Fork side of the pass near Fossil Lake, the fishing gets even better. There are a great many lakes in the Clarks Fork drainage, and this trail goes through the heart of this incredible fishery. Because of the easy access for horses, most of the lakes along the trail were stocked with brook trout in the first half of the twentieth century. The brookies tend to be on the smaller side but provide some great fishing and an easy meal.

Just off the trail, Leo Lake, Lake of the Winds, and Lake of the Clouds host cutthroat trout, while Gallery Lake also has rainbows. Fox Lake is one of those places that few people stop at, but many more should. It sports larger than average brookies, nice rainbows, and an occasional grayling that works its way down from Cliff Lake.

As an experiment, DFWP has stocked lake trout in Kersey Lake to prey on the brook trout population. It is hoped that by reducing the number of brookies, the remaining ones will grow larger. At last check, this seems to be working.

GETTING OFF THE BEATEN PATH

To get the most out of an extended trans-Beartooth trip, try some off-trail excursions. Only those proficient with compass and topo map should attempt cross-country travel. The following list of side trips has been ranked as Human (easy for almost everybody, including children), Semi-human (moderately difficult), and Animal (don't try it unless you're very fit and wilderness-wise). Refer to the chapter Using this Guidebook for more information on ratings.

Destination	Difficulty
Snow Lakes	Animal
Arch Lakes	Animal
Echo Lake	Human
Martin Lake	Animal
Medicine Lake	Animal
Fossil Lake	Human
Cairn Lake	Semi-human
Fizzle (Windy) Lake	Human
Basin (Picasso) Lake	Human
Fulcrum (Mermaid) Lake	Human
Lake of the Clouds	Semi-human
Nymph (Leo) Lake	Semi-human
Looking Glass (Stephanie) Lake	Semi-human
Rough Lake, Aero Lakes	Animal
Sky Top Lakes	Animal
Gallery Lake	Semi-human
Mariane Lake	Human
Lake of the Winds	Semi-human
Fox Lake	Human
Rock Island Lake	Human
Vernon Lake	Human
Curl Lake	Human
Aquarius Lake	Animal

21 Elk Lake

General description: A moderately long but easy day trip and possible candidate for an easy overnighter
Special attractions: Elk Lake
Type of trip: Out-and-back
Total distance: 6 miles

Difficulty: Easy
Traffic: Heavy
Maps: USGS—Alpine; RMS—Alpine–Mount Maurice
Starting point: East Rosebud Trailhead

Finding the trailhead: Refer to The Beaten Path, Hike 20.
Parking and trailhead facilities: A huge trailhead parking area with room for large horse trailers; toilet; also has a campground nearby.

The Hike

This route covers the first 3 miles of the popular trans–Beartooth trail from East Rosebud to Clarks Fork, referred to in this book as The Beaten Path. The trail is well maintained and well traveled. Expect to see lots of people.

The rocky but well-constructed trail between Elk Lake and Rimrock Lake.

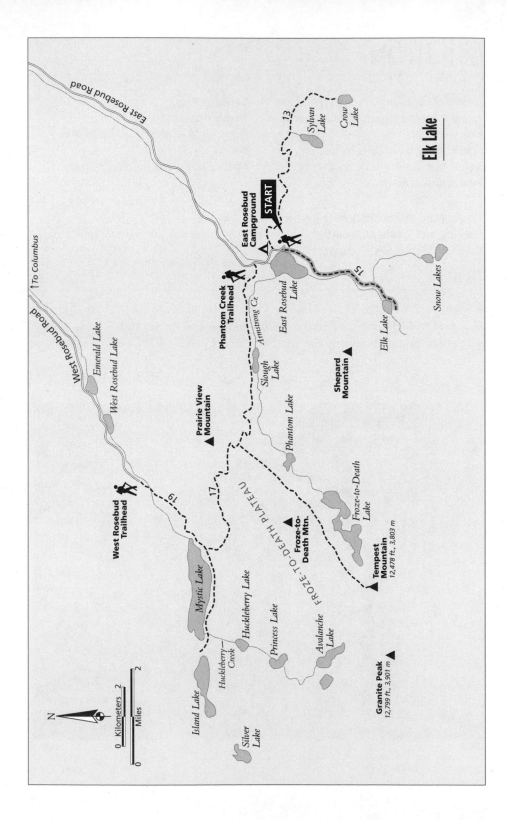

Elk Lake

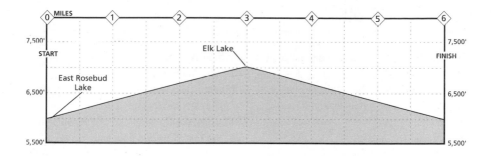

The trail starts at the huge East Rosebud Trailhead and goes through deep, un-burned forest all the way to Elk Lake. From the trail there are several great views of 10,979-foot Shepard Mountain to the west and East Rosebud Creek as it tumbles down from the Beartooth Plateau.

Elk Lake is nestled in a forested pocket just below the point where the trail starts to traverse more rocky, open terrain. As a destination, it's best suited for day trips. The upper end of the lake has a pleasant but well used spot for lunch.

In 1999 a forest fire burned through the drainage above Elk Lake.

Camping

Even though Elk Lake offers limited camping, a fair number of people spend the night here, mainly those who started too late in the day on their trans-Beartooth adventure. The main camping area at the inlet shows signs of overuse, but you can find other campsites along the eastern shore.

Fishing

Elk Lake offers both cutthroat and brook trout fishing, with the brook trout providing the largest portion of a possible dinner. Anglers day hiking to Elk Lake should plan a couple of stops to fish in the creek. At the trailhead, East Rosebud Lake holds some large brown trout, along with a mixed bag of brookies, rainbows, and cutthroats.

22 Sylvan Lake

General description: A long, hard day trip or moderate overnighter
Special attractions: One of the few easily accessible golden trout lakes in the Beartooths
Type of trip: Out-and-back
Total distance: 10 miles

Difficulty: Moderate
Traffic: Moderate
Maps: USGS—Alpine and Sylvan Lake; RMS—Alpine-Mount Maurice
Starting point: North end of the campground at the East Rosebud Trailhead

Finding the trailhead: Refer to The Beaten Path, Hike 20. As the road swings by Alpine and around the east side of East Rosebud Lake, turn left into East Rosebud Campground to reach the trailhead for Trail 13 to Sylvan Lake.
Parking and trailhead facilities: Limited parking directly at this trailhead, but ample parking at the nearby East Rosebud Trailhead.

Key Points

4.1	Top of ridge.
4.6	Junction with trail to Crow Lake; turn right.
5.0	Sylvan Lake.

The Hike

The true beauty of Sylvan Lake lies beneath the surface. There swim the gorgeous, multicolored golden trout in abundance. Biologists call the Sylvan Lake golden trout population one of the purest in the Beartooths, and they use the lake as a source of fish to plant in other lakes. However, even for the non-angler, this lake is worth the uphill trek.

Start up Trail 13 right from the East Rosebud Campground and gradually switchback up the steep slopes of the East Rosebud Plateau. It's 5 miles and almost completely uphill, but, of course, the return trip is all downhill back to the trailhead. The trail is heavily used and well maintained. It's also expertly designed so the climb doesn't seem so steep. The top of the ridge offers a fantastic view ("I climbed that!") of

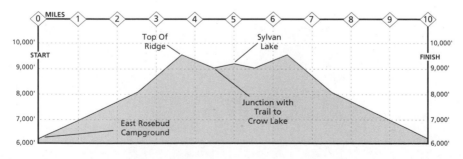

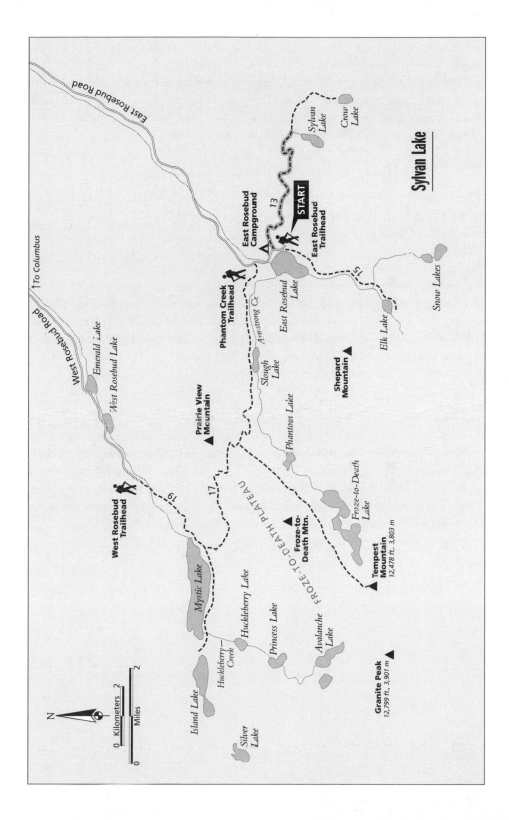

Sylvan Lake

the East Rosebud Drainage, including East Rosebud Lake about 2,400 feet straight down.

On the ridge, the trail markers fade into a series of cairns for a few hundred yards, so be alert to stay on the trail. Also, don't miss the junction where the spur trail heads up to Sylvan Lake and Trail 13 continues on to Crow Lake. The junction is well marked, but inattentive hikers could end up at the wrong lake.

Side Trips

An overnight stay at Sylvan Lake does allow time for the short side trip over to Crow Lake, which probably surpasses Sylvan Lake for beauty, at least above the surface. Below the surface, the brook trout are not nearly as beautiful as the golden trout of Sylvan Lake.

Camping

Even though it's 10 miles total, Sylvan Lake is more suited for day trips. There is one campsite on a small plateau to the right just before the trail breaks over the last ridge into the lake basin. Camp here, however, and people will be walking by the front door of your tent. There are no good campsites right at the lake. Sylvan Lake is at timberline, so please refrain from building a campfire.

Fishing

Anglers intent on pursuing the golden trout of Sylvan Lake should plan to spend the night. Goldens are shy and more easily caught in the morning and evening, precluding a day hike. The golden trout of Sylvan Lake reproduce readily, so don't worry about taking a few home, even if it's just to put one of these beauties on the wall. Anglers who make the trek to Crow Lake will find that the brook trout there are larger than average and are much easier to catch than the goldens at Sylvan.

23 Slough Lake

General description: A leisurely day trip
Special attractions: Terrific view of the upper Phantom Creek drainage and Froze-to-Death Plateau from the lake
Type of trip: Out-and-back
Total distance: 4 miles

Difficulty: Easy
Traffic: Moderate
Maps: USGS—Alpine; RMS—Alpine-Mount Maurice
Starting point: Phantom Creek Trailhead

Finding the trailhead: Refer to The Beaten Path, Hike 20. The Phantom Creek Trail 17 begins on the right (west) side of the road a quarter mile before East Rosebud Lake. This is a popular route to Froze-to-Death Plateau and Granite Peak.

Parking and trailhead facilities: A large parking lot (often full) and toilet.

Slough Lake.

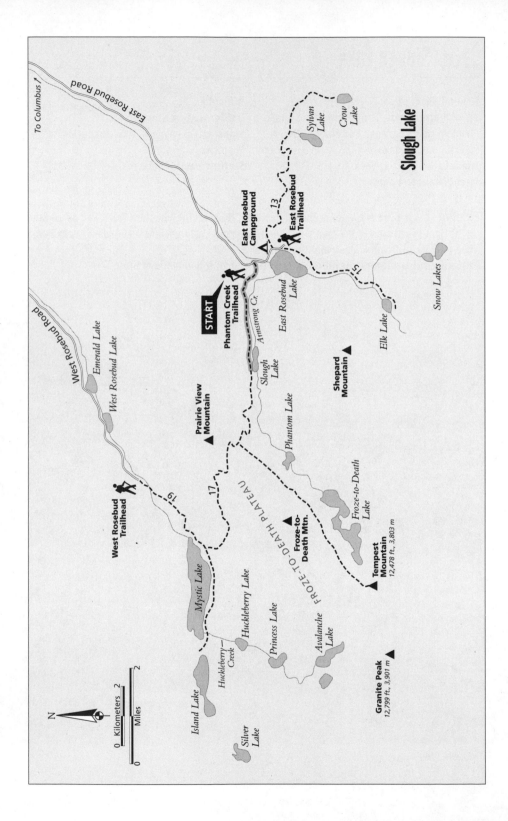

Slough Lake

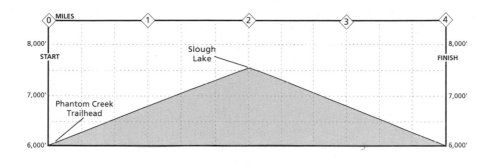

The Hike

This trail is perfectly suited for that leisurely, quiet day in the wilderness amid some great scenery.

Trail 17 climbs, with gradual switchbacks, along Armstrong Creek (yes, it probably should be called the Armstrong Creek Trailhead) for about 2.5 miles before it breaks out of the forest into a great panorama highlighted by Hole-in-the-Wall Mountain to the south. Look ahead to see how the trail climbs up to Froze-to-Death Plateau.

The trail reaches Slough Lake (no relation to the Slough Creek that drains south from Boulder River country to the west) about 0.5 mile after the forest opens up. This is a gorgeous, glacier-carved cirque, and Slough Lake sits in the midst of it like a little pearl. Actually, there are two small lakes, and there's one campsite at the upper end of the second lake, for those inclined to stay overnight.

Even though this trail receives heavy use, few people take their time along here or even stop at Slough Lake. Most are rushing to the top of Froze-to-Death Plateau to climb Granite Peak. Lucky for the rest of us that they hurry right by this pastoral pond, a perfect spot to sit on a sunny day savoring the spirit of the wilderness.

Camping

There are a couple of campsites on the north shore of Slough Creek near the trail, so this can be an easy overnighter.

Fishing

Slough Lake provides a good source of willing brookies for dinner or for fun.

Red Lodge Area

The area between Red Lodge and Beartooth Pass has several trailheads, mostly along the West Fork of Rock Creek, but also in the Lake Fork of Rock Creek and the main fork of Rock Creek below Beartooth Pass. The trails in this area provide a nice variety ranging from short, easy, flat hikes to opportunities to explore the backcountry off-trail with topo map and compass. Many lakes and other scenic areas can be reached within a few miles of a trailhead. The climbs to some lakes are often steep but usually short.

The West Fork of Rock Creek Road, known locally as the West Fork Road and officially as Forest Road 71, actually has four trailheads, all in proximity, along with three vehicle campgrounds and a sprinkling of residential developments. Since the West Fork Road starts right in Red Lodge, the lower valley is almost like the town's backyard wilderness.

The West Fork Road is paved for the first 7 miles up to Cascade Campground. This is a heavily used area, both for day trips and extended backcountry excursions. Fortunately, the area offers a wide range of trail choices and visitors tend to disperse. Trails rarely feel crowded.

The Lake Fork of Rock Creek area is similar to the West Fork. Both drainages are easily accessible from Red Lodge and receive lots of use. This high level of use in the Lake Fork may be more noticeable because everybody uses the same trail. In the West Fork, multiple trails tend to disperse the use.

The Rock Creek area is the last stop before driving up the world-famous switchbacks to the top of Beartooth Pass and into Wyoming. The two trailheads (Glacier Lake and Hellroaring) are accessed from the Forest Service campgrounds at the base of Beartooth Pass. Day hikers can camp at one of the three vehicle campgrounds and go to Hellroaring Lakes and Glacier Lake on extended one-day outings.

To access the West Fork trailheads, turn west on the West Fork Road (FR 71), which leaves U.S. Highway 212 on the south edge of Red Lodge and is marked with a ski area sign. After 2.8 miles, the road bends left and heads up the West Fork. Calculating from Red Lodge, the mileage to the trailheads in the West Fork is as follows:

Silver Run—4.4 miles
Basin Creek—7 miles
Lake Fork—9.3 miles
Timberline Lake—11.1 miles
Senia Creek—12.1 miles
Main West Fork—12.8 miles
Hellroaring Plateau—10.9 miles
Glacier Lake—10.9 miles

All West Fork trailheads are well signed and can be reached with any vehicle, with the possible exception of the Silver Run Trailhead, which is difficult to reach without a high-clearance four-wheel-drive vehicle. The West Fork Road is paved up to the Cascade Campground.

Medicine Mountain and the headwaters of the West Fork of Rock Creek.

24 Basin Creek Lakes

General description: An easy day hike well suited for families

Special attractions: An accessible, safe trail, designated as a National Recreational Trail

Type of trip: Out-and-back

Total distance: 5 miles to lower lake; 8 miles to upper lake

Difficulty: Easy

Traffic: Heavy

Maps: USGS—Bare Mountain; RMS—Alpine-Mount Maurice

Starting point: Basin Creek Trailhead

Finding the trailhead: From Red Lodge, drive 7 miles on West Fork Road (FR 71) and turn left (south) into the trailhead parking lot.

Parking and trailhead facilities: Moderately large trailhead area with toilet but too small for horse trailers; Cascade Campground just west of the trailhead.

Key Points

0.5 Basin Creek Falls.

2.5 Lower Basin Creek Lake.

4.0 Upper Basin Creek Lake.

The Hike

The Forest Service has designated Basin Creek Lakes as a National Recreational Trail, so not surprisingly, it's popular. It's so popular, in fact, that this is one of the few trails in the Beartooths restricted to hiking only—no horses are allowed until mid-September when the big-game hunting seasons get under way.

Technically, Trail 61 to Basin Creek Lakes does not lie within the Absaroka-Beartooth Wilderness, but it's a wilderness trip by all other definitions. The trail is well maintained, easy to follow, and ideal for family day trips for those who can handle the gradual, but steady, uphill gradient. The route crosses Basin Creek twice, but bridges keep your feet dry.

About a half mile up the trail, listen for Basin Creek Falls tumbling down from above. Where the trail takes a sharp right, hikers can scramble up a short, undeveloped spur trail to get a closer look at the falls, which is well worth the short detour. The rest of the trail is hazard-free, but this short climb up to see the falls might be too hazardous for small children.

The trail passes through thick forest all the way. With so much of the Beartooths burned by the 1988 fires, this peaceful walk in the woods can be a real treat. The remains of logging activity from the early 1900s are still visible along the way—but it's also apparent that nature is finally reclaiming the disturbed landscape.

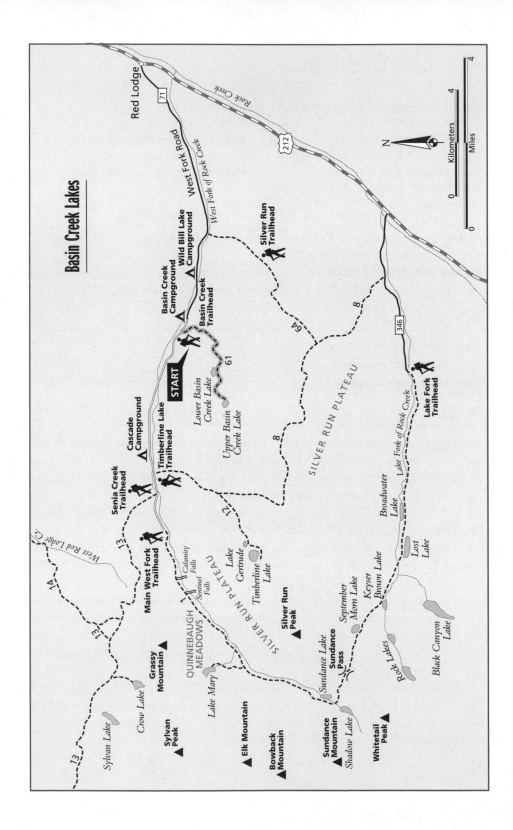

Basin Creek Lakes

Red Lodge

Rock Creek

71

West Fork Road

West Fork of Rock Creek

212

Silver Run Trailhead

Basin Creek Campground

Wild Bill Lake Campground

Basin Creek Trailhead

START

61

Lower Basin Creek Lake

Upper Basin Creek Lake

64

8

8

346

SILVER RUN PLATEAU

Lake Fork of Rock Creek

Lake Fork Trailhead

Cascade Campground

Timberline Lake Trailhead

Senia Creek Trailhead

Main West Fork Trailhead

West Red Lodge Cr.

13

13

13

14

2

Calamity Falls

Sentinel Falls

QUINNEBAUGH MEADOWS

1

Lake Gertrude

Timberline Lake

Silver Run Peak

SILVER RUN PLATEAU

Lake Mary

Sundance Lake

Sundance Pass

September Morn Lake

Keyser Brown Lake

Broadwater Lake

Lost Lake

Sylvan Lake

Crow Lake

Grassy Mountain ▲

Sylvan Peak ▲

Elk Mountain ▲

Bowback Mountain ▲

Sundance Mountain ▲

Shadow Lake

Whitetail Peak ▲

Rock Lakes

Black Canyon Lake

N

0   Kilometers   4

0   Miles   4

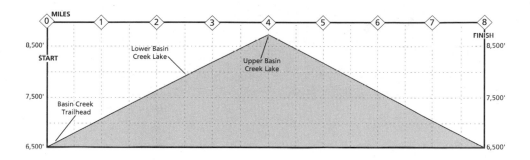

Lower Basin Lake is one of those forest-lined mountain ponds with darkish, warm water that tends to be half-covered by lily pads. Upper Basin Lake is larger, deeper, and nestled in a picturesque mountain cirque.

Camping

Although better suited as a destination for day trips, the upper lake also offers a few potential campsites. There is enough firewood for a low-impact campfire.

Fishing

While both of these lakes once supported brook trout populations, the lower lake suffered a freeze-out a few years back and currently has no fish. Since the brook trout in the stream and lake above will eventually work their way back down to Lower Basin, there is no immediate need to restock. Fishing in Upper Basin Lake is excellent for brook trout, and there has been some talk of introducing grayling.

25 Timberline Lake

General description: A moderately long day trip or easy overnighter
Special attractions: The view from Timberline Lake
Type of trip: Out-and-back
Total distance: 9 miles

Difficulty: Easy
Traffic: Moderate
Maps: USGS—Sylvan Peak and Bare Mountain; RMS—Alpine-Mount Maurice
Starting point: Timberline Lake Trailhead

Finding the trailhead: From Red Lodge, drive 11.1 miles on West Fork Road (FR 71) and turn left (south) into the trailhead parking lot.

Parking and trailhead facilities: Moderately large trailhead area with toilet but too small for horse trailers; Cascade Campground east of the trailhead.

Key Points

3.0 Junction with Beartrack Trail 8.

4.0 Lake Gertrude.

4.5 Timberline Lake.

The Hike

Similar to the nearby trail up Basin Creek, the trail to Timberline Lake passes through a forested environment. Here, however, the forest is more open and mature than along Basin Creek. As with almost all trails in the Custer National Forest section of the Absaroka-Beartooth Wilderness, this one is well maintained and marked.

The corridor to Timberline Lake was excluded from the Absaroka-Beartooth Wilderness. However, Lake Gertrude and Timberline Lake lie within the wilderness boundary, and current wilderness bills call for adding the corridor to the wilderness.

It's a short 3 miles to the junction with Beartrack Trail 8, which veers off to the left and heads up to Silver Run Plateau. Turn right and continue along Timberline Creek. If you cross the stream here, you took a wrong turn.

After another mile or so, look for Lake Gertrude nestled in a forested pocket off to the right. This is a good spot to pause for a rest while enjoying Lake Gertrude,

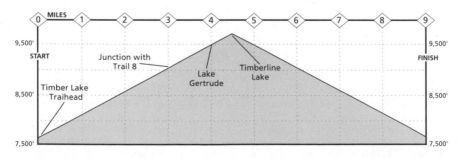

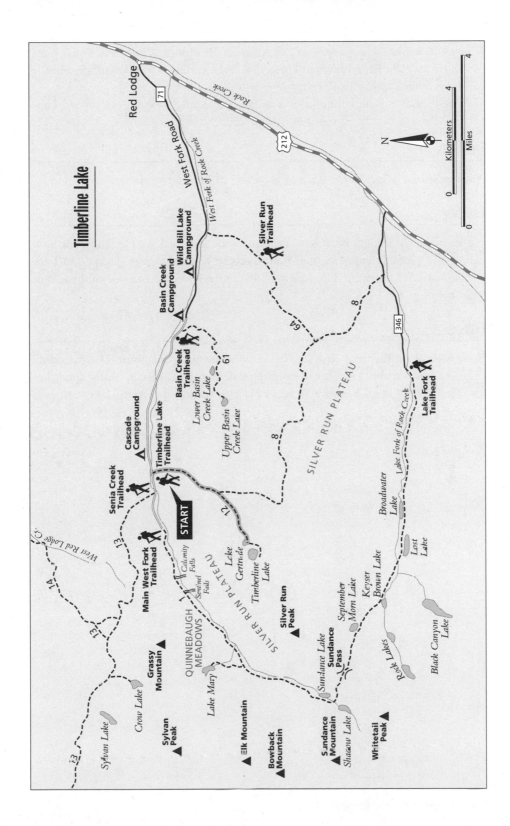

Timberline Lake

Red Lodge

Rock Creek

71

212

West Fork Road

West Fork of Rock Creek

N

Kilometers 4

Miles

0

0

Basin Creek Campground

Wild Bill Lake Campground

Silver Run Trailhead

64

8

346

Cascade Campground

Basin Creek Trailhead

61

Lower Basin Creek Lake

Upper Basin Creek Lake

8

SILVER RUN PLATEAU

Lake Fork of Rock Creek

Lake Fork Trailhead

Senia Creek Trailhead

Timberline Lake Trailhead

START

Calamity Falls

Sentinel Falls

Lake Gertrude

Timberline Lake

Silver Run Peak

Broadwater Lake

Last Lake

West Red Lodge Cr.

Main West Fork Trailhead

13

14

37

QUINNEBAUGH MEADOWS

SILVER RUN PLATEAU

Sundance Lake

Sundance Pass

September Morn Lake

Keyser Brown Lake

Rock Lakes

Black Canyon Lake

Grassy Mountain

Sylvan Peak

Crow Lake

Lake Mary

Elk Mountain

Bowback Mountain

Sundance Mountain

Shadow Lake

Whitetail Peak

13

Sylvan Lake

73

which also marks the boundary of the Absaroka-Beartooth Wilderness. Don't burn too much daylight here, however. Timberline Lake is only 0.5 mile farther, and the basin is definitely worth exploring.

The view from Timberline Lake is fantastic, especially to the south toward Timberline Glacier and 12,500-foot Silver Run Peak.

Side Trips

Adventuresome hikers might want to try a side trip up to the glacier.

Camping

For an overnight trip, it's possible to camp near the inlet of Lake Gertrude, but most people will probably enjoy the night out more by going the extra 0.5 mile to Timberline Lake. At Timberline Lake, camp on the moraine on the east side of the lake or near the inlet.

Fishing

Both lakes along this trail have healthy populations of brook trout. The fish aren't large but can probably be counted on to provide dinner. The small outlet ponds below Timberline Lake may prove an easier place to catch fish than the lake itself.

26 Silver Run Plateau

General description: An unusual, long day trip or overnighter for experienced, well-conditioned hikers only

Special attractions: An extraordinarily scenic high plateau with a challenging trail to follow

Type of trip: Shuttle

Total distance: 17 miles

Difficulty: Difficult

Traffic: Light

Maps: USGS—Sylvan Peak and Bare Mountain; RMS—Alpine-Mount Maurice

Starting point: Timberline Lake Trailhead

Finding the trailhead: From Red Lodge, drive 11.1 miles on West Fork Road (FR 71) and turn left (south) into the Timberline Lake Trailhead parking lot.

Parking and trailhead facilities: Moderately large trailhead area with toilet but too small for horse trailers.

Key Points

3.0 Junction with Beartrack Trail 8; turn left.

4.4 Silver Run Lake Basin.

5.1 Trail turns to string of cairns.

11.0 Junction with Trail 64; turn left.

14.5 End of Trail 64 turns into gravel road.

17.0 West Fork Road (FR 71).

The Hike

This is unconditionally one of the most remarkable and unusual trails in the Beartooths. It doesn't feature an endless string of lakes as do most trails here, but most hikers will be too busy enjoying the trip to notice. Only the midsection of this trail is actually within the Absaroka-Beartooth Wilderness, but the entire trip seems exceptionally wild.

Weather is always important in the Beartooths, but it's especially critical on this trail. Double-check the weather report before leaving home. Good weather is essential for this trip. And be sure to take an extra water bottle, as water is scarce, especially in late summer.

Another big issue on this trail is transportation. Arrange to be picked up or leave a vehicle (or bicycle) at the end of the trail to get back to the vehicle at the Timberline Lake Trailhead. The turnoff to Silver Run Trail 64 (near the end of this hike) is marked on the south side of the West Fork Road, about 2 miles past the turnoff to Palisades Campground. The spur road to this trailhead can be traversed by any vehicle, but a high-clearance vehicle is better.

From the Timberline Lake Trailhead, hikers share the first 3 miles with everyone going to Timberline Lake. At the junction with Beartrack Trail 8, however, go left and cross Timberline Creek and head another mile along the east side of the creek to Silver Run Basin.

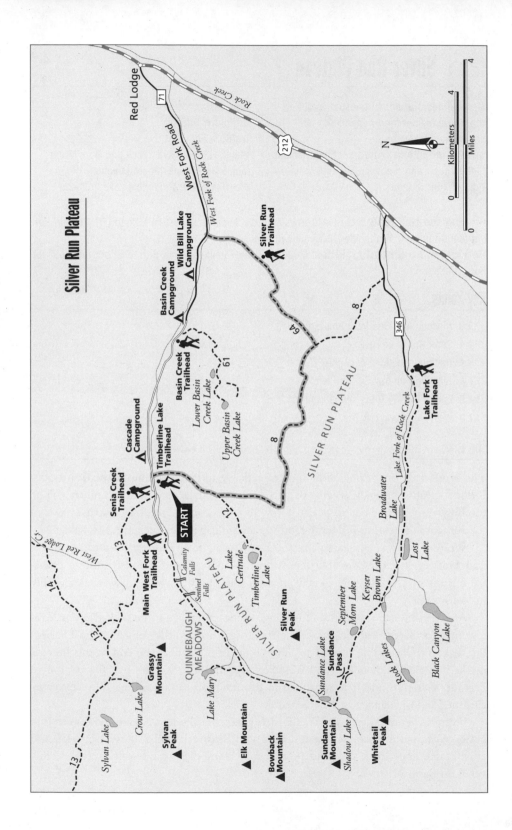

Silver Run Plateau

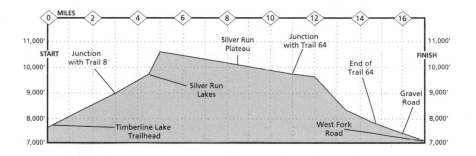

Since the tiny lakes in the Silver Run Basin aren't much of a fishery, the area doesn't get much use. However, the scenery equals any high-altitude basin in the Beartooths. Backpackers will probably want to spend their night out in the luxurious accommodations found in Silver Run Basin. It's definitely a room with a view.

The trail is easy to follow up to the basin, but in the basin, it becomes difficult to find in places. As the trail leaves the basin and starts switchbacking up a steep slope to the plateau, it becomes clearly visible again. If you lose the trail in the basin, look ahead to see where it climbs up to the plateau.

Immediately after the last switchback on the edge of the plateau, the trail disappears, and from this point on, a long string of cairns mark the way. Other trails in the Beartooths have short stretches of cairns, but in this case the cairns last for about 7 miles. Fortunately, the cairns are well placed, large, and easy to see.

The Silver Run Plateau is all above 10,000 feet and affords a fresh perspective of the Beartooths. It's nearly trackless, treeless, bugless, waterless, and peopleless, but none of these shortages detracts from its raw beauty. For example, take a minute to look over your shoulder to the west for a view of 12,500-foot Silver Run Peak. Or look down at your feet to see the rare Arctic gentian. This is one of the few places in the Beartooths where this lovely, pale green flower is found in abundance.

Traveling from cairn to cairn, do a good deed and help keep the cairns maintained. If a cairn has collapsed, take the time to rebuild it. When approaching a cairn, look for a rock or two that looks like it needs a new home, carry it the last few feet, and then use it to build up the cairn.

After following cairns for about 6 miles, watch for the junction with Silver Run Trail 64. Beartrack Trail 8 continues straight into the Lake Fork of Rock Creek. You turn left (north) on Silver Run Trail 64 and head down Silver Run Creek into the West Fork of Rock Creek.

After this junction, there's only another half mile or so of the long journey on Silver Run Plateau. Before dropping off the edge of the plateau onto a normal, forested trail, glance backward for a last look at the plateau.

The trail drops rapidly into Silver Run Creek, so steeply that doing this trip in reverse would seem foolish. Stay on this trail for 4 miles until it turns into the gravel road where you left a vehicle or bicycle or are being picked up.

Lake Fork of Rock Creek.

On the way down from the plateau, take note of STOCK DRIVEWAY signs nailed on trees. This area, including the plateau, was once heavily grazed by sheep. Since then, the grazing allotment has been closed, mainly because of potential damage to this fragile environment.

Options

Doing this shuttle in reverse would be more difficult.

Side Trips

On the way up, you could take a side trip to see Timberline Lake.

Camping

If you're staying overnight, you can camp almost anywhere in the Silver Run Basin. This is not centrally located on the route, and you can also camp on the plateau, but the only water would be small, snowmelt rivulets. Wherever you camp, follow strict zero-impact practices to keep this area as pristine as it presently is. No campfires, please.

Fishing

The only fishery along this route is Silver Run Lakes. Only one of the five small lakes, the southernmost lake, contains fish (brookies).

Arctic gentian, *a rare, pale green flower found in abundance on Silver Run Plateau.*
Photo: Michael S. Sample

27 Quinnebaugh Meadows

General description: A moderate day hike, easy overnighter, or base camp trip
Special attractions: An unusually large and beautiful mountain meadow
Type of trip: Out-and-back
Total distance: 10 miles

Difficulty: Easy
Traffic: Moderate
Maps: USGS—Sylvan Peak and Bare Mountain; RMS—Alpine-Mount Maurice
Starting point: Main West Fork Trailhead

Finding the trailhead: From Red Lodge, drive 12.8 miles to the end of the West Fork Road (FR 71) and the trailhead.
Parking and trailhead facilities: Ample parking and enough room for most horse trailers; toilet.

Key Points

1.3 Calamity Falls.

1.8 Sentinel Falls.

5.0 Junction with Lake Mary Trail and Quinnebaugh Meadows.

The Hike

The trail, like others in this region, is well maintained and marked. It closely follows the West Fork of Rock Creek, not climbing any more than the stream drops in elevation as it powers its way out of the Beartooths. Most of the trail passes through a rich forest that gradually thins out as you progress up the drainage. In a few places, the forest opens up into small meadows with rewarding vistas of Elk Mountain and Bowback Mountain on the southern horizon near the terminus of the West Fork valley.

The trail passes close by Calamity Falls and Sentinel Falls. These cascades are reminders that the West Fork is not only a peaceful stream meandering out of the wilderness, but it can be a powerful force. Short spur trails lead to both falls for better views.

The West Fork broadens out and slows down just as the trail nears Quinnebaugh

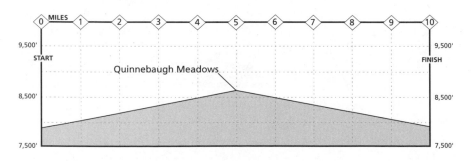

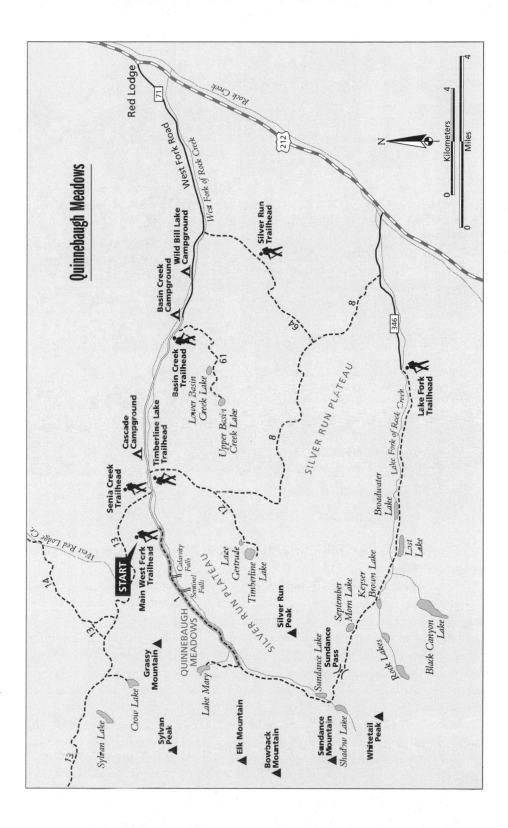

Quinnebaugh Meadows

Red Lodge

71
212

Rock Creek

West Fork of Rock Creek
West Fork Road

Basin Creek Campground
Wild Bill Lake Campground

Silver Run Trailhead

64
8

346

Cascade Campground
Timberline Lake Trailhead
Basin Creek Trailhead

61

Lower Basin Creek Lake
Upper Basin Creek Lake

SILVER RUN PLATEAU

8

Lake Fork Trailhead

Lake Fork of Rock Creek

Senia Creek Trailhead

13

West Red Lodge Cr.

14

13

START
Main West Fork Trailhead

Calamity Falls
Sentinel Falls

Timberline Lake
Gertrude Lake

12

QUINNEBAUGH MEADOWS

1

Broadwater Lake

SILVER RUN PLATEAU

Silver Run Peak

Grassy Mountain

Lake Mary

Sylvan Peak
Crow Lake
Sylvan Lake

13

Elk Mountain

Bowback Mountain

Sundance Lake
Sundance Pass

September Morn Lake
Keyser Brown Lake

Rock Lakes

Lost Lake

Black Canyon Lake

Sundance Mountain
Shadow Lake

Whitetail Peak

N

Kilometers   4
0

Miles   4
0

Quinnebaugh Meadows on the West Fork of Rock Creek.

Meadows. Look for the sign for Lake Mary just after breaking out into the enormous mountain meadow.

The extra dimension of Quinnebaugh Meadows is its attractiveness as a base camp. This site is perfect for someone who wants to camp in a lovely wilderness setting but doesn't want to carry a heavy pack very far—or up any big climbs. It's an easy 5 miles to get into the meadows, and that's 5 miles closer to many interesting destinations, mostly off-trail excursions. Strong hikers might be tempted to go 2 or 3 more miles past Quinnebaugh Meadows before setting up a base camp, but regrettably, the rest of the drainage offers much less attractive campsites than Quinnebaugh Meadows.

From this base camp, avid hikers could spend a week exploring the surrounding wilderness, taking a new route each day. Whether you're an angler, a climber, or simply out to see lots of really grand country, you won't be disappointed.

Side Trips

Lake Mary is the obvious side trip, but there are several other possibilities. Refer to Where to Go from Quinnebaugh Meadows on page 154.

Camping

Set up camp almost anywhere in Quinnebaugh Meadows. It would, in fact, be difficult to not find a great campsite. In most campsites, there should be enough wood for a campfire. This is a popular place, so expect company. Fortunately, the meadow is large enough to accommodate several parties, including backcountry horsemen.

Fishing

Although the West Fork of Rock Creek is not highly productive, anglers can find a few trout in many stretches of this stream. The stream near Quinnebaugh Meadows is no exception. The best fishing, however, is found in various basin lakes 1,000 feet higher in elevation. With the exception of Lake Mary, none of these is easy to access, but all of them may be worth the trip.

A crude trail leads to Senal and Dude Lakes between two bridges over the creek that drains them. It's a difficult side trip, but there are nice brookies and cutts in Senal and pure cutts in Dude. Cutthroats are stocked in Dude on an eight-year cycle, last done in 1999.

Ship Lake Basin contains six lakes, all of which hold fish. The highest lake in Montana with fish is Marker Lake, and it has nice aggressive cutthroats that are stocked on an eight-year cycle. Bowback, Kookoo, and Triangle Lakes are also stocked on the eight-year cycle. The reference year is 1995 for all but Bowback, which was last stocked in 1996. Ship Lake has easy-to-catch brookies, if the local cutts have stumped you.

On the main creek, Shadow, Sundance, and Silt Lakes are stocked with cutthroat trout, but these don't grow as well as those in the lakes above.

Many hikers use Sundance Pass as access to the Lake Fork of Rock Creek, where the first lake encountered is September Morn Lake. September Morn has an abundance of brookies.

WHERE TO GO FROM QUINNEBAUGH MEADOWS

Anybody who ventures off the trail in this area (or anywhere, for that matter) should be proficient with compass and topo map. The following destinations are ranked for difficulty as follows: Human (almost anybody can do it), Semi-human (moderately difficult), or Animal (don't do it unless you're very fit and wilderness-wise). Also refer to more detailed rating information in the chapter Using this Guidebook.

Destination	Difficulty
Lake Mary	Human
Crow Lake	Animal
Sundance Lake	Human
Sundance Pass	Human
Dude Lake	Animal
Shadow Lake	Human
Kookoo Lake	Animal
Ship Lake Basin	Animal
Marker Lake	Animal

28 Lake Mary

General description: A steep climb to a gorgeous mountain lake, well suited for a weekend overnight trip

Special attractions: A special view of the entire West Fork of Rock Creek valley

Type of trip: Out-and-back

Total distance: 12 miles

Difficulty: Easy for the first 5 miles, very steep for the last mile

Traffic: Moderate

Maps: USGS—Sylvan Peak and Bare Mountain; RMS—Alpine-Mount Maurice

Starting point: Main West Fork Trailhead

Finding the trailhead: From Red Lodge, drive 12.8 miles to the end of the West Fork Road (FR 71) and the trailhead.

Parking and trailhead facilities: Ample parking and enough room for most horse trailers; toilet.

Key Points

1.3 Calamity Falls.

1.8 Sentinel Falls.

5.0 Quinnebaugh Meadows.

5.1 Junction with Lake Mary Trail; turn right.

6.0 Lake Mary.

The Hike

The first 5 miles of the trail into Lake Mary is described under Quinnebaugh Meadows, Hike 27.

This hike comes in two distinct parts. The first half is the first 5 miles, and the second half is the last mile. Those carrying a big pack can plan on two hours for the first 5 miles and two hours for the last mile.

Stroll on up to Quinnebaugh Meadows. Enjoy a nice long rest and relish the picturesque openness of the meadow. Then take a deep breath and psych yourself up before starting the ascent. The trail is well constructed with frequent switchbacks to minimize the grade, but it's still a grind. It climbs 1,200 feet in only 1 mile, a Category H hill, one of the toughest in the Beartooths. Even though Lake Mary sits at 9,900 feet, the trail doesn't break out of the forest until just before the lake. The good news is that Lake Mary is worth the effort.

Options

If the climb is too intimidating with a pack, there is the option of pitching camp in Quinnebaugh Meadows and hiking up to the lake with just a day pack.

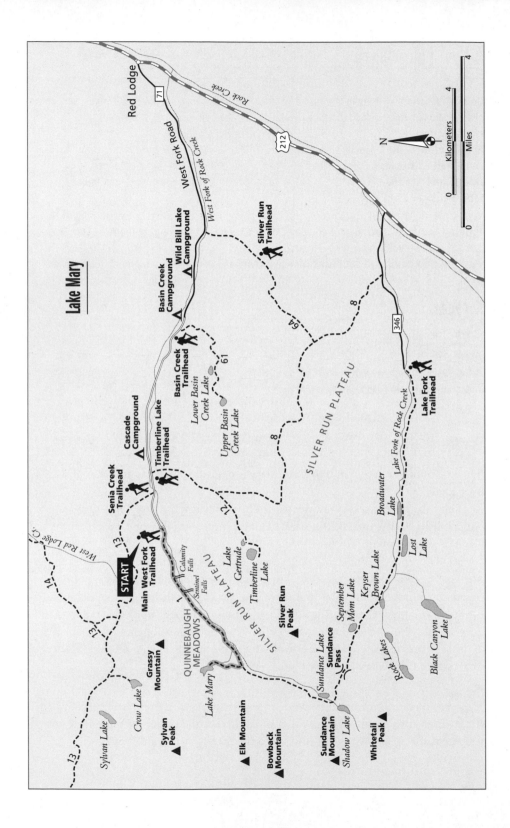

Lake Mary

Red Lodge

Rock Creek

West Fork Road

West Fork of Rock Creek

71

212

346

Basin Creek Campground

Wild Bill Lake Campground

Silver Run Trailhead

Cascade Campground

Timberline Lake Trailhead

Basin Creek Trailhead

Lower Basin Creek Lake

Upper Basin Creek Lake

61

64

8

8

SILVER RUN PLATEAU

Lake Fork Trailhead

Lake Fork of Rock Creek

Broadwater Lake

Lost Lake

Black Canyon Lake

Keyser Brown Lake

September Mom Lake

Rock Lakes

Senia Creek Trailhead

West Red Lodge C.

13

14

13

START

Main West Fork Trailhead

Calamity Falls

Sentinel Falls

1

QUINNEBAUGH MEADOWS

Lake Gertrude

Timberline Lake

72

SILVER RUN PLATEAU

Lake Mary

Grassy Mountain

Crow Lake

Sylvan Lake

Sylvan Peak

Elk Mountain

Bowback Mountain

Silver Run Peak

Sundance Lake

Sundance Pass

Sundance Mountain

Shadow Lake

Whitetail Peak

13

N

Kilometers

Miles

0   4

0   4

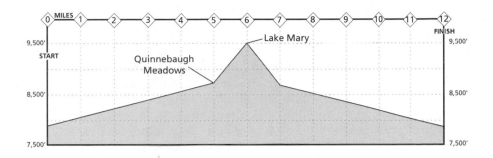

You can also make a loop out of this trip by bushwhacking over to Crow Lake and out to the Senia Creek Trailhead, but if you decide to take this loop option, you would be smart to start at Senia Creek and hike down the Category H hill to the West Fork.

Side Trips

If you have some extra time, you can climb up on the saddle between Lake Mary and Crow Lake.

Camping

There are campsites on either side of Lake Mary, which is actually two lakes. Especially agile hikers can cross the shallow section separating the lakes with some precarious rock-hopping. Since Lake Mary is above timberline, please refrain from building campfires.

Fishing

The West Fork of Rock Creek is characterized by beautiful cascades and sparkling pools, all of which are exceptionally photogenic, but most of which provide few fish. The very cold water, restricted sunlight, and rapid current make life difficult for fish. Cutthroat trout are more able to cope with these factors, although anglers will also find a few brook trout.

Lake Mary harbors a nice population of brook trout, comparable to those found elsewhere in the Beartooths. Count on them for dinner.

29 Crow Lake

General description: An overnighter into a seldom visited area

Special attractions: A delightful, remote, little-used mountain lake

Type of trip: Out-and-back

Total distance: 14 miles

Difficulty: Moderate, except for the difficult trip to Lake Mary (optional)

Traffic: Moderate

Maps: USGS—Sylvan Peak and Bare Mountain; RMS—Alpine-Mount Maurice

Starting point: Senia Creek Trailhead

Finding the trailhead: From Red Lodge, drive 12.1 miles (about 1 mile before the end of the West Fork Road). Park in a pulloff on the right (north) side of the road near the Senia Creek summer homes.

Parking and trailhead facilities: Very limited parking (only room for 5 or 6 vehicles) with no room for horse trailers; no toilet.

Key Points

4.2 Junction cutoff to Trail 14 down West Red Lodge Creek; turn left.

6.5 Junction with Crow Lake Trail; turn left.

7.0 Crow Lake.

The Hike

Before starting up Trail 13, make sure the water bottles are full. It's a long, steep 4 miles until they can be refilled.

From the trailhead, the route switchbacks up to the Red Lodge Creek Plateau, climbing about 1,800 feet in 2.6 miles, a steep Category 1 climb. At that point (at higher than 9,500 feet), the trail breaks out of the timber onto the plateau. The first part of this trail is a grind, but after catching your breath, you'll find the scenic vistas from this high-altitude plateau a fitting reward.

The trail up to the plateau is well defined, but after about a half mile on the plateau, it fades away in places. Stay alert and follow cairns to stay on the route. Try

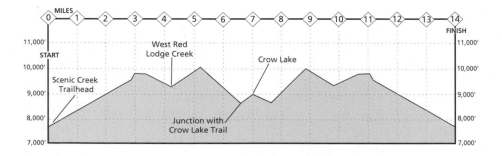

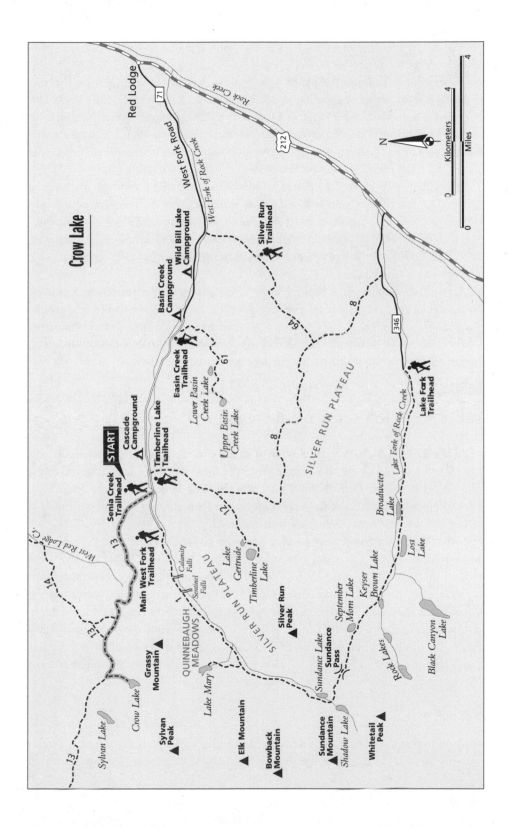

Crow Lake

to stay on the trail to protect the fragile vegetation clinging to existence in this austere environment.

After about a mile on the plateau, the trail reaches its highest point on this trip (9,980 feet) just before descending about 500 feet into West Red Lodge Creek. This is a great place to stop for a lengthy rest and to refill your empty water bottles.

About a quarter mile after crossing the creek, there's a well-signed junction with a trail cutting off to the northwest and joining up with Trail 14 down West Red Lodge Creek. Turn left (west), staying on Trail 13.

After the junction, Trail 13 descends over the course of 1.8 miles to Hellroaring Creek. The first half mile or so is still above timberline. Just off the plateau and into the timber, watch for a glimpse of Crow Lake to the southwest. The trail soon crosses Hellroaring Creek and meets the trail to Crow Lake. Trail 13 keeps on heading west to Sylvan Lake. To get to Crow Lake, turn left (south) and follow the stream about a half mile up to the lake.

Crow Lake doesn't get as many visitors as some lakes in the Beartooths, but that's changing. In the past few years, the lake has seen more use, especially from backcountry horsemen. There is, of course, a good reason for the new-found popularity. Crow Lake is well worth the trip. It lies in a beautiful forested pocket with several unnamed crags to the south, giving the lake a panoramic backdrop.

Options

You can also reach Crow Lake from the East Rosebud Trailhead. It's about the same distance, and both routes start with big hills.

For a little adventure and to avoid backtracking to the Senia Creek Trailhead, you can make a loop out of this trip by going over the ridge south of Crow Lake and dropping into Lake Mary. Then follow Trail 1 out the West Fork back to the Main West Fork Trailhead at the end of the road. This requires a mile-long walk down the road to get to your vehicle at the Senia Creek Trailhead.

The off-trail section (about 2 miles) between Crow Lake and Lake Mary covers some rough country. This should only be attempted by those capable of navigating with compass and topo map. Also, be wary of what looks like the easiest route from the lake, a low pass to the right. Instead, check the topo map carefully before leaving Crow Lake, and you'll see the best route is to the east over a ridge that looks more difficult than the other route but really isn't. The last half-mile into the Lake Mary basin goes through a pile of oversized rocks, so go slowly and carefully.

Taking the off-trail loop option allows you to spend your second night at Lake Mary, leaving an easy 6 miles for the last day.

Side Trips

A base camp at Crow Lake allows hikers to day hike to Sylvan Lake, about 1.8 miles west on Trail 13. Head back down along Hellroaring Creek to the junction with Trail

Crow Lake.

13, turn left (west), and go about 1 mile. Just after crossing the outlet stream, the trail up to Sylvan Lake takes off to the left (south).

Camping

There are campsites at the outlet of Crow Lake, but those who still have some energy might want to carefully cross the stream at the outlet and follow an angler's trail along the east side of the lake to a selection of better campsites on the west side of the inlet.

Fishing

Crow Lake is not as popular a place as some lakes, and the brook trout found here are larger than average. Also make a fishing expedition over to Sylvan Lake, if you have time. It holds a thriving golden trout population.

30 SUNDANCE PASS

General description: A fairly rugged, two- or three-day hike for experienced hikers

Special attractions: Spectacular mountain scenery, especially the view from Sundance Pass

Type of trip: Shuttle

Total distance: 21 miles, not counting side trips

Difficulty: Difficult

Traffic: Heavy

Maps: USGS—Black Pyramid Mountain, Silver Run Peak, and Sylvan Peak; RMS—Alpine-Mount Maurice

Starting point: Lake Fork Trailhead

Finding the trailhead: From Red Lodge, drive southwest for 9.3 miles on U.S. Highway 212. Turn west at the well-marked road up the Lake Fork of Rock Creek. A 2-mile paved road leads to a turnaround and the trailhead.

Parking and trailhead facilities: A huge trailhead area with plenty of parking and room for horse trailers, but even this large lot gets full on busy weekends; toilet.

Key Points

3.5 Broadwater Lake.

5.0 Trail to Lost Lake; turn right.

5.2 Trail to Black Canyon Lake; turn right.

6.5 Turn to Keyser Brown Lake; turn right.

8.5 September Morn Lake.

11.3 Sundance Pass.

13.0 West Fork of Rock Creek.

13.5 Sundance Lake.

15.9 Junction with trail to Lake Mary; turn right.

16.0 Quinnebaugh Meadows.

21.0 Main West Fork Trailhead.

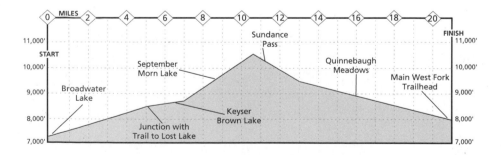

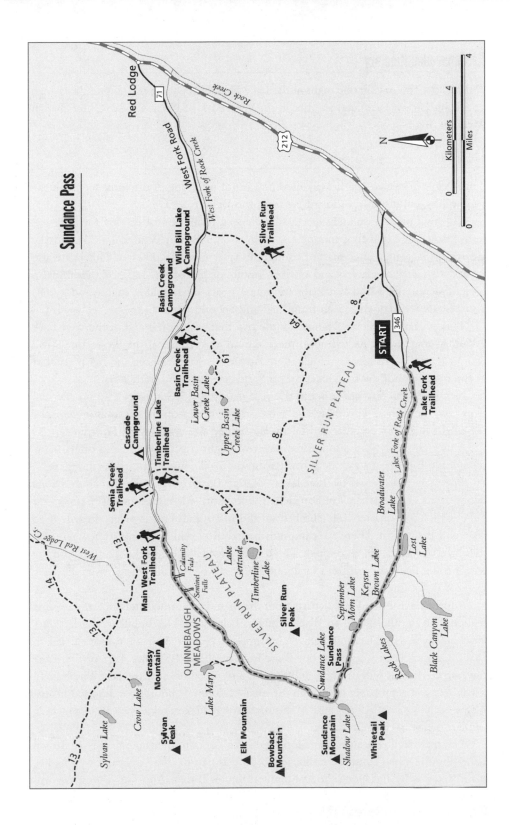

Sundance Pass

Recommended Itinerary

A three-day trip staying one night in the Lake Fork of Rock Creek (September Morn or Keyser Brown Lake) and another in the West Fork of Rock Creek (Quinnebaugh Meadows).

The Hike

This well-maintained and heavily used trail is not only one of the most scenic in the Beartooths, but it's only a short drive from the Billings area.

This trail offers absolutely spectacular scenery. From Sundance Pass, for example, vistas include 12,000-foot mountains, such as 12,548-foot Whitetail Peak, and the Beartooth Plateau, a huge mass of contiguous land above 10,000 feet. Hikers are also treated to views of glaciers and obvious results of glaciation, exposed Precambrian rock, and waterfalls. And watch for mountain goats, deer, golden eagles, and gyrfalcons. Goats are frequently seen from First and Second Rock Lakes.

This is a fairly difficult, 21-mile shuttle trip that ends at the end of the West Fork Road. Arrange to be picked up at the trailhead at the end of the West Fork Road (Forest Road 71), or leave a vehicle there. An alternative is to have another party start at the other end of the trail, meet up on Sundance Pass, and trade keys.

Plan to do this trip no earlier in the year than July 15. Sundance Pass usually isn't snow-free until then. This delay also avoids the peak season for mosquitoes and no-see-ums, which can be quite bad in this area, especially on the West Fork side.

Although nicely suited to a three-day/two-night trip, the route also offers many scenic side trips. Plan an extra day or two in the backcountry for exploring these.

The main route passes by three lakes—Keyser Brown, September Morn, and Sundance—but several others can be reached with short side trips. One of these is Lost Lake, which is a quarter-mile climb from the main trail. This is a very heavily used lake, and it shows it. There are campsites here, but consider staying somewhere else that hasn't been trampled so much. The trail to Lost Lake leaves the main trail on the left, 5 miles from the trailhead or about 200 yards before the bridge over the Lake Fork of Rock Creek.

Another lake-bound trail departs from the main trail immediately before the same bridge. The unofficial trail to Black Canyon Lake scrambles uphill to the left also. Black Canyon Lake lies just below Grasshopper Glacier. The undeveloped trail to Black Canyon Lake is a rough but short hike of about 1.5 miles. Part of the route traverses rock talus with no trail, and there is a steep climb near the lake. The hike to Black Canyon is probably too tough for small children or poorly conditioned hikers. There is almost no place to camp at this high, rugged lake, and it's usually very windy at Black Canyon during midday.

The main trail continues west along the Lake Fork another mile to Keyser Brown Lake, about 7 miles from the trailhead. To do this trip in three days and two nights, plan to start early and spend the first night at Keyser Brown. Although the wood sup-

Lost Lake. Photo: Michael S. Sample

ply is ample enough around Keyser Brown, this is one of the most heavily used camp sites in the Beartooths. Please consider doing without a campfire here.

The lake is about a quarter mile to the left (southwest), so watch carefully for the side trail. It is an official trail, and it's signed. The lake itself comes into view from the main trail, but if you can see it you've missed the junction and need to backtrack about 200 yards to the trail to the lake. An anglers' trail leads south from the far end of Keyser Brown to First and Second Rock Lakes. This side trip involves some difficult boulder-hopping.

For another campsite option, continue 1.5 miles up the main trail to September Morn Lake. The campsite selection is much more limited here than at Keyser Brown, but it is closer to Sundance Pass.

Get a good night's sleep and a hearty breakfast before starting the second day. From Keyser Brown it's a 1,660-foot, Category 2 climb to the top of Sundance Pass. The scenery is so incredible, however, that hikers might not notice how much work it is getting to the top. To the north and east stretch the twin lobes of the Silver Run Plateau, rising to their apex at 12,500-foot Silver Run Peak. Directly south of the pass, 11,647-foot Mount Lockhart partially shields the pyramid of 12,548-foot Whitetail Peak. Remember to carry extra water on this stretch—it is scarce on the pass.

Coming down from Sundance Pass into the West Fork won't take long. A series of switchbacks drops about 1,000 feet in 1 mile or so to a bridge over the headwaters of the West Fork.

Although there are campsites in a meadow about a quarter mile down the trail from the Sundance Bridge, Quinnebaugh Meadows is probably the best choice for the second night out. It offers plenty of excellent campsites, and there's enough downed wood for a campfire. It's a long 8 miles from Keyser Brown to Quinnebaugh Meadows, but there aren't many good campsites between September Morn Lake and Quinnebaugh Meadows. Camping at the meadows leaves an easy 5 miles for the last day out. It might also allow enough time for a side trip up to Lake Mary or Dude Lake. Dude Lake is 1 mile west via a rough, steep trail from Quinnebaugh Meadows. And there's a steep but good trail from Quinnebaugh Meadows to Lake Mary. Some people use the saddle to the north of Lake Mary as a cross-country route to Crow, Sylvan, and East Rosebud Lakes.

The final day of hiking follows the trail along the north bank of the West Fork all the way to the trailhead. Sentinel and Calamity Falls both offer good places to drop the pack and relax.

Both the Lake Fork and the West Fork are probably used as heavily as any wild area in Montana. Consequently, the Forest Service has rangers out enforcing several protective regulations. These special regulations are listed at a sign on the trailhead. Be sure to read them carefully, and then, of course, obey them. They are necessary to protect these fragile environs.

This trip also works well in reverse. In fact, starting from the West Fork results in about 600 feet less overall elevation gain. However, Sundance Pass is tougher to climb from the West Fork side.

Options

This trip can be done from either trailhead with no noticeable difference. Climbing Sundance Pass is a lung-buster from either side.

Side Trips

This hike offers an abundant variety of side trips, including: Lost Lake (Human), Black Canyon Lake (Animal), Rock Lakes (Semi-human), Whitetail Peak (Animal), Sundance Mountain (Animal), Sundance Lake (Human), Marker Lake (Animal), Ship Lake Basin (Animal), Kookoo Lake (Animal), Shadow Lake (Human), Dude Lake (Animal), Lake Mary (Semi-human), and Crow Lake (Animal). Refer to Quinnebaugh Meadows, Hike 27, for more suggested side trips.

Camping

There are no designated campsites in this area. Since this area gets heavy use, please make sure you have zero-impact campsites.

Fishing at Black Canyon Lake.

Fishing

The lakes found along the Lake Fork provide some of the easiest fishing in the Beartooths. Anglers will find plenty of hungry brookies in September Morn, Keyser Brown, and First and Second Rock Lakes. Overnight campers can count on these lakes to supply dinner. Keyser Brown and Second Rock Lakes also support healthy cutthroat fisheries.

For those with something other than brook trout on their mind, Lost Lake supports a few cutthroat trout of surprising size. Grayling also have been planted in Lost Lake, and they grow large as well.

The scramble up to Black Canyon Lake rewards anglers with plenty of cutthroats near the glacial moraine that blocks the outlet. While this lake once grew exceptionally large fish, a probable change in food organisms, caused by the fish themselves, now keeps them in the slightly above-average range. This lake offers the best chance for catching a 15-inch or larger trout in the Lake Fork drainage.

From the crest of Sundance Pass, look to the lakes in the high basin across the West Fork to the northwest. Ship Lake is the largest of these. There are plenty of fish in these waters for hikers who don't mind climbing up the other side of the valley after coming down Sundance Pass.

31 Broadwater Lake

General description: An easy day trip
Special attractions: Early in the year, watch for waterfalls cascading off the high plateau from the south
Type of trip: Out-and-back
Total distance: 7 miles

Difficulty: Easy
Traffic: Heavy
Maps: USGS—Black Pyramid Mountain; RMS—Alpine-Mount Maurice
Starting point: Lake Fork Trailhead

Finding the trailhead: Refer to Sundance Pass, Hike 30.
Parking and trailhead facilities: Refer to Sundance Pass, Hike 30.

The Hike

From the trailhead, immediately cross a bridge over the Lake Fork of Rock Creek, turn right (west), and head upstream along the Lake Fork. The trail stays close to the stream all the way. The trail is easy to follow, well maintained, hazard-free, and usually dry. Plus, there are no steep hills, and the trail stays on the south side of the stream the entire way to Broadwater Lake, so there are no fords.

All of these advantages make this trip near-perfect for an easy day hike with children. Perhaps the best part of the trip into Broadwater Lake is constantly being near a clean, natural mountain stream. Hikers can stop at dozens of places and just sit back against a tree, relax, and soak in the sound of the rushing water. Along the way, watch for water ouzels playing in the blue-green waters of the Lake Fork and expect to see lots of wildflowers along the stream.

Broadwater Lake is beautiful, but not well named. It's not really a lake at all, but a long "glide" where the stream widens and slows for a few moments before hurrying out of the mountains.

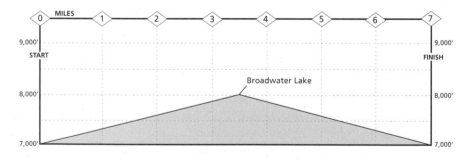

Camping

There aren't really any good campsites in the area, so it's best to consider this a nice day trip.

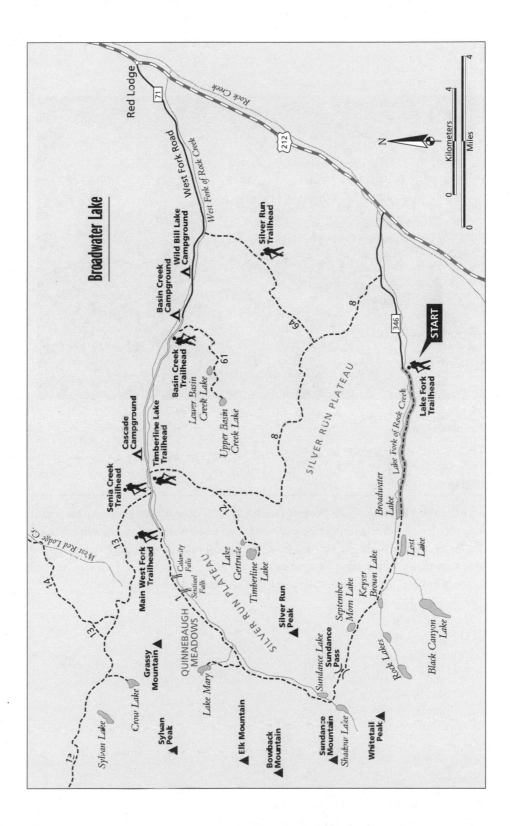

Broadwater Lake

Red Lodge

Rock Creek

71

West Fork Road

West Fork of Rock Creek

212

N

Kilometers

Miles

0   4

0   4

Basin Creek Campground

Wild Bill Lake Campground

Silver Run Trailhead

Cascade Campground

Timberline Lake Trailhead

Basin Creek Trailhead

Lower Basin Creek Lake

Upper Basin Creek Lake

61

64

8

8

SILVER RUN PLATEAU

346

START

Lake Fork Trailhead

Lake Fork of Rock Creek

Broadwater Lake

Lost Lake

Senia Creek Trailhead

Main West Fork Trailhead

W West Red Lodge Cr.

Calamity Falls

Sentinel Falls

QUINNEBAUGH MEADOWS

Lake Mary

SILVER RUN PLATEAU

Lake Gertrude

Timberline Lake

Silver Run Peak

Sundance Lake

Sundance Pass

September Morn Lake

Keyser Brown Lake

Rock Lakes

Black Canyon Lake

Grassy Mountain

Sylvan Lake

Crow Lake

Sylvan Peak

Elk Mountain

Bowback Mountain

Sundance Mountain

Shadow Lake

Whitetail Peak

13

14

13

12

12

1

2

The Lake Fork of Rock Creek with Thunder Mountain as a backdrop.
Photo: Michael S. Sample

Fishing

Like the West Fork, the Lake Fork of Rock Creek is exceptionally photogenic, but it supports fewer fish than might be expected. The cold water, restricted sunlight, and fast current don't make life easy for fish. The Lake Fork supports both cutthroat and brook trout, but with some exceptions, the numbers are not high. Fish concentrate in the slower sections of the stream, and Broadwater Lake is one of these.

32 Hellroaring Lakes

General description: A short, mostly off-trail trip into a high-elevation basin filled with lakes; best suited for day hiking

Special attractions: So much to see on such a short hike

Type of trip: Out-and-back, with loop option

Total distance: 4 to 8 miles, depending on how much exploring you do

Difficulty: Moderate to difficult if you go into the basin; easy if you stay on the plateau

Traffic: Moderate

Maps: USGS—Black Pyramid Mountain; RMS—Alpine-Mount Maurice

Starting point: Hellroaring Plateau Trailhead

Finding the trailhead: Drive south from Red Lodge on U.S. Highway 212 for 10.9 miles. Watch for a well-marked turnoff on the right (west) to three Forest Service campgrounds. Stay on this paved road for 0.9 mile until you cross a bridge near the entrance to Limberpine Campground. Immediately after the bridge, the pavement ends and you reach a fork in the road. For Hellroaring Lakes, turn right (north then sharply turning southwest). You need a high-clearance four-wheel-drive vehicle to get to this trailhead. Snow usually blocks this gravel road until at least early July. Once on the road to the Hellroaring Lakes parking area, there's only one fork in the road, about a half mile before the trailhead where you go left. It's a rough 5.8 miles to the end of the road and the trailhead, which is on the edge of the Hellroaring Plateau. To be blunt, this road isn't for faint-hearted drivers or horse trailers.

Parking and trailhead facilities: Moderately large parking area; no toilet.

The Hike

From the trailhead, follow an old, closed-off jeep road (Trail 11) about a mile along the Hellroaring Plateau. Lower Hellroaring Lakes are soon visible in the valley off to right (north). You are better off continuing along the plateau instead of going down to the lakes from this point. If you drop off the plateau too early, the terrain gets very steep and you have to fight through a maze of alpine willows and small streams. Instead, continue along the plateau for another half mile or so. The scenery is worth it. Wander over to the south edge of the plateau on the left to see the main fork of Rock Creek.

At about the 1.5-mile mark and just before a huge snowbank on the right (northwest), head down to the lakes. Take a close look at the topo map before dropping off the plateau, and keep the map handy until you climb back out of the basin.

The climb down to the lakes is more gradual from this point. Watch for game trails on the way down, but be prepared for essentially off-trail hiking. Once at the lakes, the hiking is much easier. There are fairly well defined anglers' trails between the lakes.

This is a heavenly basin filled with lakes, mostly above 10,000 feet. Hairpin Lake, for example, is definitely worth seeing. It has a series of beautiful bays, and a waterfall

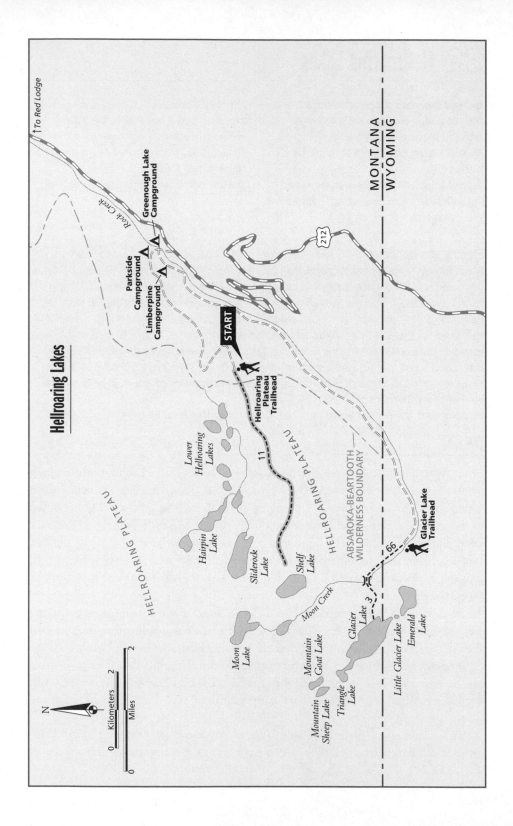

Hellroaring Lakes

To Red Lodge

Rock Creek

Greenough Lake Campground

Parkside Campground

Limberpine Campground

START

Hellroaring Plateau Trailhead

212

11

HELLROARING PLATEAU

Lower Hellroaring Lakes

Hairpin Lake

Sliderock Lake

Shelf Lake

HELLROARING PLATEAU

ABSAROKA-BEARTOOTH WILDERNESS BOUNDARY

66

Glacier Lake Trailhead

Moon Creek

Glacier Lake 3

Moon Lake

Mountain Goat Lake

Triangle Lake

Little Glacier Lake

Emerald Lake

Mountain Sheep Lake

MONTANA
WYOMING

N

Kilometers

Miles

0 2

0 2

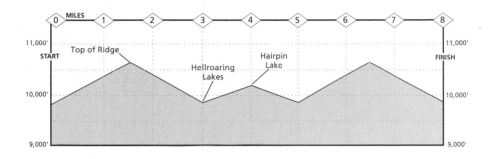

plunges into the lake from the northwest. There are plenty of grand places to explore and all within a short distance.

After a few hours exploring the basin, climb back up to the plateau and back to your vehicle.

While exploring the basin, watch the weather. It's all too easy—and dangerous—to get caught on the plateau by one of the severe thunderstorms that often roll through here in the afternoon.

Options

To make a short loop out of the trip, hike down to the lower lakes and then up to the plateau. Bear in mind that the climb back to the plateau from the lower basin is brutal. It's much easier to retrace your steps up the valley and then take the more gradual climb to the plateau just east of the large snowbank. Another short loop can be made by heading west to Sliderock Lake and then climbing back to the plateau on the west side of the snowbank.

Side Trips

The entire purpose of this hike is side trips. Simply get out your topo map and find a vantage point to decide where to go.

Camping

The basin is best suited for an extended day hike, but a few people camp there. The best choice for a campsite is around one of the lower lakes where there are more level spots and trees to break the wind. This is alpine country, so please don't burn up the aesthetic wood supply by using it for campfires.

Fishing

There are thirteen Hellroaring Lakes in the basin, and most offer fishing opportunities. Three lakes are fishless, and please leave them that way. If you prepare for mosquitoes, the lower lakes are the perfect place to take your son or daughter for his or

Off-trail hiking on the Hellroaring Plateau.

her first mountain backpacking trip. Each small lake has its own personality, and most support brook trout and cutthroat trout, both of which are willing to be caught. The trees here provide cover from the wind and a visual break from the rocky terrain above. When you're tired of catching the numerous smaller trout in the lower lakes, head up the drainage. Hairpin Lake has nice cutts, some of which could break a line. On the way back out, make the side trip to Sliderock Lake for some of the healthiest brook trout anywhere in the Beartooths. Pack them in snow while you finish fishing, and then take them home for dinner.

33 Glacier Lake

General description: A steep but short day trip or overnighter

Special attractions: A spectacular area accessible with a short hike

Type of trip: Out-and-back

Total distance: 4 miles, plus side trips

Difficulty: Moderately strenuous but short to Glacier Lake; some side trips and exploring can be difficult

Traffic: Moderate

Maps: USGS—Beartooth Butte and Silver Run Peak; RMS—Alpine-Mount Maurice and Wyoming Beartooths

Starting point: Glacier Lake Trailhead

Finding the trailhead: Drive south from Red Lodge on U.S. Highway 212 for 10.9 miles. Watch for a well-marked turnoff on the right (west) to three Forest Service campgrounds. Stay on this paved road for 0.9 mile until you cross a bridge near the entrance to Limberpine Campground. Immediately after the bridge, the pavement ends and you reach a fork in the road. For Glacier Lake, turn left (southwest). You really want a high-clearance vehicle to get to this trailhead, but you can get there slowly with any vehicle. Snow usually blocks this gravel road until at least early July. Once on the road to the Glacier Lake parking area, there's no chance of making a wrong turn because there are no other forks or spur roads. It's a long, slow, bumpy 7.6 miles to the trailhead.

Parking and trailhead facilities: Small parking area is frequently full, so be careful not to take more than one space; pit toilet at trailhead, along with a National Weather Service precipitation gauge; plenty of undeveloped camping areas and one developed campground along this road, as well as plenty of vehicle camping at the start of the road to Glacier Lake.

The Hike

Although this route could be done as an overnighter, the Glacier Lake area seems nicely suited to a long day of exploring, fishing, photographing, and simply enjoying high-elevation majestic vistas. It's easily accessible by a 2-mile trail. The Forest Service has restricted stock use on this trail due to hazardous conditions for horses.

The trail to Glacier Lake is short but very steep. The trailhead is at 8,680 feet and the lake is at 9,702 feet, but the route actually climbs more than the difference (1,022 feet) in the 2 miles to Glacier Lake. That's because there's a ridge in the middle that's about 800 feet higher than the lake, making the first part of the trail a Category 1 climb.

After climbing for about a half mile, the trail crosses Moon Creek on a bridge. After Moon Creek, the trail gets even steeper—and the higher it goes, the better the scenery. Shortly after Moon Creek, a faint, unofficial trail veers off to the north to Moon Lake and Shelf Lake. Turn left (west) and stay on what is obviously the main trail. For most of the way, the trail is rough and rock-studded, but it remains easy to follow and without hazards.

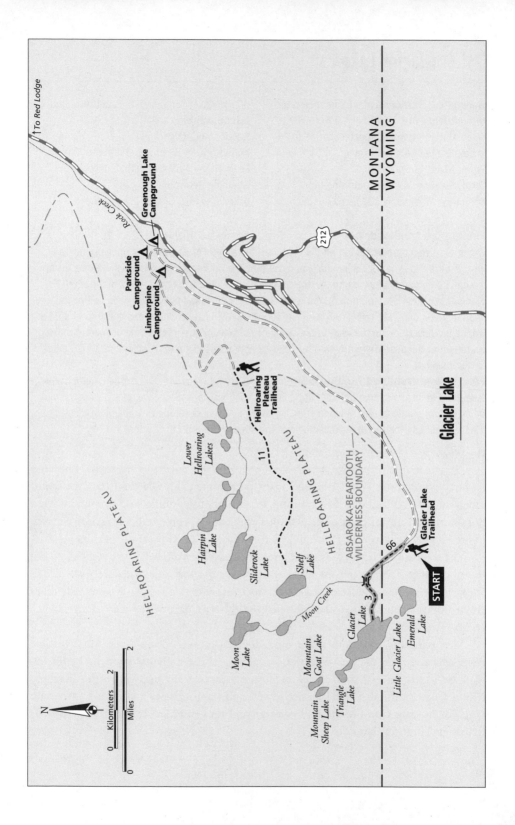

Glacier Lake

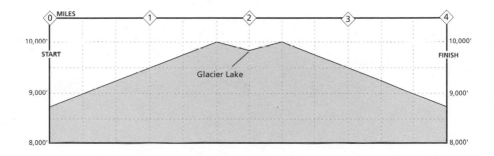

Once atop the ridge, cross some rock shelves on the way down to massive Glacier Lake. Even though the lake sits at 9,702 feet (above timberline), some large trees stand along the shoreline.

The trail reaches the lake at a small dam built long ago to increase the depth of Glacier Lake. A faint trail heads off to the right and goes about halfway around the lake. After a large point jutting out into the lake, the trail degenerates into a series of boulder fields and talus slopes. Watch for the amazing numbers of pikas that inhabit the area.

Bearing right along the north shore of the lake affords views of Triangle Lake and access to Mountain Sheep Lake and Mountain Goat Lake at the head of the basin. Bearing left and across the dam around the south shore of the lake leads directly to Little Glacier Lake, a small jewel just barely separated from Glacier Lake. Continuing south on this trail over a small ridge treats wanderers to the sight of lovely Emerald Lake.

If you're fishing, be sure to keep track of which state you're in, and make sure you have the right license. The state line goes right through Glacier Lake. Little Glacier and Emerald Lakes are in Wyoming.

Because of topography, Glacier Lake tends to become remarkably windy during midday, so try to arrive early to catch the scenery before the winds start ripping through this valley. Emerald Lake is not quite as windy.

Side Trips

Mountain Goat and Mountain Sheep Lakes can be reached with a reasonable effort, but Moon and Shelf Lakes are strenuous side trips.

Camping

All of the potential campsites along the north shore of Glacier Lake are cramped and marginal at best and probably too close to the lake. For those planning to stay overnight, there are several quality campsites on the north side of Emerald Lake. The south side of the lake is spectacularly steep. This is high alpine country, so please resist the temptation to have a campfire.

Glacier Lake. Photo: Michael S. Sample

Fishing

The ice-cold, swift-running water and high canyon walls make Rock Creek extremely attractive to look at, but these conditions also make life hard for fish. Rock Creek is home to small populations of cutthroat and brook trout. Fish concentrate in the slower water, so look for good holding places out of the current. The main fork of Rock Creek winds in and out of Wyoming and Montana, so anglers need to know which state they're in and have the appropriate license.

Glacier Lake supports cutthroat and brook trout, both of which grow to above-average size. The fish tend to school, with cutthroats working rocky shorelines, so anglers should work the shoreline as well. When water levels are high, water flows between Glacier and Little Glacier Lakes, so the fishery is the same in both. But the fish are easier to find in Little Glacier. Emerald Lake supports both cutts and brookies as well, though slightly smaller than those in Glacier.

Plan on seeing other anglers. The tough hike around Glacier Lake probably spreads out the competition. Cutts are stocked in Mountain Goat Lake and work their way down to Mountain Sheep Lake. Count on more fish in the upper lake and larger ones in the lower.

Fewer hikers go to Moon and Shelf Lakes, as the trail seems steeper and longer than it is. Shelf Lake harbors hefty brookies, while Moon grows above-average cutts.

The Beartooth Highway

Driving the Beartooth Highway (U.S. Highway 212) is an adventure for some people. In addition to offering up outstanding scenery, the lofty roadway provides the unique opportunity to start hiking trips well above timberline at 9,500 to 10,000 feet elevation. Gardner Lake has the distinction of being the highest trailhead I've ever used—10,536 feet. Some trailheads, like Island Lake, Beartooth Lake, Clay Butte, and Clarks Fork, get heavy use, but most get minimal use. For experienced hikers who can hike off-trail, the open, treeless terrain is a wide-open invitation to start hiking at virtually any pullout along the highway.

Hikers often ignore the undesignated wilderness south of the Beartooth Highway and flock to the heavily used trails in the designated Absaroka-Beartooth Wilderness north of the road. Yet, the area south of the highway is equally wild and scenic and less crowded. Although not designated as wilderness, the Forest Service manages the area with a priority on backcountry recreation. Unlike trails north of the highway, some trails heading south are open to mountain biking. Also, backcountry horsemen commonly use the trails south of the highway.

A mile west of the Island Lake Trailhead, check out the aptly named Top of the World Store. Looking in all directions from the store certainly makes it easy to see why it got its name. It's hard to believe this landscape wasn't included in the designated wilderness, which coincides with the Montana–Wyoming border. Fortunately, though, the Forest Service manages it as though it was included.

Hikers can find dozens of lakes within a short walk of the Beartooth Highway trailheads. Many trails are at least partly in Wyoming, so if you plan to fish, be sure you have the correct fishing license—or in some cases, one from both states.

Many lakes were stocked with brook trout in the first half of the twentieth century. The rationale was that brookies are hearty, reproduce easily, and could establish reproducing populations, which they certainly did. Today, brookies provide excellent fishing for great numbers of aggressive, hungry trout. However, brookies tend to over-populate these lakes, resulting in smaller, stunted fish. On the positive side, 8- to 9-inch brookies may be the tastiest trout of the Beartooths, and don't feel bad about keeping some for dinner. You're actually doing the environment a favor.

The Forest Service has developed several excellent vehicle campgrounds along the highway, often strategically located near trailheads—and often full, too. Campers who prefer undeveloped camping can also find good sites on short spur roads off the highway, particularly on the west side of Beartooth Pass.

Beartooth Lake lies in the shadow of famous 10,514-foot Beartooth Butte, which dominates the western horizon on the west side of the pass. Beartooth Butte is an enigma, a tiny island of sedimentary rock in a sea of granite making up the Beartooth Mountains. Beartooth Butte and neighboring Clay Butte to the east and Table Mountain to the south are the only outcrops on the entire Beartooth Plateau still covered with sedimentary rock. Erosion removed the sedimentary rock from the rest of the area, but for some reason, still somewhat unclear to geologists, these three remnants survived. Geologists do know, however, that Beartooth Butte contains fossils of some the oldest known plants ever found in North America.

Most people are in a big hurry to hit the trail when they get to the trailhead, but at the Clay Butte Trailhead, it's worth taking an extra 15 minutes to drive to the top of Clay Butte for the view. It's only another mile to the lookout, where—at 9,811 feet—you'll find a splendid view of the Beartooth Plateau. From this vista, much of the terrain covered by the trails leaving from this trailhead can be seen.

Anyone who has been to the Clarks Fork Trailhead could mount a strong argument that it's the most beautiful trailhead in the Beartooths. It rests on the south shoreline of the Clarks Fork of the Yellowstone as the river leaves the Beartooths right at a spectacular falls and large pool, perfect for a dip after a long, hot week in the wilderness. The large grassy area with picnic tables is especially nice for people wanting a leisurely picnic in a gorgeous setting followed by a short day hike. In fact, a worthwhile attraction lies just beyond the trailhead, where a major footbridge spans the Clarks Fork where it has cut a narrow gorge.

With the exception of Lake Abundance and Fisher Creek, all Beartooth Highway trailheads are easy to find and are located right on the highway. The mileage along U.S. Highway 212 from Red Lodge or Cooke City is as follows:

Lake Abundance—0.5 mile from Cooke City, 61 miles from Red Lodge
Fisher Creek—2 miles from Cooke City, 59.5 miles from Red Lodge
Clarks Fork of the Yellowstone—3.4 miles from Cooke City, 58.1 miles from
    Red Lodge
Crazy Creek—11 miles from Cooke City, 50.5 miles from Red Lodge
Muddy Creek—18 miles from Cooke City, 43.5 miles from Red Lodge
Clay Butte—21.2 miles from Cooke City, 40.3 miles from Red Lodge
Beartooth Lake—22.7 miles from Cooke City, 38.8 miles from Red Lodge
Island Lake—25.8 miles from Cooke City, 35.7 miles from Red Lodge
Long Lake—27.3 miles from Cooke City, 34.2 miles from Red Lodge
Gardner Lake—34.1 miles from Cooke City, 27.4 miles from Red Lodge

Hiking the Beartooth High Lakes Trail.

Rock Creek—50.6 miles from Cooke City, 10.9 miles from Red Lodge

Lake Fork of Rock Creek—52.5 miles from Cooke City, 9.3 miles from Red Lodge

West Fork of Rock Creek—61.4 miles from Cooke City, 0.1 mile from Red Lodge

34 Gardner Lake

General description: A steep but short day trip

Special attractions: A high-elevation lake within sight of the Beartooth Highway

Type of trip: Out-and-back

Total distance: 1.5 miles

Difficulty: Easy

Traffic: Light

Maps: USGS—Deep Lake; RMS—Wyoming Beartooths

Starting point: Gardner Lake Trailhead

Finding the trailhead: A large pullout on the south side of the Beartooth Highway (U.S. 212) 34.1 miles east of Cooke City and 27.4 miles west of Red Lodge.

Parking and trailhead facilities: Plenty of parking; no toilet.

The Hike

The trail to Gardner Lake is the beginning of the Beartooth Loop National Recreation Trail, a long backpacking route.

Gardner Lake is the fairly large lake you can see from the trailhead. You can also see that even though it's only 0.75 mile to the lake, it's all downhill to get there and all uphill to get back to your vehicle.

This is high country. The trail starts at 10,936 feet and drops to 9,950 feet at the lake, making it a Category H climb to get back to the trailhead from the lake. This elevation prevents tree growth, so the entire hike goes through open alpine terrain. Along the trail you can note many species of delicate alpine wildflowers.

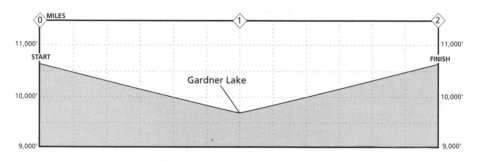

Camping

Although it's possible and legal to camp at Gardner Lake, very few people do, mainly because your tent would be within sight of passing motorists.

Fishing

Gardner Lake has a good population of easy-to-catch brookies.

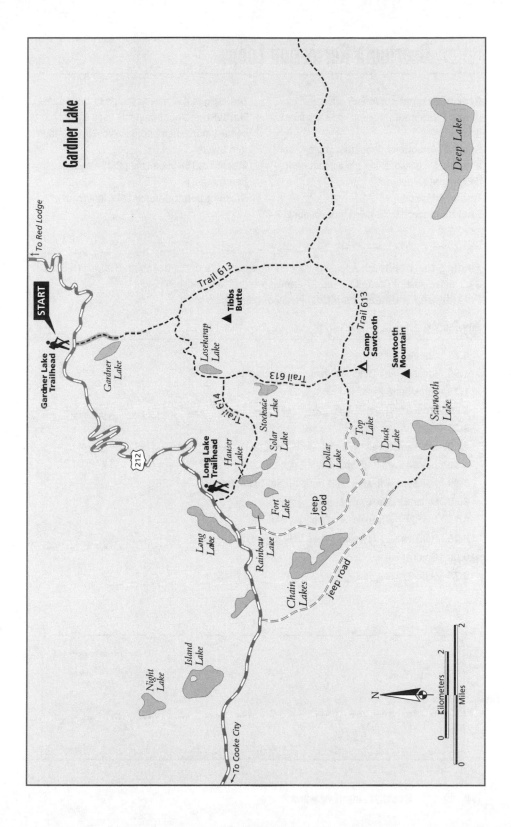

Gardner Lake

35 Beartooth Recreation Loop

General description: A fairly short, easy, uncrowded trip with multiple side trip possibilities

Special attractions: Proof that you can have a wonderful backpacking trip without having designated wilderness

Type of trip: Loop

Total distance: 10.75 miles, not counting side trips

Difficulty: Easy, unless you go to Deep Lake

Traffic: Light, but frequently used by backcountry horsemen and occasionally by mountain bikers

Maps: USGS—Deep Lake; RMS—Wyoming Beartooths

Starting point: Gardner Lake Trailhead

Finding the trailhead: A large pullout on the south side of the Beartooth Highway (U.S. 212) 34.1 miles east of Cooke City and 27.4 miles west of Red Lodge.

Parking and trailhead facilities: Plenty of parking; no toilet.

Key Points

- **0.75**   Gardner Lake.
- **1.50**   Junction with Littlerock Creek Trail; turn right.
- **1.75**   Tibbs Butte Pass.
- **3.00**   Losekamp Lake.
- **3.25**   Junction with Hauser Lake Trail; turn left.
- **4.00**   Stockade Lake.
- **4.50**   Junction with trail from Chain Lake; turn left.
- **5.50**   Junctions with spur trails to Camp Sawtooth; turn left.
- **6.50**   Littlerock Creek Valley.
- **6.75**   Junction with Lower Highline Trail; turn left.
- **9.25**   Junction with Losekamp Lake Trail; turn right.
- **10.00**   Gardner Lake.
- **10.75**   Gardner Lake Trailhead.

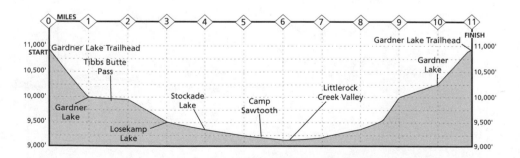

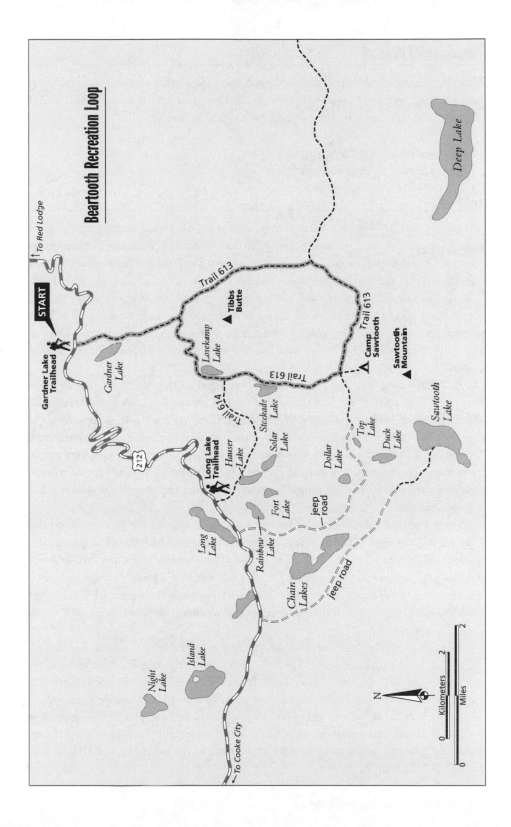

Beartooth Recreation Loop

START

Gardner Lake Trailhead

To Red Lodge

Gardner Lake

212

Long Lake Trailhead

Trail 613

Losekamp Lake

▲ Tibbs Butte

Trail 614

Stockade Lake

Hauser Lake

Solar Lake

Fort Lake

Rainbow Lake

jeep road

Dollar Lake

Top Lake

Duck Lake

△ Camp Sawtooth

Trail 613

Trail 613

▲ Sawtooth Mountain

Sawtooth Lake

Long Lake

Chair Lakes

jeep road

Island Lake

Night Lake

To Cooke City

Deep Lake

N

Kilometers   2

0

Miles   2

0

Recommended Itinerary

Like any route, this trip could be lengthened, but unlike most routes, this could be an easy overnighter. You're here—why not spend some time hiking around, fishing, and enjoying the wilderness before heading back to the highway?

First night: Camp Sawtooth
Second night: Same campsite

The Hike

This could be a day hike, but because there is so much to see along the way, it's nicely suited for an easy—or perhaps somebody's first— backpacking trip. The route is mostly flat and scenic, mostly above timberline, with no steep climbs except a short calf-stretcher at the end of the hike—and no hazards, unless you go to Deep Lake. The trail is well defined all the way with good signage, plenty of good campsites, and lots of lakes and streams filled with little brookies that love to get caught by kids. In general, this is not an austere place. Instead, it's a gentle, elegant, peaceful place, just as wild and beautiful as the Tetons you can see on the western horizon, but not so rugged.

At 10,950 feet, this may be the highest trailhead in the Northern Rockies, but that changes quickly, as the trail plunges down to Gardner Lake. It's a good trail with no switchbacks, which you might want when climbing back up to your vehicle. At Gardner Lake, the trail levels out and stays that way most of the trip. It's amazing how fast the wilderness takes over from civilization. Even at Gardner Lake, less than a mile away from the highway, you get the feeling you're in the middle of a great wilderness. You can look up and see motor homes cruising the highway in the distance, but try to avoid this.

From Gardner Lake, the trail goes south for 0.75 mile to the junction with the Littlerock Creek Trail (Trail 613) that you use to complete the loop, which essentially circles 10,676-foot Tibbs Butte. Turn right (west) here and gain about a hundred feet elevation to 10,060-foot Tibbs Butte Pass. It's not much of a pass—but not a place to get caught in a lightning storm, as we did. Start enjoying the carpet of wildflowers that follows most of the route—lupine, bottle cleaners, elephant head, and many more.

After Tibbs Butte Pass, you drop down a few hundred feet, almost to timberline, where you find Losekamp Lake. The trail goes around the lake to the right and on the other side you see the Hauser Lake Trail coming in from the north. Turn left (south) here. In another 0.75 mile, slightly downhill, you hit Stockade Lake with a small "stockade" at the north end of lake. At both lakes, you can plan on being greeted by clouds of mosquitoes unless you waited until late summer to take this trip. From Stockade Lake, you get a great view of Tibbs Butte to the northeast and 10,262-foot Sawtooth Mountain to the south.

Littlerock Creek Valley.

After Stockade the trail goes through scattered stands of conifers interspersed with a series of beautiful meadows complete with a small, unnamed meandering stream. Watch for moose and elk. You also drop slightly below timberline and stay there until after you leave Camp Sawtooth.

The trail from Chain Lake joins the loop 0.5 mile below the south end of Stockade Lake. Turn left (east) here and continue hiking through a open forested landscape for another mile to the spur trail leading to Camp Sawtooth, a good choice for your overnight stay.

Camp Sawtooth is on the north edge of a huge, gorgeous meadow about a half mile south of the main trail. Unless spring runoff has already washed it away, you can cross Littlerock Creek on a rapidly deteriorating old bridge. You can find many good campsites and the remains of several old structures at Camp Sawtooth. If you don't camp here, drop your pack for an hour or so and go visit it.

Back on the main trail, turn right (east) and hike about another quarter mile to another sign for another spur trail leading to Camp Sawtooth. Either spur trail will take you to Camp Sawtooth, but the first one seemed more heavily used—and when I was there, it had a great trail sign that had been chewed on by a bear.

After leaving Camp Sawtooth behind, you go though a big wet meadow and then up a small, 200-foot hill and into the lower end of the delightful Littlerock Creek Valley, a truly wonderful high-altitude mountain basin. When you reach the junction with the Lower Highline Trail, turn left (north). You actually gain some elevation hiking through the Littlerock Creek Valley, but it's so pleasant and seemingly flat that you don't notice. You cross Littlerock Creek twice—no bridges, but late in the year, you can usually cross on rocks without getting wet feet.

At the upper end of the valley, you come back to the junction south of Gardner Lake. Turn right (north) here and retrace your steps past Gardner Lake to your vehicle. Allow a little extra time to get up the Category H hill from the lake to the highway.

Options

You could do this loop in reverse with no added difficulty. If you do it in reverse, you could make a shuttle out of it by going out to Chain Lake or Hauser Lake.

Side Trips

The logical side trip is to Deep Lake, but this transforms a walk in the park into a difficult, strenuous hike. Deep Lake is austere and ruggedly beautiful. Three inlet streams come in at the same place at the north end of the lake, which is a good place to visit but not to camp. The terrain more or less forces all visitors to go to the same place right at the inlet, creating the potential for conflict and overuse. In late summer you can cross the inlet stream and hike a short way along the east side of Deep Lake.

In general, the trip to Deep Lake is not for families with small kids or the fainthearted. To get there, fight through the brush and several small streams in the monstrous meadow south of Camp Sawtooth. At the other end of the meadow, just west of where an unnamed stream comes in from two small tarns, you start up a hill, a gradual, 400-foot, 1.5-mile climb on a good unofficial trail. Then, it's a 1,150-foot drop to the lake in less than a mile with no trail and lots of rocks—it's very tough going and outright hazardous in a few spots. A few cairns mark the way, but it's basically route-finding. Don't try it unless you are experienced and fit and have lots of time. And keep in mind that after your visit to Deep Lake, you face this Category H climb to get back to your base camp. Other side trip opportunities are Hauser, Dollar, and Christmas Lakes.

Camping

The entire route is lined with great campsites, so you'd have to work hard at finding a bad campsite. Stockade Lake has a big outfitter camp on the east side of the lake, but you can still find a good campsite on the west side of the lake. Camp Sawtooth is a

Deep Lake, a demanding off-trail side trip.

conveniently located camping area with a great view and plenty of room for several parties without feeling like your privacy has been lost. You can find enough downed wood for a campfire at several campsites, but try to resist. If you have one, keep the fire small and as close to zero impact as possible.

Fishing

Most lakes and streams along this route have small brookies. Deep Lake has larger brookies and cutthroats.

36 Hauser Lake

General description: A short but seemingly remote day trip or overnighter
Special attractions: A very spectacular area accessible with a short hike
Type of trip: Out-and-back or easy base camp
Total distance: 1.5 miles

Difficulty: Easy
Traffic: Light
Maps: USGS—Deep Lake; RMS—Wyoming Beartooths
Starting point: Long Lake Trailhead

Finding the trailhead: A small pullout on the north side of the Beartooth Highway (U.S. 212) along Long Lake about 27.3 miles east of Cooke City and 34.2 miles southwest of Red Lodge.
Parking and trailhead facilities: Room to park five to ten vehicles; no toilet.

The Hike

This trail is similar to the Gardner Lake hike (Hike 34) without the big hill. This trip is ideal for beginning backpackers who like to fish or families with young children out for their first night in the wilderness.

There's a trailhead information sign on the south side of the road for the Beartooth Recreation Loop (Hike 35), which can be hiked from this trailhead as easily as from Gardner Lake Trailhead. The trail is not well-defined in the meadow along the road, so keep your eyes peeled for a few big cairns that mark the trail.

Once you get near the trees, the trail becomes easy to follow and stays so all the way to Hauser Lake. The elevation on this hike is much lower than the trail to Gardner Lake—starting at 9,841 feet and going to the lake at 9,650 feet. The area is mostly open—and very scenic.

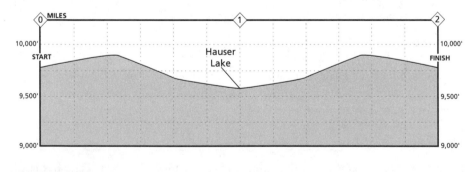

Side Trips

If you have some extra time and energy (and don't mind off-trail hiking), you can visit three more lakes with very short walks from Hauser Lake—Solar, Fort, and Rainbow Lakes.

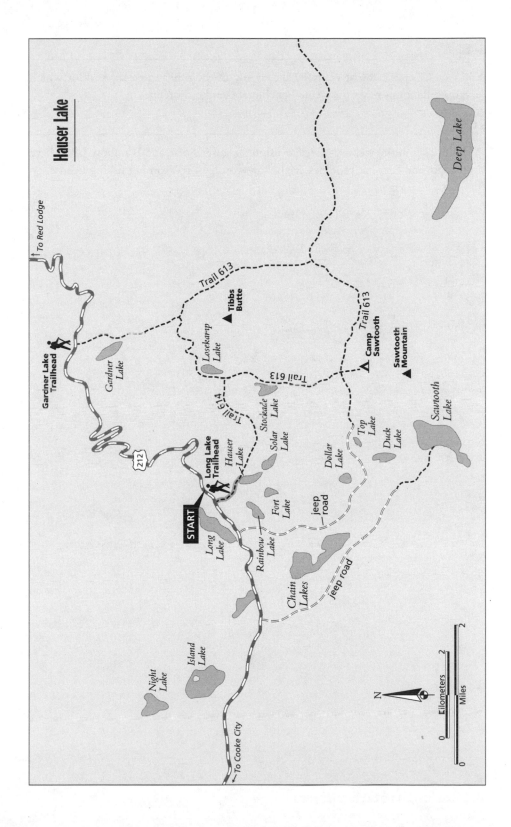

Hauser Lake

To Red Lodge

Garciner Lake
Trailhead

Gardner
Lake

212

Long Lake
Trailhead

START

Long
Lake

Night
Lake

Island
Lake

To Cooke City

Trail 613

Tibbs
Butte

Losekarp
Lake

Trail 614

Stockade
Lake

Solar
Lake

Hauser
Lake

Fort
Lake

Rainbow
Lake

Chain
Lakes

jeep road

jeep
road

Dollar
Lake

Camp
Sawtooth

Trail 613

Trail 613

Sawtooth
Mountain

Sawtooth
Lake

Top
Lake

Duck
Lake

Deep Lake

N

Kilometers 2
Miles

0   2
0   2

Camping

You can set up a camp at Hauser Lake or any of the other three lakes, all of which have excellent campsites on scenic benches above the shorelines.

Fishing

All four lakes in the vicinity offer fair fishing. Hauser, Solar, and Rainbow Lakes have cutthroats, and Fort has brookies. Make sure you have a Wyoming fishing license.

Becker Lake. ▶

37 Becker Lake

General description: An easy day hike, overnighter, or base camp

Special attractions: A remarkable number of lakes in such a short route

Type of trip: Out-and-back

Total distance: 7.5 miles

Difficulty: Easy

Traffic: Heavy

Maps: USGS—Beartooth Butte; RMS—Wyoming Beartooths

Starting point: Island Lake Trailhead

Finding the trailhead: From Cooke City, drive 25.8 miles east on the Beartooth Highway (U.S. 212), or from Red Lodge, drive 35.7 miles; take the short access road to the Island Lake Campground on the north side of the highway. The trailhead is at the end of the road.

Parking and trailhead facilities: A large parking lot; toilets; camping in the campground at the trailhead.

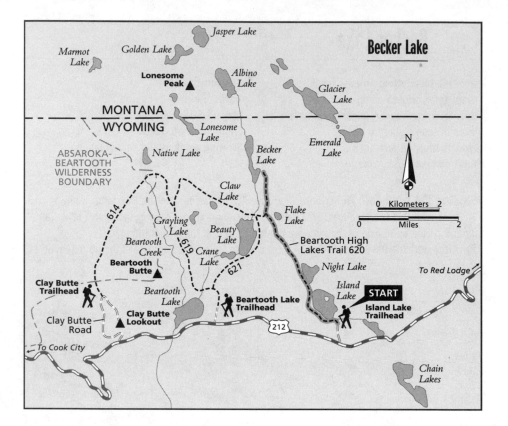

Key Points

1.0 Night Lake.

2.5 Flake Lake.

2.7 Turn off Beartooth High Lakes Trail 620.

3.2 Mutt and Jeff Lakes.

3.5 Becker Lake.

The Hike

This is not only a great day hike, but also a perfect choice for that first overnight camping experience with family or children. The trail gains only 175 feet in elevation over 3.5 miles, but just because it's flat doesn't mean it's lacking in scenery. To the contrary, this is one of the most scenic routes in the Beartooths.

From the trailhead the trail closely follows the west shore of Island Lake for most of the first mile. Then it leads less than 0.25 mile over to Night Lake and once again follows the west shore. Small children love this section of trail, but they tend to go slowly because there are so many discoveries for them to make.

Continue past Flake Lake, also to the east, until you leave Trail 620 and head straight north (to the right) toward Becker Lake. Be alert not to miss the trail heading to Becker Lake—this is not an official Forest Service trail, nor does it show up on the Forest Service or USGS maps.

The trail turns off in a wet meadow just after you leave Flake Lake behind and Trail 620 turns to the west. The first 50 feet or so is overgrown and hard to see. Then it becomes an excellent trail, almost as well-used as Trail 620. If you miss the trail, simply head off cross-country along the continuous lake between Flake Lake and Jeff Lake. Stay on the west side of the lakes, and you'll soon see the trail.

Go between Mutt Lake and Jeff Lake, crossing over a small stream between the lakes. The two lakes are essentially one lake since the elevation drop between them is about 5 inches. Just past Mutt and Jeff, navigate through a small boulder field. The trail disappears here, so look ahead to where it is clearly defined.

After climbing a small hill (the only one on this trip), hikers are treated with their first view of Becker Lake, with incredibly sheer cliffs on the west bank and 11,409-foot Lonesome Mountain dominating the northern horizon. From this point, you get your first view of the wilderness jewel known as Becker Lake.

Side Trips

A base camp here offers plenty of choices for day trips, all of them off-trail. Anglers like the short trip to Albino, Golden, and Jasper Lakes (all fairly easy off-trail routes), and peak baggers like the climb up Lonesome Mountain.

Camping

Campsites can be found at Jeff Lake, off to the right just as you first see Jeff Lake. However, most people prefer to go on to Becker Lake. When you reach the bench where you can first see the lake, leave the trail and head off along the south shore of the lake. It's fairly easy to find a good campsite for one or two tents, but campsites suitable for large parties are difficult to find.

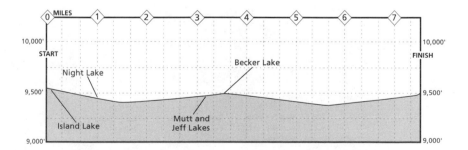

Fishing

This route has become very popular with anglers, in part because there is very little elevation gain to fight along the way. The fishing here tends to lean toward brook trout, a good fish for youngsters learning to fish as well as oldsters looking for lots of action. Keep in mind that brook trout are often easier to catch on hardware (lures) than hackle (flies). Island and Night Lakes have been stocked with rainbows, but now these two lakes are primarily brook trout fisheries. Becker Lake may hold some cutthroats that have migrated down from Albino Lake.

For some variety and a chance to hook cutthroat trout, head up over the saddle at the end of Becker Lake into Montana and Albino Lake. It is stocked on a four-year basis and has some natural reproduction as well to provide some variation in size.

Golden and Jasper Lakes, just over the hill from Albino, harbor slightly larger cutts. Heading west cross-country, anglers can try the Cloverleaf Lakes, sporting some of the best cutthroat fishing in the Beartooths.

38 Beartooth High Lakes

General description: A truly spectacular trail, best suited for long day trips

Special attractions: Perhaps the best opportunity to travel through the unique high lake country

Type of trip: Shuttle

Total distance: 8.5 miles

Difficulty: Moderate

Traffic: Heavy

Maps: USGS—Beartooth Butte; RMS—Wyoming Beartooths

Starting point: Island Lake Trailhead

Finding the trailhead: From Cooke City, drive 25.8 miles east on U.S. Highway 212, or from Red Lodge, drive 35.7 miles; take the short access road to the Island Lake Campground on the north side of the highway. The trailhead is at the end of the road.

Parking and trailhead facilities: A large parking lot; toilets; camping in the campground at the trailhead.

Beartooth Butte overlooking Beartooth Lake.

Key Points

1.0 Night Lake.

2.5 Flake Lake.

3.2 Junction with Trail 621 to Beartooth Lake Trailhead; stay to the right.

3.3 Beauty Lake.

4.5 Claw Lake.

4.9 Shallow Lake.

5.1 Marmot Lake.

5.3 Horseshoe Lake.

5.8 Junction with Trail 619 to Beartooth Lake Trailhead; turn left.

8.5 Beartooth Lake Trailhead.

The Hike

This is one of those shuttle trails that requires arranging transportation in advance. Leave a vehicle at the Beartooth Lake Trailhead, or arrange with another party to start at Beartooth Lake and meet at Claw Lake or Beauty Lake for lunch so you can trade keys.

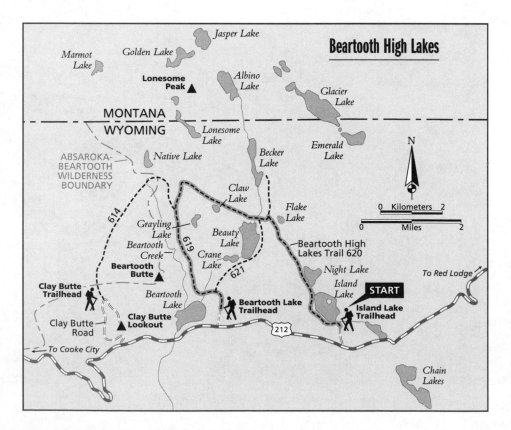

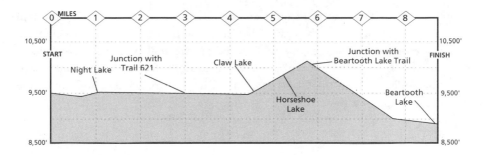

Although relatively long and sometimes used for an easy overnighter, this route is also well suited for a day trip, but plan on taking the entire day to cover the distance, leaving plenty of time to enjoy the scenery. Carry a water filter to save weight rather than packing several full water bottles; the route follows streams and lakes virtually every step of the way.

The first section of this trail goes along Island, Night, and Flake Lakes, as described in the Becker Lake trip (Hike 37). It's flat and scenic, and it stays that way for the rest of the trip.

The trail turns west just after Flake Lake and soon drops down into Beauty Lake, where the scenery matches the name. Just before the lake, look for Trail 621 heading off to the south along the east shore of Beauty Lake. This route offers a shorter hike for those so inclined, but it also misses some great vistas by cutting the trip short.

After a short climb out of the Beauty Lake Basin, continue through an open, alpine plateau to Claw Lake. For an overnight stay, this lake and Grayling Lake (just to the south) probably offer the best choices for campsites. Wood is scarce, so please do without campfires here.

After passing Claw Lake and laboring up another small hill, follow a string of lakes (Shallow, Marmot, Horseshoe, and others). This stretch of trail embodies the essence of the Beartooth high lakes country—water in every direction with Lonesome Mountain dominating the northern horizon and Beartooth Butte on the western horizon. It really doesn't get much better than this, especially on such an accessible trail.

After Horseshoe Lake, the trail turns south toward Beartooth Lake. For about 0.25 mile, the trail fades away, but it's marked by clearly visible cairns. At the well-marked junction with Trail 619, turn left (south) and continue 2.7 miles in the shadow of Beartooth Butte to the Beartooth Lake Trailhead on U.S. 212.

Options

This shuttle trip can be done in reverse with no added difficulty.

If this route isn't a long enough hike, consider the option of leaving a vehicle at the Clay Butte Trailhead and adding about 3 miles to the trip. For this option, turn right at the junction with Trail 619, and head north around the north side of

Beartooth Butte. This option includes another (and longer) section where the trail fades away to nothing more than cairns, but once you hit Trail 614 to Clay Butte, the trail is well-defined. On the way to Clay Butte, the trail passes through a huge meadow that is one of the best places in the Beartooths for wildflower enthusiasts. The downside of taking the Clay Butte option is a tough, 2-mile climb up to the trailhead from the meadow.

Side Trips

If you have the time, this trip offers a nearly endless selection of side trips, including the chance to simply wander through the open, trail-less terrain with no particular destination in mind.

Camping

Although most hikers day hike this route, it has plenty of good campsites, such as the north end of Beauty Lake, the south end of Claw Lake near Grayling Lake, or somewhere in the vicinity of Horseshoe, Finger, or T Lake.

Fishing

Fishing along this trail leans toward brook trout, although several other species have been planted over the brook trout populations. Fishing is usually excellent in lakes with brookies, but some days even these fish are hard to catch—and sometimes hardware users will outfish the fly fishermen. Beauty Lake has had cutts stocked over the brookies. Claw, Horseshoe, and Beartooth Lakes have all had lake trout planted to feed on the brookies to control their population. Beartooth Lake has had several other species introduced, including rainbows, cutts, goldens, and grayling.

Beauty Lake. ▶

39 Beauty Lake

General description: A nice day hike suitable for children

Special attractions: A good choice for families

Type of trip: Out-and-back

Total distance: 4.8 miles

Difficulty: Easy

Traffic: Heavy

Maps: USGS—Beartooth Butte; RMS—Wyoming Beartooths

Starting point: Beartooth Lake Trailhead

Finding the trailhead: From Cooke City, drive east 22.7 miles on U.S. Highway 212 or 38.8 miles from Red Lodge to a well-marked turnoff for Beartooth Lake Campground. Once in the campground, it might take a few minutes to find the trailhead. The likely looking spot on the left just past the entrance is actually a picnic area and boat launch. The trailhead is at the north end of the campground. The last 100 yards to the trailhead is a narrow dirt road.

Parking and trailhead facilities: Small parking area so take only one space; toilets and camping in the campground at the trailhead.

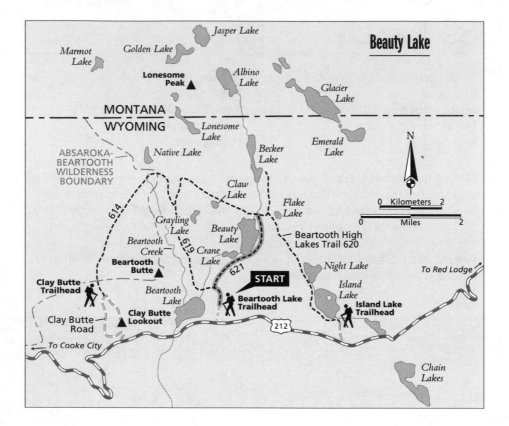

Key Points

0.2 Junction with trail to Beauty Lake; turn right.

1.4 Junction with trail to Crane Lake; turn right.

1.6 South edge of Beauty Lake.

2.4 Junction with Beartooth High Lakes Trail 620.

The Hike

This trail leaves from a major vehicle campground and is one of the most accessible trails in the Beartooths. Consequently, the trail to Beauty Lake receives heavy use compared to most other trails in the Beartooths, but not heavy compared to short day hikes in most national parks.

Right at the trailhead the trail is faint. After crossing Beartooth Creek, however, the trail becomes well defined and stays that way all the way to Beauty Lake. In less than 0.25 mile from the trailhead, the trail splits. Trail 619 veers off to the left toward Beartooth Butte. Go right (north) on Trail 621 to Beauty Lake.

From this junction the trail gradually climbs about 500 feet through lush forest

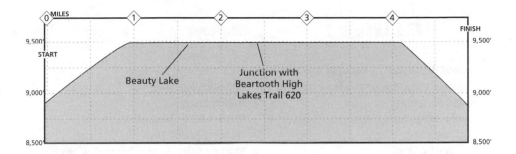

with lots of wildflowers and mushrooms. The trail is rocky in a few places but is still nicely suited for families with small children. It's rare for such great scenery to grace such a short hike. And it's all downhill on the way back to the trailhead.

After 1.4 miles look for Crane Lake off to the left (west) and a trail splitting off in that direction. Those looking for a place to stay overnight will find better campsites along the south shore of Crane Lake than at Beauty Lake.

To get to Beauty Lake, take the right fork in the trail and continue north for less than 0.25 mile. Undoubtedly, visitors here will all agree that this lake lives up to its name. This large, clear, alpine lake boasts several sandy beaches just right for wading on a warm day.

Camping

Most people consider Beauty Lake a leisurely day trip. Others hurry by on their way to some more remote spot. But it's also a nice spot to camp. If you do, however, please resist the temptation to build a campfire.

Fishing

Beartooth Lake has been stocked with lake trout, which have thinned the brook trout population. The remaining brookies are larger than average size. Beartooth Lake has had several introductions of other species including rainbows, cutts, goldens, and grayling.

Even though other species have been planted in Beauty Lake, the fishing is still dominated by brook trout. Crane Lake has had cutts stocked over the brookies. Fishing in both lakes is excellent.

40 Claw Lake

General description: A moderate day hike or easy overnighter, a good choice for that first backpacking trip
Special attractions: A rare, short loop returning to the same trailhead
Type of trip: Loop

Total distance: 8.3 miles
Difficulty: Moderate
Traffic: Heavy
Maps: USGS—Beartooth Butte; RMS—Wyoming Beartooths
Starting point: Beartooth Lake Trailhead

Finding the trailhead: From Cooke City, drive east 22.7 miles on U.S. Highway 212 or 38.8 miles from Red Lodge to a well-marked turnoff for Beartooth Lake Campground. Once in the campground, it might take a few minutes to find the trailhead. The likely looking spot on the left just past the entrance is actually a picnic area and boat launch. The trailhead is at the north end of the campground. The last 100 yards to the trailhead is a narrow dirt road.

Parking and trailhead facilities: Small parking area so be careful to take only one space; toilets and camping in the campground at the trailhead.

Key Points

0.2 Junction with Trail 621 to Beauty Lake; turn left on Trail 619.

2.9 Junction with Beartooth High Lakes Trail 620; turn right.

3.9 Horseshoe Lake.

4.1 Marmot Lake.

4.3 Shallow Lake.

4.7 Claw Lake.

5.9 Junction with Trail 621; turn right.

6.7 South end of Beauty Lake.

6.9 Crane Lake.

8.3 Beartooth Lake Trailhead.

The Hike

This is one of the rare opportunities to trace a short loop returning to the same trailhead. Most trips of this length are shuttle or out-and-back trails.

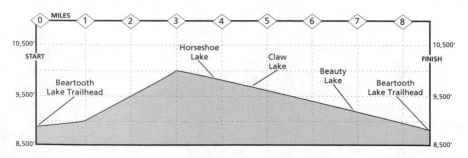

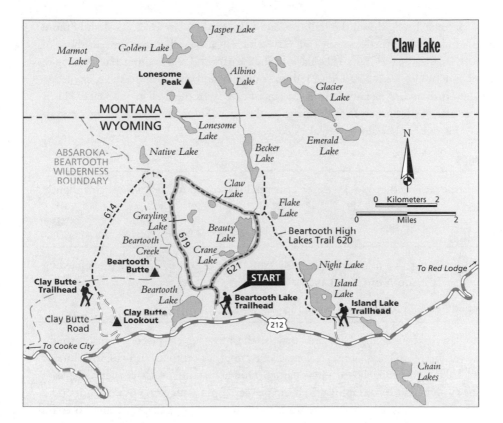

Perhaps the most troublesome spot on the entire trip is the stream crossing right at the trailhead. Earlier in the season, in June and July, this stream carries lots of water, so be careful. Even though children might have some difficulty crossing this stream, the rest of the trip is quite safe. There are five more stream crossings, but none of them is hazardous, and it's usually possible to cross on rocks to keep your feet dry.

Less than 0.25 mile from the trailhead, watch for the junction with Trail 621 to Beauty Lake. To do this trip clockwise, turn left to stay on Trail 619 and head for Beartooth Butte. The return route of this loop comes down Trail 621 to this junction on the final leg to the trailhead.

The first part of the trail hugs the north shoreline of beautiful Beartooth Lake. Some parts of the trail can get quite marshy, especially in June and July. Then, after crossing Beartooth Creek, the trail turns north through the shadow of spectacular Beartooth Butte for another 2 miles to the junction with Beartooth High Lakes Trail 620.

Turn right onto the Beartooth High Lakes Trail, and don't be surprised when the trail fades away for about 0.25 mile. A series of cairns clearly marks the way. At the top of a small ridge (the highest point on this trail, about 9,900 feet), the trail becomes well defined again. From this point on to Claw Lake, the trail skirts the south edge of a chain of lakes. Beyond the lakes to the north looms awesome, 11,409-foot Lonesome Mountain.

Continue 1 mile down the trail to Claw Lake. From Claw Lake, it's slightly more than a mile to the junction with Trail 621, which heads south along the east shore of Beauty Lake and past Crane Lake back to the Beartooth Lake Trailhead. When you're at the junction of Trails 620 and 621, drop your pack and walk over to the rocky ledge on the north end of Beauty Lake for a fantastic view of the well-named lake. This is a great place to eat lunch for day hikers on this loop. There are several more views to equal this one farther along the lake's edge.

Options

This trip works either clockwise or counterclockwise, but clockwise seems slightly easier.

Side Trips

The route offers a wide variety of side trips, such as a trek around the sprawling Grayling Lake, south of Claw Lake.

Camping

The Claw Lake–Grayling Lake area may be the most logical place for an overnight camp on this loop. There are several excellent campsites on the southwestern shore of Claw Lake, some suitable for large parties. Downed wood is scarce here so please refrain from building a campfire. For more privacy, move your camp out of sight of the trail by going a few hundred more yards south to Grayling Lake. You can also camp along Horseshoe and Finger Lakes as well as several other places along this route.

Fishing

Claw, Horseshoe, and Beartooth Lakes have all been planted with lake trout to act as predators to the brook trout populations. For the most part, the fishing along this route is the standard brook trout fare. Sorry, there aren't any grayling left in Grayling Lake.

41 Native Lake

General description: An easily accessible base camp

Special attractions: Incredible number of alpine lakes within a short distance of base camp

Type of trip: Out-and-back or shuttle

Total distance: 8 miles, not counting side trips

Difficulty: Easy

Traffic: Heavy

Maps: USGS—Beartooth Butte, Muddy Creek, Castle Mountain, and Silver Run Peak; RMS—Wyoming Beartooths and Alpine–Mount Maurice

Starting point: Beartooth Lake Trailhead

Finding the trailhead: From Cooke City, drive east 22.7 miles on U.S. Highway 212 or 38.8 miles from Red Lodge to a well-marked turnoff for Beartooth Lake Campground. Once in the campground, it might take a few minutes to find the trailhead. The likely looking spot on the left just past the entrance is actually a picnic area and boat launch. The trailhead is at the north end of the campground. The last 100 yards to the trailhead is on a narrow dirt road.

Parking and trailhead facilities: Small parking area so be careful to take only one space; toilets and camping in the campground at the trailhead.

Key Points

0.2 Junction with Trail 621 to Beauty Lake; turn left.

2.9 Junction with Beartooth High Lakes Trail 620; turn left.

3.6 Turnoff to Clay Butte Trailhead; turn right.

4.0 Native Lake.

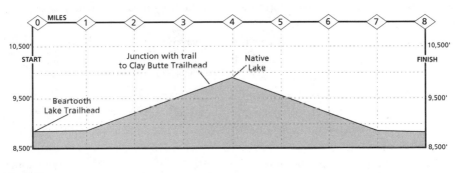

The Hike

You can, of course, set up a base camp at many places on the Beartooth Plateau, but Native Lake is an ideal place for a base camp for those who don't want to carry their big packs very far but still want get into some remote wilderness. Unlike some base camp locations, you can easily reach many remote destinations from Native both on trail and off trail.

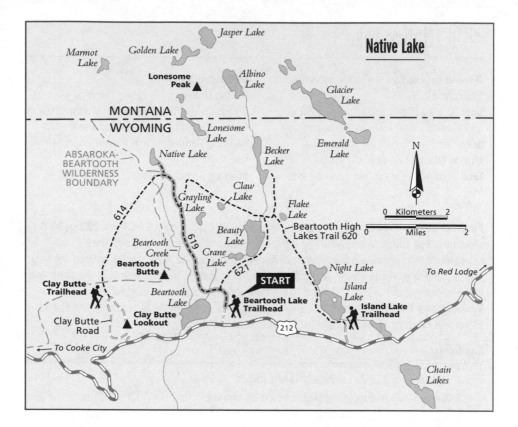

How to get to Native Lake, however, can be a tough decision. Going in at the Beartooth Lake Trailhead is the shortest way. But the Clay Butte and Island Lake Trailheads also offer access to this area.

Regardless of which trailhead you use, the way into Native Lake can be nearly effortless compared to many trails in the Beartooths. All three trails go through gorgeous, open, alpine country, dotted with lakes and carpeted with wildflowers.

From Beartooth Lake Trailhead, head north on Trail 619. There are two trails that leave the trailhead, so be careful not to get on Trail 621 to Beauty Lake. If you do, the punishment will be 2 extra miles of famous Beartooth high lakes country before reaching Native Lake.

Start out hiking around the north edge of Beartooth Lake on the edge of some moist meadows. Beartooth Butte provides a magnificent backdrop on the western horizon most of the way into Native Lake. The trail crosses Beartooth Creek twice, but it's usually easy to find a way across on rocks without getting your feet wet.

At the junction with Beartooth High Lakes Trail 620, bear left and keep going north on Trail 619. About 0.5 mile after the junction, watch for a trail and a string of cairns going off to the west through the pass on the north side of Beartooth Butte. These cairns lead down to Trail 614 to Clay Butte.

Continue northwest on the main trail another 0.5 mile to Native Lake. The trail is well-defined the entire way.

From Native Lake, there are plenty of options for adventurous side trips. Set up camp and start exploring the area. This is a great place to practice using a compass and topo map.

Options

You can reach Native Lake from three major trailheads: Beartooth Lake, Clay Butte, and Island Lake.

Consider arranging a shuttle at a different trailhead to avoid retracing your steps on the way out. With two vehicles, it's best to leave a vehicle at Beartooth Lake and then go in at the Clay Butte Trailhead. Then the entire trip is downhill, with the exception of a minor hill just before Native Lake. The start at Clay Butte is at 9,600 feet, and the end at Beartooth Lake is at 8,900.

Side Trips

Please refer to Where to Go from Native Lake on page 210.

Camping

Camp on the bench above the trail on the west side of the lake. There are several excellent campsites here, and they're spacious enough for large parties. This campsite is at 9,500 feet, above timberline; even though there is a limited supply of firewood in this area, please don't give in to the temptation of starting a fire.

Fishing

Native Lake is a cutthroat exception to the brook trout theme found throughout this area. If the cutts are being stubborn, many of the lakes in the area sport voracious populations of brookies. The nearby Beartooth High Lakes Trail provides access to many of these, with lake trout having been added to both T and Lamb Lakes.

The Montana state line is about 1 mile north of Native Lake, so anglers must make sure they have the proper state license(s). North of Lonesome Lake, heading cross-country, are Golden and Jasper Lakes, both offering cutthroat trout fishing. Just to the west is the Cloverleaf chain of lakes, with a sgreat cutthroat fishery.

WHERE TO GO FROM NATIVE LAKE
The Beartooth high lakes area provides abundant opportunities for moderately easy, off-trail side trips. Day trips in this area are less advanced than in other areas of the Beartooths, and they provide a good chance to familiarize yourself with off-trail travel without getting in over your head. Here's a list of suggestions rated for difficulty as follows: Human (easy for almost everyone, including children), Semi-human (moderately difficult), or Animal (don't try it unless you're very fit and wilderness-wise). Also refer to more detailed rating information in the chapter Using this Guidebook.

Destination	Difficulty
Box Lakes	Human
Surprise Lake	Human
Mule Lake	Human
Thiel Lake	Human
Martin Lake Basin	Human
Hidden Lake	Semi-human
Swede Lake	Semi-human
Lonesome Mountain	Animal
Cloverleaf Lakes	Animal
Jasper and Golden Lakes	Animal
T Lake	Semi-human
Lonesome Lake	Semi-human
Beartooth Butte	Animal
Claw and Grayling Lakes	Human

42 Upper Granite Lake

General description: An out-and-back trip on a well-used trail suitable for a long day trip or an overnighter

Special attractions: One of the largest, deepest, most majestic mountain lakes in the Beartooths

Type of trip: Out-and-back

Total distance: 10.4 miles

Difficulty: Moderate

Traffic: Moderate

Maps: USGS—Muddy Creek and Castle Mountain; RMS—Wyoming Beartooths and Alpine–Mount Maurice

Starting point: Clay Butte Trailhead

Finding the trailhead: The well-marked Clay Butte Road 142 turns north off the Beartooth Highway 21.2 miles east of Cooke City or 40.3 miles west of Red Lodge. Any passenger car can make it up the moderately steep, well-maintained gravel road to Clay Butte Lookout, but it's not recommended for vehicles pulling trailers. The road to the trailhead turns off to the left 2 miles from the Beartooth Highway.

Parking and trailhead facilities: Small parking area (way too small for its popularity); no toilet.

Upper Granite Lake.

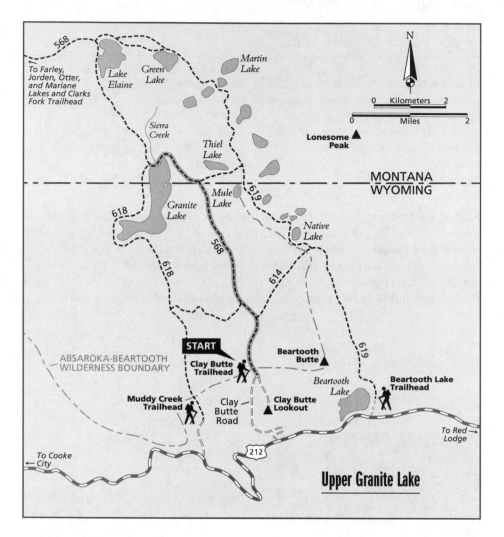

Upper Granite Lake

Key Points

- **1.2** Junction with Trail 614 to Native Lake; turn left.
- **1.7** Junction with connecting trail to Muddy Creek Trailhead; turn right.
- **4.1** Junction with trail to Thiel Lake; turn left.
- **5.2** Upper Granite Lake.

The Hike

This is the typical hike in the mountains, only in reverse. It's downhill all the way to the lake and uphill all the way out. Because the trail to Upper Granite Lake stays moist until late in the season, it's not suited for use by backcountry horsemen.

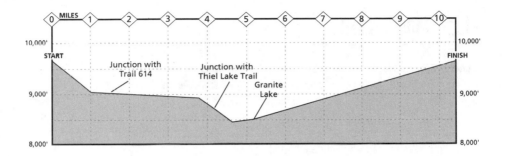

The route is, however, popular with backpackers, and when you get to Granite Lake the reason for this becomes clear. It's hard to believe such a large, beautiful lake so close to a paved highway doesn't have a road to it, vehicle campgrounds, cabins lining the shoreline, and motorboats pulling water-skiers. Instead, visitors find a pristine, forested lake straddling the Montana-Wyoming border, protected on all sides by the Absaroka-Beartooth Wilderness.

The first 2 miles of the trail go through open meadows rich in wildflowers, especially early in the season. For wildflower buffs, this is one of the best trails in the Beartooths. And if you ever grow weary of wildflowers, look up. In every direction, on every horizon, the rich greens of the high mountain meadows rise to a panorama of snow-capped peaks. Lonesome Mountain looms to the northeast and Pilot and Index Peaks mark the western view.

This trail has some wet sections that get churned by horses, making travel difficult for hikers. Later in the season, however, the boggy areas dry up.

Camping

Upper Granite Lake has a few good campsites, but because it's in a location that becomes a logical overnight stay, it gets heavy use. Stock parties frequently use this camping area and magnify the impact. You might be able to find enough downed wood for a campfire.

Fishing

Granite Lake straddles the Wyoming-Montana border, but there is no official agreement between the states on this joint jurisdiction. Technically, anglers should be careful to fish only in the state for which they carry a license. Perhaps the safest approach is to carry licenses from both states.

Granite Lake supports brook trout, rainbows, and cutthroats. There is also talk of planting lake trout. Brook trout dominate the fishery, but there are plenty of other fish. The Montana Department of Fish, Wildlife & Parks also stocks grayling, when available, in Spaghetti and Skeeter Lakes.

43 Martin Lake

General description: An excellent base camp trip into one of the most scenic sections of the Beartooths, with many opportunities for side trips

Special attractions: Multitudes of scenic, trout-filled lakes and a high-altitude waterfall

Type of trip: Out-and-back

Total distance: 12.5 miles

Difficulty: Moderate

Traffic: Moderate

Maps: USGS—Muddy Creek, Beartooth Butte, Castle Mountain, and Silver Run Peak; RMS—Wyoming Beartooths and Alpine–Mount Maurice

Starting point: Clay Butte Trailhead

Finding the trailhead: The well-marked Clay Butte Road 142 turns north off the Beartooth Highway 21.2 miles east of Cooke City or 40.3 miles west of Red Lodge. Any passenger car can make it up the moderately steep, well-maintained gravel road to Clay Butte Lookout, but it's not recommended for vehicles pulling trailers. The road to the trailhead turns off to the left 2 miles from the Beartooth Highway.

Parking and trailhead facilities: Small parking area (way too small for its popularity); no toilet.

Key Points

1.2 Junction with Trail 568 to Upper Granite Lake; turn right.

2.9 Junction with Trail 619 from Beartooth Lake Trailhead; turn left.

3.1 Native Lake.

4.2 Mule Lake.

4.7 Thiel Lake.

6.5 Martin Lake Basin.

The Hike

For those who like to spend one moderately hard day getting into a beautiful base camp and then spend several days doing scenic day trips, this is an ideal choice.

Trail 614 starts out downhill but turns uphill after 1 mile at the junction of Trail 568 to Upper Granite Lake. Turn right and stay on Trail 614. For the first 2.5 miles,

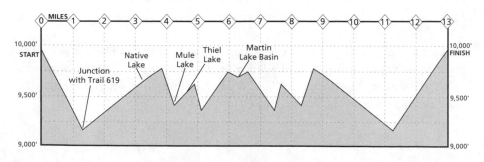

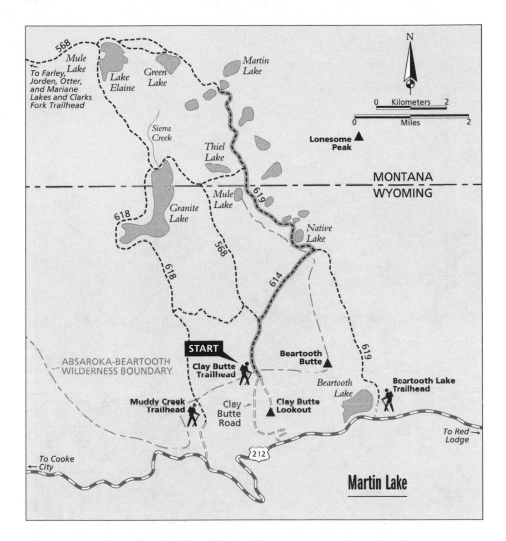

Martin Lake

the trail travels through an enormous, high-altitude meadow carpeted with wildflowers. At one point, the trail fades away into a string of cairns, so watch carefully for the next trail marker.

About 0.25 mile before Native Lake the trail meets Trail 619 coming from Beartooth Lake. Turn left (west) on Trail 619. Native Lake is the beginning of a long string of lakes. It's tempting to look for campsites along the way, but the best is yet to come at Martin Lake. Be prepared for short, steep climbs just before and after Mule Lake and a long, strenuous climb into the Martin Lake Basin that starts just after Thiel Lake. Be careful not to miss Thiel Lake. It's off to the left (south) at the bottom of the hill after Mule Lake, just after the trail breaks out into a lush meadow.

Spogen Lake and falls.

Martin Lake Basin is one of the most fascinating places in the Beartooths. Four major lakes (Martin, Wright, Spogen, and Whitcomb) are linked by a trout-filled stream, and there's a spectacular, high-altitude waterfall between Wright and Spogen Lakes. The waterfall seems larger and more majestic here at 9,600 feet.

As is plain from the topo map, this is lake country. Dozens of lakes lie within a day's trek from this basin. Even avid explorers could spend a week here and not see the same lake twice. Don't forget to spend one of those days simply hiking around the four lakes in the basin to fully appreciate a place that would put most national parks to shame.

Options

You can make a long loop out of this by following the route described under the Green Lake trip, Hike 44.

Another reason Martin Lake is a better base camp than most is that hikers don't have to retrace the exact same route on the way out. On the return trip, from the bottom of the big hill to Thiel Lake, leave Trail 619 and follow a well-used trail that traverses the east side of Thiel Lake. This isn't an official Forest Service trail and doesn't show on the topo or national forest maps, but it's well-maintained and well-signed at the south end. In less than 1 mile, it intersects with Trail 568, which goes to Upper Granite Lake. Turn left (south) at this junction and follow this well-used trail back to the trailhead. This still means retracing your steps the last uphill mile to the trailhead from the junction of Trails 568 and 614, but most of the trip will be new country.

Side Trips

From Martin Lake, hikers have a large number of choices for day trips. Refer to Where to Go from Martin Lake on page 218.

Camping

You can camp almost anywhere in the basin, but the most convenient sites are around Wright and Martin Lakes. This is like a five-star hotel: Every room has a view. You could call it nature's penthouse. Firewood, however, is in short supply and essential to the extraordinary charm of this basin, so resist the temptation to have a campfire.

Fishing

Most of the lakes in this area were stocked with brook trout, and the chain of lakes in Martin Lake Basin is named after the men who hauled in the brook trout. The brookies here are average for the Beartooths, with Whitcomb Lake and Lake Estelle having slightly larger fish.

For variation, Trail Lake (appropriately named) has cutthroats that are stocked but also reproduce. Head upstream from Martin Lake to reach the cutthroat hotbed found in the Cloverleaf Lakes.

Earlier along the route in, a side trip to Swede and Hidden Lakes is worthwhile for the cutthroats found there. Goldens were once found in Hidden Lake, and a few may still remain.

WHERE TO GO FROM MARTIN LAKE
The Martin Lake Basin provides abundant opportunities for moderately easy off-trail side trips. Here's a list of suggestions rated for difficulty as follows: Human (easy for almost everyone, including children), Semi-human (moderately difficult), or Animal (don't try it unless you're very fit and wilderness-wise). Also refer to more detailed rating information in the chapter Using this Guidebook.

Destination	Difficulty
Box Lakes	Human
Surprise Lake	Human
Mule Lake	Human
Thiel Lake	Human
Around Martin Lake Basin	Human
Hidden Lake	Semi-human
Swede Lake	Semi-human
Cloverleaf Lakes	Animal
Kidney Lake	Human
Marmot Lake	Semi-human
Trail Lake	Human
Green Lake	Human
Lake Estelle	Semi-human
Sierra Creek	Semi-human

44 Green Lake

General description: A long loop on the southwest edge of the Beartooth Plateau, best suited for at least two nights out, with one short off-trail section; a short section is impassable for horses

Special attractions: The short, easy, off-trail section can be a confidence builder, and unlike some trips, there are plenty of opportunities to get your feet wet

Type of trip: Loop

Total distance: 19.4 miles

Difficulty: Difficult

Traffic: Heavy near the Martin Lake Basin and Granite Lake, but light along the rest of the route

Maps: USGS—Muddy Creek, Beartooth Butte, Castle Mountain, and Silver Run Peak; RMS—Wyoming Beartooths and Alpine–Mount Maurice

Starting point: Clay Butte Trailhead

Finding the trailhead: The well-marked Clay Butte Road 142 turns north off the Beartooth Highway 21.2 miles east of Cooke City or 40.3 miles west of Red Lodge. Any passenger car can make it up the moderately steep, well-maintained gravel road to Clay Butte Lookout, but it's not recommended for vehicles pulling trailers. The road to the trailhead turns off to the left 2 miles from the Beartooth Highway.

Parking and trailhead facilities: Small parking area (way too small for its popularity); no toilet.

Key Points

1.2 Junction with Trail 568 to Granite Lake; turn right.

2.9 Junction with Trail 619 from Beartooth Lake Trailhead; turn left.

3.1 Native Lake.

4.3 Mule Lake.

4.6 Thiel Lake.

6.5 Martin Lake Basin.

7.8 Green Lake.

8.8 Sierra Creek.

10.1 Upper Lake Elaine and junction with Trail 568 to Farley Lake; turn left.

10.9 Lower Lake Elaine.

13.7 Upper Granite Lake and junction with Trail 618; turn left.

14.9 Junction with trail to Thiel Lake; turn right.

17.9 Junction with connecting trail to Muddy Creek Trailhead; turn left.

18.2 Junction with Trail 614; turn right.

19.4 Clay Butte Trailhead.

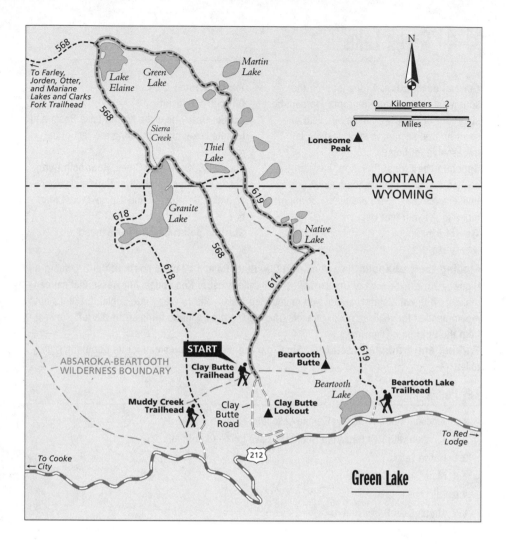

Green Lake

Recommended Itinerary

This is one of those hikes that you don't have to plan extensively. There are so many places to see and camp that you can sort of "play it by ear," and when you get ready to camp, you can usually find a good spot in an hour or two. You should take at least three days to do this loop, but you can spend much longer by setting up base camps at several points such as around Native Lake, Martin Lake, Green Lake, or Lake Elaine.

The Hike

Clay Butte is one of those rare trailheads that allow backpackers to go downhill instead of up at the beginning of a trip. In fact, the trailhead, at 9,600 feet, is almost the high-

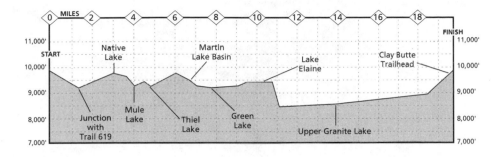

est point on any trail leaving from it. The trail edges a few feet over 10,000 just before reaching Martin Lake, but most of the trip is at a lower elevation than the trailhead.

Clay Butte and neighboring Beartooth Butte to the east and Table Mountain to the south are the only outcrops on the entire Beartooth Plateau still covered with sedimentary rock. Erosion removed the sedimentary rock from the rest of the area, but for some reason, still somewhat unclear to geologists, these three remnants survived.

Most people are in a big hurry to hit the trail when they get to the trailhead, but here it's worth taking an extra fifteen minutes to drive to the top of Clay Butte for the view. It's only another mile drive to the lookout, where (at 9,811 feet) a splendid view is had of the Beartooth Plateau. From this vista, much of the terrain covered on this hike can be seen. As at other trailheads along the Beartooth Highway, anglers need to know which state they are in so they can be sure to have the appropriate fishing license(s) and regulations.

Trail 614 starts out downhill but turns uphill after 1 mile at the junction of Trail 568 to Upper Granite Lake. Turn right and stay on Trail 614. For the first 2.5 miles, the trail travels through an enormous, high-altitude meadow carpeted with wildflowers. At one point the trail fades away into a string of cairns, so watch carefully for the next trail marker.

About a quarter mile before Native Lake, the trail meets Trail 619 coming from Beartooth Lake. Turn left (west) onto Trail 619. Native Lake is the beginning of a long string of lakes. Native, Box, Mule, and Thiel Lakes all boast excellent campsites. Thiel Lake is a frequent overnight stay for backcountry horsemen; be careful not to miss it. Thiel Lake is off to the left (south) at the bottom of the hill after Mule Lake, just after the trail breaks out into a lush meadow.

Regardless of where you spend your first night, continue along Trail 619 the next morning. Just after Thiel Lake, start a long, strenuous climb into the Martin Lake Basin. It's a fairly tough, Category 3 grind, but the reward at the end is well worth it. Martin Lake Basin is one of the most alluring spots in the Beartooths. Four major lakes (Martin, Wright, Spogen, and Whitcomb) stair-step through this magnificent basin, and there's a spectacular, high-altitude waterfall between Wright and Spogen Lakes. The waterfall seems larger and more majestic here at 9,600 feet

Fishing the Cloverleaf Lakes.

You can camp almost anywhere in the basin, especially around Wright and Martin Lakes. This is like a five-star hotel where every room has a view—nature's penthouse. Firewood, however, is in short supply and essential to the extraordinary charm of this basin, so resist the temptation to have a campfire.

As is obvious with a quick look at the topo map, this is lake country. Dozens of lakes lie within a day's trek from this basin. Even avid explorers could spend a week here and not see the same lake twice. Don't forget to spend one of those days simply hiking around the four lakes in the basin to fully appreciate a place that would put most national parks to shame.

Because this is one of the most spectacular spots in the Beartooths, plan to spend the night in this basin. For those who hiked all the way in on their first day, this area is worth a two-night stay. There are plenty of enticing day trips you can take from Martin Lake Basin.

The creek between Wright and Spogen Lakes must be forded. When selecting a campsite consider whether you want wet feet that night or first thing the next morning.

After spending a night in the Martin Lake Basin, you might have to force yourself to hit the trail the next morning. After a small hill to get out of the basin, the route skirts Trail Lake before heading down a steep hill into the gorgeous Green Lake valley. Going down this grade is all the argument needed against doing this trip in reverse. This hill makes the climb from Thiel Lake to Martin Lake Basin seem mild.

At Green Lake do not continue around the lake to the south, even though the trail appears to head in that direction. Instead, turn north, cross the inlet stream, and head around the north side of Green Lake on a less-defined trail. This isn't an official Forest Service trail, nor is it on the national forest map or topo map, but it's an easily followed pathway around the lake to Sierra Creek. If you decide not to camp in the Martin Lake Basin, camp instead at the head of Green Lake or after crossing Sierra Creek.

The Sierra Creek ford can be fairly difficult early in the season, so be careful. After the ford the trail leaves the Green Lake shoreline and heads straight west to Lake Elaine. Again, this isn't an official trail, and it is not maintained or marked, but it's still fairly easy to navigate. The trail through this section fades away in several wet meadows. Stay on the south edge of these meadows.

At Lake Elaine traverse the north shoreline—including a short boulder field—until you hit well-used Trail 568. Be careful in the boulder field; it can be dangerous, especially if you're carrying a big pack or if the rocks are wet. Turn left (south) on Trail 568, which hugs the west shore of Lake Elaine for about 1 mile.

Shortly after leaving Lake Elaine, the trail heads down a steep hill, another good reason not to do this trip in reverse. This downhill grade receives heavy horse traffic, which has ground up the rock into a fine dust that can make footing precarious, so watch your step. From the bottom of this climb, it's a pleasant 2 miles to upper Granite Lake.

Granite Lake is a huge mountain lake fed by massive Lake Creek, which splinters into six channels just before tumbling into Granite Lake. Some folks moan and groan about having to cross six streams, but imagine how difficult the crossing would be if Lake Creek stayed in one channel.

The first view of Granite Lake is all the enticement most people need to stay, so why not? Choose from any of the numerous campsites at the upper end of the lake.

From Granite Lake, the trail gradually climbs all the way to the Clay Butte Trailhead. This final stretch can become fairly muddy in frequent boggy sections. The hardest part of the trip, it seems, is the last uphill mile, which seemed so pleasant three or four days ago.

Options

This loop can be done in reverse, but that route would require a steep climb just south of Lake Elaine and another up from Green Lake. This trip is also a good choice for backpackers who like to set up base camps and explore some of the surrounding terrain without a big pack.

Actually, this trip can be done as a shuttle by leaving a vehicle at the Muddy Creek Trailhead. This avoids the uphill grind back to the Clay Butte Trailhead. The trail along the west side of Granite Lake leads out of Muddy Creek. Another option is to continue toward Clay Butte, but then turn off on a trail that heads west about 1 mile before the trailhead and drops steeply down to Muddy Creek. If you go around Granite Lake, you must make a difficult ford of Lake Creek as it leaves Granite Lake.

Side Trips

Refer to Where to Go from Martin Lake on page 218.

Camping

There are no designated campsites, but there are delightful places to camp everywhere along this route, with the possible exception of Lake Elaine where campsites are marginal. Be sure to set up a zero-impact camp.

Fishing

Most of the lakes in this area were stocked with brook trout, and the chain of lakes in Martin Lake Basin is named after the men who hauled in the brook trout. The brookies here are average for the Beartooths, with Whitcomb Lake having slightly larger fish.

For variation, Trail Lake (appropriately named) has cutthroats that are stocked but also reproduce. Head upstream from Martin Lake to reach the cutthroat hotbed found in the Cloverleaf Lakes.

Earlier along the route in, a side trip to Swede and Hidden Lakes is worthwhile for the cutthroats found there. Goldens were once found in Hidden Lake, and a few may still remain.

45 Jorden Lake

General description: A long shuttle on the southwest edge of the Beartooth Plateau, best suited for at least three nights out for hikers and one night for backcountry horsemen
Special attractions: A series of large, trout-filled lakes and a variety of scenery; a popular trip for backcountry horsemen
Type of trip: Shuttle

Total distance: 23.9 miles
Difficulty: Moderate
Traffic: Moderate
Maps: USGS—Muddy Creek, Castle Mountain, and Fossil Lake; RMS—Wyoming Beartooths, Alpine-Mount Maurice, and Cooke City-Cutoff Mountain
Starting point: Clay Butte Trailhead

Finding the trailhead: The well-marked Clay Butte Road 142 turns north off the Beartooth Highway 21.2 miles east of Cooke City or 40.3 miles west of Red Lodge. Any passenger car can make it up the moderately steep, well-maintained gravel road to Clay Butte Lookout, but it's not recommended for vehicles pulling trailers. The road to the trailhead turns off to the left 2 miles from the Beartooth Highway.

Parking and trailhead facilities: Small parking area (way too small for its popularity); no toilet.

Key Points

1.2 Junction with Trail 568 to Upper Granite Lake; turn left.
1.7 Junction with connecting trail down to Muddy Creek Trailhead; turn right.
4.1 Junction with trail to Thiel Lake; turn left.
5.2 Upper Granite Lake and junction with Trail 618; turn right.
7.5 Lower Lake Elaine.
9.8 Farley Lake and junction with trail to Jorden Lake; turn right.
11.1 Jorden Lake.
12.6 Otter Lake.
13.7 Mariane Lake.
15.7 Junction with Trail 567; turn left.
15.9 Russell Lake.
18.7 Junction with trail to Fox Lake; turn right.
19.9 Junction with Crazy Lakes Trail 3; turn right.
20.1 Junction with Rock Island Lake Trail 566; turn right.
21.7 Kersey Lake.
22.1 Junction with Vernon Lake Trail 565; turn right.
22.8 Junction with Curl Lake Trail 564; turn left.
23.9 Clarks Fork Trailhead.

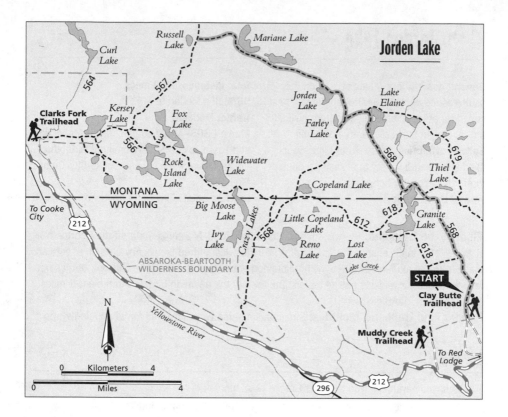

Recommended Itinerary

If you want to extend this trip, set up a base camp at Jorden Lake and spend a day or two exploring the area.

First night: Upper Granite Lake
Second night: Jorden Lake
Third night: Fox Lake or Rock Island Lake

The Hike

The first 5.2 miles of this trip are identical to the Upper Granite Lake trip, Hike 42, described earlier in this section. Head downhill from the Clay Butte Trailhead, through open mountain parks and forest to Upper Granite Lake. This is a good place to camp the first night out, particularly for those who started late in the day. Lake Elaine offers only limited camping, especially for large parties, and it would be a long day with a backpack to get to Farley or Jorden Lake for the first night out.

From Granite Lake, the trail climbs gradually along Lake Creek until just before Lake Elaine. Here it goes madly uphill with poor footing. Heavy horse traffic has pounded this section into dust, making it slippery even when it isn't wet.

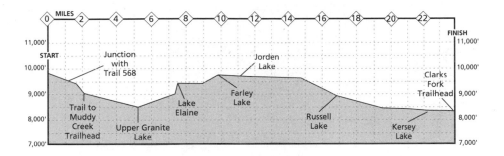

At the top of the hill, the forest opens up to beautiful Lake Elaine. Follow the west shore of the lake for about 1 mile until the trail veers off to the left (northwest) at the upper end of the lake. There are two campsites along the west shore.

Shortly after leaving Lake Elaine, climb just enough to break out above timberline. It's about 2 miles to Farley Lake, but it's a little over a mile to Jorden Lake. Both lakes have plenty of quality campsites and are similar in appearance, with Jorden Lake the larger of the two. Jorden Lake is a popular destination for backcountry horsemen. This is a good place to set up a base camp and extend your trip for a day or two.

From Jorden Lake, you start a highly enjoyable trek along a string of beautiful lakes in both forested and subalpine environments to Trail 567 coming down from Fossil Lake. Follow the trail 1.5 miles northwest to Otter Lake. The trail from Otter to Russell Lake isn't on the national forest or topo map, but it's well-defined on the ground most of the way. In a few places around Otter and Mariane Lakes, the trail fades away, but the route is still easy to follow. After dropping down a steep grade from Mariane Lake to Russell Lake, the route dips below timberline into a fairly moist forested landscape. It then meets The Beaten Path (i.e., the main thoroughfare through the Beartooths, Trail 567) about a quarter mile from Russell Lake. Turn left (south) on Trail 567.

Approaching Kersey Lake, the aftermath of the dramatic fires of 1988 becomes apparent, but the rest of the trip travels through unburned forest. Also, be sure to watch for the point where the trail splits into horse and footpaths just after Kersey Lake. Parties with stock go right (west) to a separate trailhead, and parties on foot stay left (east).

Options

At Farley Lake, you can turn left on Trail 568 and exit at either the Crazy Creek Trailhead or make a loop out of this by going back to Clay Butte. You can also turn south at Lower Granite Lake and head out Muddy Creek.

Side Trips

If you have extra time at Farley Lake, check out Hipshot or Wade Lake. If you set up a base camp at Jorden Lake, spend a day visiting the Desolation Lake area, but make sure you have good weather. On the way out, you might save some time to visit Fox, Rock Island, or Vernon Lake.

Camping

Upper Granite Lake has a few good campsites, but because it's in a location that becomes a logical overnight stay, it gets heavy use. Stock parties frequently use this camping area and magnify the impact.

Jorden Lake has a large selection of good campsites, so it shouldn't be difficult finding a good one for a base camp.

Russell Lake offers a conveniently located campsite for the third night out. Perhaps because of its convenient location, however, Russell Lake is very heavily used. The Forest Service discourages camping here, especially by backcountry horsemen because of the heavy impact stock has had on this area and the limited forage. You can camp at either the upper end or lower end of the lake but may have to cross the stream to reach the best campsites. You can also push on to Fox or Rock Island Lake to camp. Both lakes have a limited number of campsites that are not well-suited for horses. However, there's a good chance that these campsites will be occupied; both Fox and Rock Island are popular overnight camping destinations from the Clarks Fork Trailhead.

Fishing

Jorden Lake holds a reproducing population of cutthroat trout that adequately complements the scenery. There are two creeks that enter the north side of Jorden Lake, both of which originate at Widowed Lake. Starting with Desolation Lake and ending with Widowed Lake, Montana's Department of Fish, Wildlife & Parks is trying to establish a reproducing population of golden trout. The trout are there in low numbers, but this experiment cannot yet be declared a success. Many of the lakes along this route contain brook trout, but anglers willing to get off the trail can find other species. Keep in mind, however, that not all lakes contain fish. Fox Lake sports larger-than-average brookies, nice rainbows, and an occasional grayling that works its way down from Cliff Lake.

46 Lower Granite Lake

General description: A fairly long, but not strenuous, out-and-back day hike or an easy overnight backpack

Special attractions: A sprawling subalpine lake with good fishing

Type of trip: Out-and-back

Total distance: 10.4 miles

Difficulty: Moderate (unless you ford Lake Creek)

Traffic: Light

Maps: USGS—Muddy Creek; RMS—Wyoming Beartooths

Starting point: Muddy Creek Trailhead

Finding the trailhead: The trailhead is well-signed on the north side of the Beartooth Highway (U.S. Highway 212), 18 miles east of Cooke City or 43.5 west of Red Lodge. The short access road is fairly rough.

Parking and trailhead facilities: Adequate parking; no toilet; undeveloped camping sites near trailhead.

Key Points

0.8 End of jeep road.

2.8 Connecting trail to Clay Butte; turn left.

5.2 Lower Granite Lake.

The Hike

Going up Muddy Creek is the easiest—but the muddiest—way to reach monstrous Granite Lake. You can also get to the lower end of Granite Lake from Clay Butte, but the route back to the trailhead has a Category 1 climb—a near-vertical climb (720 feet elevation gain in 0.8 mile) out of Muddy Creek to connect with Clay Butte Trail 568 and then another 560-foot climb to get to the Clay Butte Trailhead.

The trail starts out from the Muddy Creek Trailhead as a rough jeep road, and vehicles are sometimes parked anywhere along the first 0.8 mile of the trail. Then the trail opens up into an expansive and beautiful meadow. It's also a wet meadow. The best time to take this hike is late August when the water level in the meadow has dropped. In a few places, the trail can be difficult to find through the tall grass, but the gradient remains almost flat until just before Granite Lake. Here the trail climbs about 200 feet and then drops into the Lake Creek drainage.

The trail arrives at the south end of Granite Lake and turns west to ford the outlet stream, Lake Creek. But beware: Fording Lake Creek can be dangerous. A tremendous amount of water leaves Granite Lake, and the flow can be powerful and chest-deep on a short person. This is one of the most hazardous fords in the Beartooths.

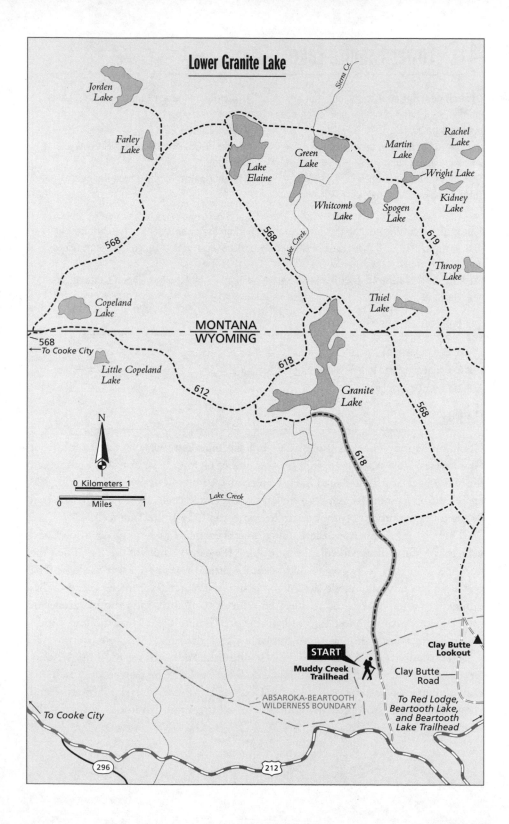

Lower Granite Lake

Jorden Lake

Farley Lake

Sierra Cr.

Martin Lake

Rachel Lake

Green Lake

Lake Elaine

Wright Lake

Whitcomb Lake

Spogen Lake

Kidney Lake

568

568

Lake Creek

619

Throop Lake

Thiel Lake

Copeland Lake

MONTANA
WYOMING

568
← *To Cooke City*

Little Copeland Lake

612

618

Granite Lake

568

N

0 Kilometers 1

0 Miles 1

618

Lake Creek

START
Muddy Creek Trailhead

Clay Butte Lookout

Clay Butte Road

To Red Lodge, Beartooth Lake, and Beartooth Lake Trailhead

ABSAROKA-BEARTOOTH
WILDERNESS BOUNDARY

To Cooke City

296

212

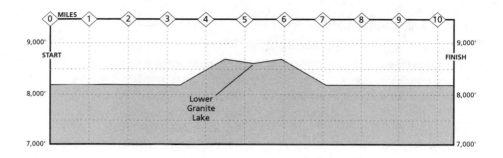

Options

You could start at Clay Butte and end at Muddy Creek Trailhead, but this would require two vehicles.

Side Trips

If you have extra time and have the courage to ford Lake Creek, try the pleasant hike along the west shore of the lake.

Camping

There are excellent campsites on both sides of Lake Creek where it leaves the lake.

Fishing

Granite Lake supports rainbows and cutthroats, but brook trout dominate the fishery. Fisheries managers are currently discussing the possibility of introducing lake trout to Granite Lake.

47 Copeland Lake

General description: A long loop suited for a three- or four-night backpack
Special attractions: Several large wilderness lakes
Type of trip: Loop
Total distance: 26.5 miles
Difficulty: Moderately difficult, with two diffi-cult stream crossings and one steep hill
Traffic: Light to moderate
Maps: USGS—Muddy Creek and Castle Mountain; RMS—Wyoming Beartooths and Alpine-Mount Maurice
Starting point: Muddy Creek Trailhead

Finding the trailhead: The trailhead is well-signed on the north side of the Beartooth Highway (U.S. 212), 18 miles east of Cooke City or 43.5 west of Red Lodge. The short access road is fairly rough.
Parking and trailhead facilities: Adequate parking; no toilet; undeveloped camping sites near trailhead.

Key Points

0.8 End of jeep road.

2.8 Connecting trail to Clay Butte; turn left.

5.2 Lower Granite Lake and Lake Creek ford.

6.1 Junction with Trail 612; turn right.

7.7 Upper Granite Lake.

7.8 Junction with Clay Butte Trail 568; turn left.

10.4 Lower end of Lake Elaine.

11.3 Upper end of Lake Elaine.

12.5 Farley Lake and junction with trail to Jorden Lake; turn left.

16.6 Junction with Cooke City Trail 624; turn left.

16.8 Copeland Lake.

17.8 Little Copeland Lake.

20.4 Junction with Granite Lake Trail 612; turn right.

21.3 Lower end of Granite Lake and Lake Creek ford.

23.7 Connecting trail to Clay Butte; turn right.

25.7 Jeep road.

26.5 Muddy Creek Trailhead.

Recommended Itinerary

To do this loop in three days requires at least one double-digit mileage day on the trail unless you risk finding space to camp the first night at the upper end of Granite Lake. From the upper end of Granite Lake, it's just more than 9 miles to Copeland

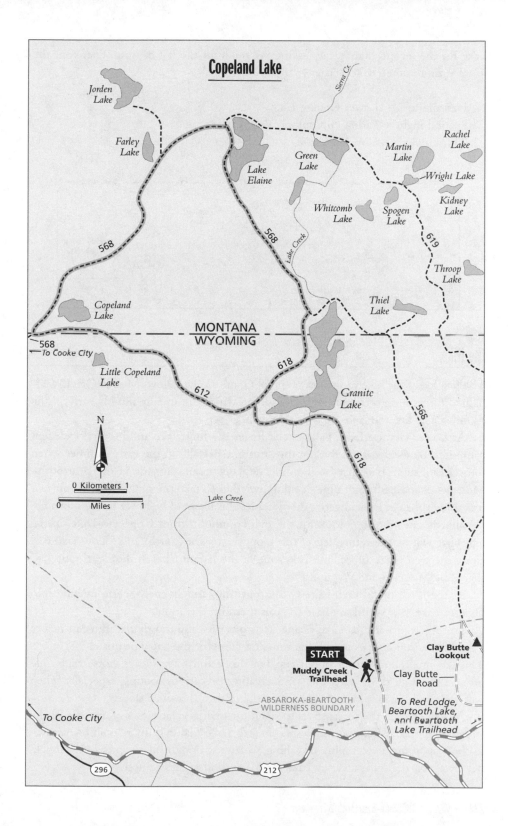

Copeland Lake

Jorden
Lake

Farley
Lake

Sierra Cr.

Lake
Elaine

Green
Lake

Martin
Lake

Rachel
Lake

Wright Lake

Kidney
Lake

Whitcomb
Lake

Spogen
Lake

568

568

Lake Creek

619

Throop
Lake

Copeland
Lake

Thiel
Lake

**MONTANA
WYOMING**

568
← To Cooke City

Little Copeland
Lake

612

618

Granite
Lake

565

N

618

0 Kilometers 1

0   Miles   1

Lake Creek

**START
Muddy Creek
Trailhead**

**Clay Butte
Lookout**

Clay Butte
Road

*To Red Lodge,
Beartooth Lake,
and Beartooth
Lake Trailhead*

ABSAROKA-BEARTOOTH
WILDERNESS BOUNDARY

To Cooke City

296

212

Lake for the second night's stay, leaving 9.7 miles for the last day out. Therefore, the route is more suited to four days.

First night: Lower Granite Lake
Second night: Farley, Hipshot, or Wade Lake
Third night: Copeland Lake

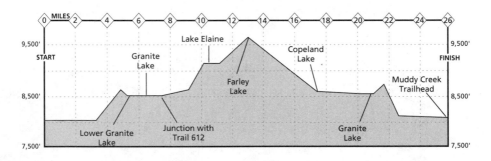

The Hike

The first leg of the hike to the lower end of Granite Lake follows Muddy Creek, well-named for its long series of boggy meadows, which are usually muddy early in the summer. The first 0.8 mile is on a seldom-used jeep road.

At Lower Granite Lake, Lake Creek leaves the huge lake amid several excellent campsites. Be extra careful fording this stream, especially in the early summer when the water is high. This may be the most difficult stream-crossing in the Beartooths. Most people have a tough time deciding whether to take the plunge that evening or first thing the next morning, but the water level is likely to be lower in the morning.

Shortly after the ford, look for the trail coming in from Copeland Lake on the left. That will be the return leg of this loop. Turn right (north) and follow Trail 618 along the west shore of Granite Lake, one of the largest lakes in the Beartooths and shared by Montana and Wyoming.

At the lake's upper end, Lake Creek splits into six channels before melting into Granite Lake. But you don't have to cross them on this route.

From here the trip to Lake Elaine starts out easy and mostly flat. But just before Lake Elaine, you are faced with the toughest climb of the trip. Fortunately, it's short. This 0.3-mile climb is not only steep, but dusty and slick. Heavy horse traffic has ground the rock down to a fine sand, creating precarious footing, especially when wet. Believe it or not, it's easier going up than down this steep slope.

At Lake Elaine the forest starts to open up, giving great views of another of the largest lakes in the Beartooths. Despite its size, Lake Elaine really doesn't offer much in the way of quality camping or fishing, so after soaking in the scenery over lunch, head west on the trail to Farley Lake for the second night's campsite.

Just before Farley Lake the trail meets the trail going right (north) to Jorden Lake. Turn left to Farley Lake, which has several campsites but not enough wood for a campfire. Those with energy to spare and who don't mind getting off the trail can go another mile to the more secluded Hipshot or Wade Lake. It's a short cross-country trip to these lakes, so check the topo map carefully before heading off-trail. Both lakes are about 0.5 mile south of Farley Lake—Wade Lake to the east of the trail and Hipshot to the west.

From Farley Lake the trail goes south, and just before Copeland Lake it meets a trail on the right coming in from the Crazy Creek Trailhead. Turn left (east) and continue 0.5 mile to Copeland Lake, which is nestled in a forested pocket with lots of wood for campfires—and a few more mosquitoes than any lake deserves. There's also a large outfitter camp here, so at times Copeland Lake could be crowded. If you camp at Copeland for the third night, you have a 9.7-mile trek out to the Muddy Creek trailhead for the final day. The grade is easy down to Granite Lake and the Lake Creek ford. From here, retrace your steps back to the Muddy Creek Trailhead.

Options

If you prefer to hike down the Lake Elaine hill, you can hike this route in reverse.

Upper Lake Elaine.

Side Trips

Attractive side trips include Jorden, Hipshot, and Wade Lakes. If you're especially ambitious, stay an extra night at Farley Lake and spend the down day exploring the Desolation Lake area.

Camping

You will probably want to spend the first night at the lower end of Granite Lake where there are several scenic campsites. It might be tempting to march on for another 2.5 miles to the upper end of Granite Lake, but there are fewer first-class campsites there, and they might be taken. The upper end of the lake gets more use than the lower end. There's also a large horse camp at the upper end. Rich forests surround aesthetic Granite Lake, and there is ample fuel for building a low-impact campfire.

For the second night out, you can choose from a large selection of campsites at Farley, Hipshot, or Wade Lake.

On the third night, Copeland Lake is the best choice, even though good campsites are limited and hard to see through the clouds of mosquitoes.

Fishing

Most lakes along this route, including Lake Elaine, contain brook trout. However, Hipshot Lake contains stocked cutthroat trout, and Jorden Lake has natural cutts. Farley Lake provides the best brook trout eatery, with the fish being an inch or so larger than nearby lakes.

48 Ivy Lake

General description: A moderately long day hike or easy overnighter

Special attractions: Crazy Falls and a better chance to see wildlife than most places in the Beartooths

Type of trip: Out-and-back

Total distance: 9 miles

Difficulty: Moderate

Traffic: Light

Maps: USGS–Jim Smith Peak; RMS–Wyoming Beartooths

Starting point: Crazy Creek Trailhead

Finding the trailhead: The Crazy Creek Trailhead is 11 miles east of Cooke City on the Beartooth Highway (U.S. 212) or 50.5 miles west of Red Lodge. The trailhead is a turnoff on the north side of the highway across from the Crazy Creek Campground.

Parking and trailhead facilities: Small parking area; no toilet; vehicle campground next door.

Key Points

3.5 Little Moose Lake.

3.7 Junction with jeep road coming in from Lily Lake area.

4.0 Turn off jeep road onto trail to Ivy Lake.

4.5 Ivy Lake.

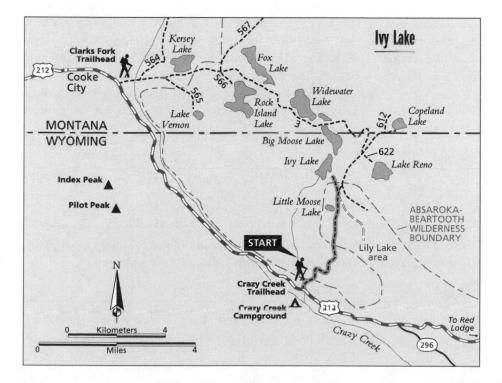

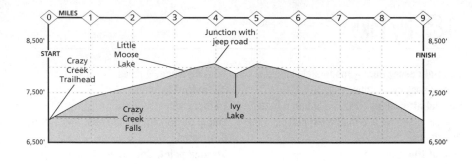

The Hike

The Ivy Lake trail starts off with a bang. The first 0.25 mile is paralleled by cascading Crazy Creek Falls. You'll want to stop and marvel at it two or three times along the way.

Much of this trail goes through a drier, sagebrush-type environment with Pilot and Index Peaks highlighting the western horizon. Plan to hike this route in early morning or evening to avoid the heat—and for a better chance of seeing those elk and moose that have been sleeping during the hot midday. Just after the trail breaks out of the forest, about 1.5 miles from the trailhead, there's one confusing spot. A good (but unofficial) trail juts off to the right. Bear left and head uphill.

About halfway to Ivy Lake the trail wanders through a big wet meadow. Earlier in the season (June and July), it can be difficult to cross this high-altitude marsh without getting your feet wet.

At the 3.5-mile mark, look to the left, down the hill to Little Moose Lake. For a short side trip, drop down and note the unusual "floating shoreline" here.

Less than 0.25 mile after Little Moose Lake, the trail meets a jeep road coming from the Lily Lake area to the east. Continue north along the jeep road for another 0.25 mile before the trail veers off to the left down to Ivy Lake.

Side Trips

Try the short spur trail to Little Moose Lake.

Camping

There are campsites on the left and right just before the lake. This area was partly burned during the 1988 fires, so there's plenty of wood for a campfire.

Fishing

Ivy Lake is the lowest of a chain of lakes on Crazy Creek. This chain of lakes harbors both brook trout and rainbow trout, and the variety provides for some nice (though

Crazy Creek Falls.

not exceptional) fishing. The rainbows are much harder to catch than brookies. Little Moose Lake is stocked occasionally with cutthroat trout. The weedy nature of the lake makes it a good home for food organisms, so fish may grow large here as they get older.

49 Crazy Lakes

General description: A two- or three-night, late summer shuttle trip

Special attractions: Large beautiful, forested lakes

Type of trip: Shuttle

Total distance: 15.2 miles

Difficulty: Moderate

Traffic: Light

Maps: USGS—Jim Smith Peak and Fossil Lake; RMS—Wyoming Beartooths and Cooke City-Cutoff Mountain

Starting point: Crazy Creek Trailhead

Finding the trailhead: The Crazy Creek Trailhead is 11 miles east of Cooke City on the Beartooth Highway (U.S. Highway 212) or 50.5 miles west of Red Lodge. The trailhead is a turnoff on the north side of the highway across from the Crazy Creek Campground.

Parking and trailhead facilities: Small parking area; no toilet; vehicle campground next door.

Key Points

3.5 Little Moose Lake.

3.7 Junction with jeep road coming in from Lily Lake area; turn left.

3.8 Junction with Crazy Lakes Trail 612; turn right.

5.6 Junction with Trail 3 and Trail 622 to Lake Reno; turn left.

7.8 Big Moose Lake.

11.7 Junction with Trail 567; turn left.

11.9 Junction with Trail 566 to Rock Island Lake; turn right.

12.9 Kersey Lake.

13.7 Junction with Trail 565 to Lake Vernon; turn right.

15.2 Clarks Fork Trailhead.

The Hike

The first order of business is leaving a vehicle at the Clarks Fork Trailhead. Keep in mind that the Clarks Fork Trailhead is split into two trailheads, one for backpackers and one for backcountry horsemen, so make sure to leave your vehicle at the right

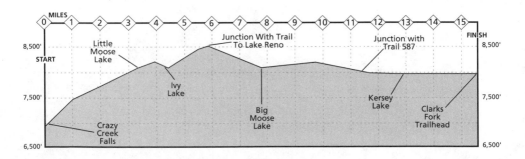

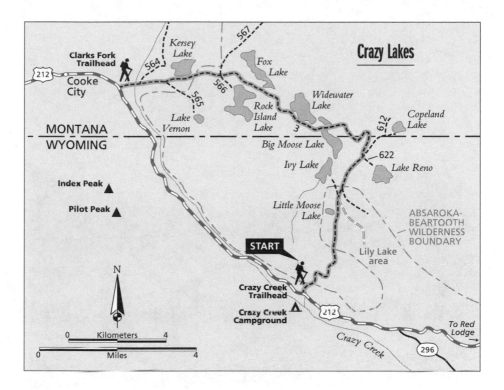

one. If you are trading keys with another party, plan on joining up at approximately the halfway point on the west shore of Big Moose Lake.

As described in the Ivy Lake trip, Hike 48, the first 4 miles of the trail start out in a grand manner with Crazy Creek Falls and then go through sagebrush and open forest, with a marsh or two, until meeting the jeep road coming in from the Lily Lake area. At this point, it's easy to get off track.

Actually, if you're out for two nights, make a note of this junction and continue on up the road to Ivy Lake, a good spot for the first night out. Come back to this confusing intersection the next morning. At the junction where the jeep road heads off to the east, continue north on the jeep road for about 100 yards. At that point a trail angles off the road at about two o'clock. Take this trail, even though it isn't marked. If you stay on the road, you'll end up at Ivy Lake.

Turn left on Trail 3, which angles off at about ten o'clock about 200 yards before the junction for Lake Reno. Shortly thereafter, the trail seems to end abruptly, but instead, it goes off to the right at about one o'clock. It's another 2 miles to Big Moose Lake.

You get to Big Moose Lake by continuing on Trail 612 to the junction with Trail 3 and Trail 622 to Lake Reno. This is a very confusing intersection, so allow an extra half hour to slowly find your way.

Fishing at Big Moose Lake, one of the Crazy Lakes.

At Big Moose Lake it becomes clear why this trip isn't recommended for early in the season, even though the snow burns off of this lower elevation area earlier than most of the Beartooths. Big Moose Lake is, more or less, a big, wide, shallow section of Crazy Creek. To continue the trek, hikers must, in essence, ford Big Moose Lake. In June this turns into an exhilarating experience, to say the least. In August it's not too bad. But even in August don't ford Big Moose Lake where the trail meets the shoreline. It's better to go slightly north where the water has some current and isn't so deep.

From Big Moose Lake, it's almost 4 miles to the junction with Trail 567. Turn left (west) here and go about 200 yards to the junction with Trail 566 to Rock Island Lake. Turn right (west) and head for Kersey Lake. Just past this lake, turn right (west) at the junction with the trail to Lake Vernon. From Big Moose Lake the trail is in excellent shape and easy to follow. From Rock Island Lake it's a leisurely 3 miles out to the Clarks Fork Trailhead.

Options

This shuttle trip can be started at the Clarks Fork Trailhead with no extra difficulty.

Side Trips

If there's time for a side trip, it's only 0.5 mile over to Lake Reno. If you camp at Rock Island Lake, you might want to set aside several hours of free time to walk around this lake.

Camping

There are several places to camp at Ivy Lake; the best site is on the left just before the lake. Camping at Lake Reno is limited, and the area tends to be marshy. At Big Moose Lake the best campsite is on the west side of the lake, just north of the trail. There's room for a large party or several parties without anybody losing much privacy. Remember that Forest Service regulations limit the size of parties with stock animals. Another good choice for the second night out is Rock Island Lake. Camping is somewhat limited at Rock Island, but once you find a spot big enough for a tent, you'll relish your stay at this gorgeous, forested lake that seems to sprawl everywhere.

Fishing

The Crazy Lakes are a chain of lakes starting with Fox and Widewater Lakes in Montana, Moose Lake straddling the border, and Ivy Lake in Wyoming. The chain of lakes has both brook and rainbow trout and a few grayling. The streams between the lakes sport the same type of fish, and they are easier to locate.

Fox Lake has some above-average brookies and some nice rainbows. Rock Island has a nice mix of cutts and brookies, but many people know this, and anglers can count on some competition, as it is an easy day hike from the Clarks Fork Trailhead to Rock Island Lake.

50 Curl Lake

General description: A seldom-used trail suitable for day trips or an overnight stay
Special attractions: The Broadwater River
Type of trip: Out-and-back
Total distance: 7 miles

Difficulty: Moderate to difficult
Traffic: Light
Maps: USGS—Fossil Lake; RMS—Cooke City-Cutoff Mountain
Starting point: Clarks Fork Trailhead

Finding the trailhead: Take U.S. Highway 212 east from Cooke City for 3.4 miles or 58.1 miles from Red Lodge and turn north onto Forest Road 306. Drive about a half mile to the trailhead.
Parking and trailhead facilities: A large trailhead with plenty of parking; toilet; picnic area.

Key Points

- **0.5** Kersey Lake jeep road.
- **1.1** Junction with Trail 564 to Curl Lake; turn left.
- **2.7** Broadwater Meadow Lakes.
- **3.5** Curl Lake.

The Hike

For a moderately short trip to an infrequently visited lake, Curl Lake hike is a good choice. The lack of use shows on the trail. It's difficult to follow in places, especially just before the lake, and early in the year hikers must skirt their way around several bogs to keep their feet dry. With the exception of the first mile, the trail goes through forests burned by the 1988 fires, including along the entire shoreline of Curl Lake.

The good news is hardly anyone goes into Curl Lake, so you will likely have the trail all to yourself.

To find Curl Lake, take Trail 3 from the Clarks Fork Trailhead. After about 0.5 mile, turn left (northeast) at the well-marked junction with the Kersey Lake jeep road. From this point on, it's a moderate uphill grade all the way to Curl Lake. Follow the road for another 0.5 mile and turn left (north) on Trail 564.

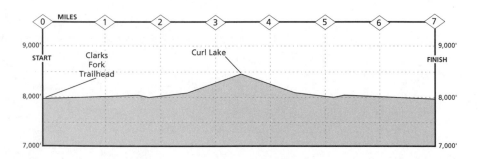

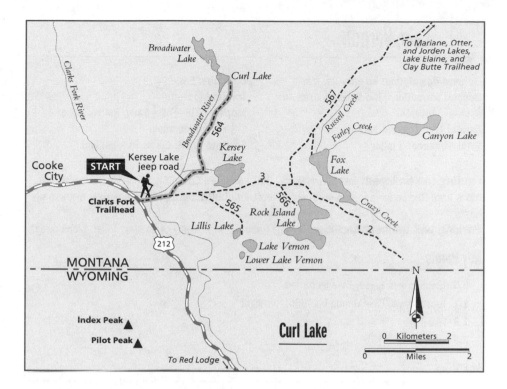

Curl Lake

Trail 564 passes through partially burnt forest and several wet meadows. Then, off to the left, watch for the Broadwater River rushing down to meet the Clarks Fork. Follow this beautiful cascading stream the rest of the way to Curl Lake. Along the way lies one of the Broadwater Meadow Lakes, essentially a scenic wide spot in the stream.

Stay alert at the head of Broadwater Meadow Lake. Just past this point, the trail gets more difficult to find, especially just before Curl Lake.

Camping

The shoreline of Curl Lake is steep and rocky, but there are places to camp.

Fishing

The Broadwater River provides a beautiful setting to fish a mountain stream. The Broadwater Meadow Lakes are known for their brook trout, providing a good opportunity to work on fly casting. Curl and Broadwater Lakes are both brook trout fisheries.

51 Lake Vernon

General description: An easy day hike
Special attractions: Two forested lakes on such a short hike
Type of trip: Out-and-back
Total distance: 5 miles

Difficulty: Easy
Traffic: Moderate
Maps: USGS—Fossil Lake; RMS—Cooke City-Cutoff Mountain
Starting point: Clarks Fork Trailhead

Finding the trailhead: Take U.S. Highway 212 east from Cooke City for 3.4 miles or 58.1 miles from Red Lodge and turn north onto Forest Road 306. Drive about a half mile to the trailhead.

Parking and trailhead facilities: A large trailhead with plenty of parking; toilet; picnic area.

Key Points

0.5 Junction with Kersey Lake jeep road.
1.2 Junction with Lake Vernon Trail 565; turn right.
1.8 Lillis Lake.
2.5 Lake Vernon.

The Hike

Lake Vernon is a great choice for a day hike with small children. The trail is well-maintained and easy to follow all the way. It passes through a rich, unburned forest, and there are no major hills. Keep a sharp eye out for moose, especially in the big meadow just before Lillis Lake.

The trail doesn't have abundant drinking water, so bring an extra bottle. Like all trails in this area, mosquitoes can be bothersome, especially early in the summer.

To reach Lake Vernon, take Trail 3 from the Clarks Fork Trailhead for about 1.2 miles to a well-signed junction with Trail 565 to Lake Vernon. Turn right (south) and head up a moderate grade. After another 0.5 mile or so look for little, jewel-like Lillis Lake in the foreground with majestic Pilot Peak and Index Peak as a backdrop.

The trail continues around the northwest shoreline of Lillis Lake less than a mile more to the destination, Lake Vernon. This forest-lined lake is larger than Lillis but

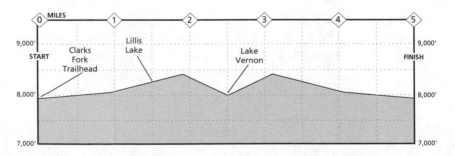

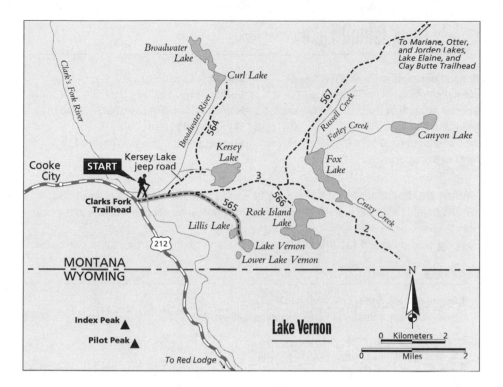

Lake Vernon

offers a similar view of Pilot and Index. Just south of Lake Vernon is Lower Lake Vernon, more appropriately called Reed Lake on some maps since it's little more than a scenic marsh.

Although better suited for day hiking, Lake Vernon also has a few campsites. Perhaps the best campsite is on the left just before the trail hits the lake.

On the way out of Lake Vernon, the trail climbs the biggest hill of the trip, about a half-mile long. Once at the top, however, it's downhill all the way to the trailhead.

Camping

A fairly short hike for an overnighter, but you can camp at Lake Vernon.

Fishing

This short day hike offers some surprising fishing. Brook trout have trouble reproducing in Lillis Lake, and the smaller population translates into bigger brookies. Be sure to stop at this small lake on the way to Vernon, which hosts both cutthroat and brook trout. Just over the hill, you could find yourself alone catching stocked cutthroats at Margaret Lake.

52 Rock Island Lake

General description: An easy day hike or overnighter
Special attractions: An unusually large forest-lined lake
Type of trip: Out-and-back
Total distance: 6 miles

Difficulty: Easy
Traffic: Heavy
Maps: USGS–Fossil Lake; RMS–Cooke City-Cutoff Mountain
Starting point: Clarks Fork Trailhead

Finding the trailhead: Take U.S. Highway 212 east from Cooke City for 3.4 miles or 58.1 miles from Red Lodge and turn north onto Forest Road 306. Drive about a half mile to the trailhead.

Parking and trailhead facilities: A large trailhead with plenty of parking; toilet; picnic area.

Key Points

0.5 Junction with Kersey Lake Jeep Road.

1.2 Junction with Trail 565 to Lake Vernon; turn left.

1.5 Kersey Lake.

2.4 Junction with Trail 566 to Rock Island Lake; turn right.

3.0 Rock Island Lake.

The Hike

Rock Island Lake differs from many high-elevation lakes. Instead of forming a small, concise oval in a cirque, it sprawls through flat and forested terrain, seemingly branching off in every direction. Visitors can spend an entire day just walking around it.

To get to Rock Island Lake, take Trail 3 from the Clarks Fork Trailhead to the junction with Trail 566 to Rock Island Lake. Turn right (east) here for about another 0.5 mile to the lake. The trail is well-used and well-maintained the entire way with only one hill (near Kersey Lake). The 1988 fires scorched the area around Kersey Lake but missed Rock Island Lake.

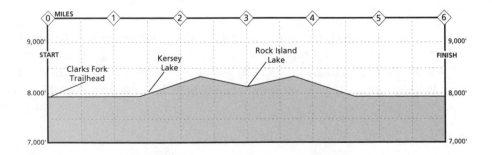

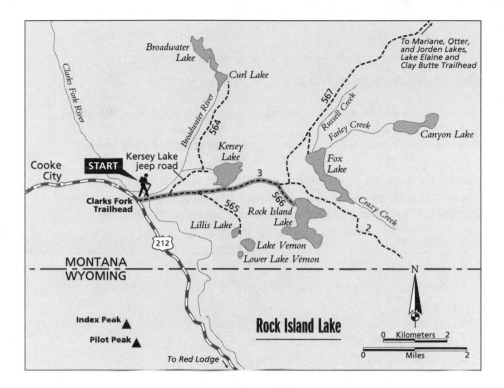

Because Rock Island Lake is so easy to reach (3 miles on a near-level trail), it's a perfect choice for a family's first trip into the Absaroka–Beartooth Wilderness. Drinking water is readily available on the trail and at the lake (it must be boiled or filtered), but the mosquitoes can be thick in early summer.

Camping

Those planning an overnight stay can camp at one of several places along the west side of the lake. However, camping spots are more limited than many other lakes in the Beartooths, and you might have to search a while to find an unoccupied spot. Although there might be enough wood for a campfire at the lake, consider using a stove for cooking. The area receives heavy use, and if everyone had a fire, the area would soon show signs of overuse.

Fishing

This popular lake has a combination of home-grown brookies and cutthroats stocked on a three-year rotation, both of which grow well in this lake. The fishing should generally be good enough to count on for dinner.

53 Fox Lake

General description: A moderately easy overnighter

Special attractions: A large and beautiful lake

Type of trip: Out-and-back

Total distance: 8 miles

Difficulty: Moderate

Traffic: Moderate

Maps: USGS–Fossil Lake; RMS–Cooke City–Cutoff Mountain

Starting point: Clarks Fork Trailhead

Finding the trailhead: Take U.S. Highway 212 east from Cooke City for 3.4 miles or 58.1 miles from Red Lodge and turn north onto Forest Road 306. Drive about a half mile to the trailhead.

Parking and trailhead facilities: A large trailhead with plenty of parking; toilet; picnic area.

Key Points

0.5 Junction with Kersey Lake jeep road.

1.2 Junction with Trail 565 to Lake Vernon; turn left.

1.5 Kersey Lake.

2.4 Junction with Trail 566 to Rock Island Lake; turn left.

2.6 Junction with Trail 567 to Russell Creek; turn left.

3.6 Junction with trail down to Fox Lake; turn right.

4.0 Fox Lake

The Hike

Fox Lake is the first of a long chain of lakes called Crazy Lakes, and it's a good choice for a moderate overnight trip.

To get to Fox Lake, take Trail 3 from the Clarks Fork Trailhead. The trail passes through mostly unburned forest (except for a section by Kersey Lake) for about 2.6 miles. Turn left onto Trail 567 to Russell Creek. Then look for a trail heading right (southeast) to Fox Lake. Be careful not to take two earlier right-hand turns to Rock Island Lake or Crazy Lakes.

The trail climbs gradually as it heads toward the high plateau. The turn onto the Fox Lake trail leads to a steep, half-mile downhill to the lake.

Fox Lake is large and striking. Explorers can follow the shoreline around to the

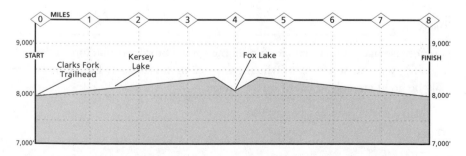

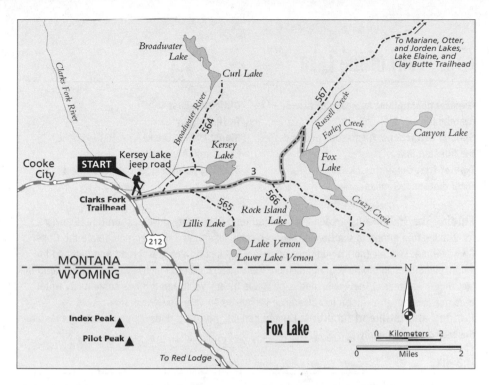

Fox Lake

right (west) but not to the left where steep climbs jut up from the lake.

Farley Creek also tumbles into Fox Lake just to the east of Russell Creek. These two streams merge in Fox Lake and leave the lake as Crazy Creek.

On the way out of Fox Lake, be prepared to climb that major hill you came down on the way in. But from that point, it's downhill to the trailhead except for a short slope along Kersey Lake.

Side Trips

For a fairly rough side trip, follow a crude anglers' trail up Farley Creek to Canyon Lake. This is a steep, difficult-to-follow trail for experienced hikers only.

Camping

There's a large camping area on the west side of where Russell Creek slips into Fox Lake. This is the only campsite, but it's suitable for a large party or more than one small group. The site is not suited for backcountry horsemen.

Fishing

Fox Lake is a personal favorite, although close to the trailhead. Most day hikers stop at Kersey or head over to Rock Island. Overnighters generally pass by on The Beaten Path (Trail 567, Hike 20). Fox has oversized brookies, nice rainbows, and an occasional grayling that slipped down from Cliff Lake. Cliff Lake is a worthwhile side trip for the hearty (no trail). It has an abundance of 8- to 12-inch grayling.

54 Lady of the Lake

General description: An easy day hike or overnighter

Special attractions: A gorgeous and accessible forested lake

Type of trip: Out-and-back

Total distance: 3 miles

Difficulty: Easy

Traffic: Heavy

Maps: USGS—Cooke City; RMS—Cooke City-Cutoff Mountain

Starting point: Fisher Creek Trailhead

Finding the trailhead: To reach the trailhead from Cooke City, drive east on U.S. Highway 212 for 2 miles to a turnoff to the Goose Lake jeep road, less than a quarter mile before the Colter Campground. Turn left (north) and drive northeast 2 miles on this gravel road and pull into the inconspicuous trailhead on your right. (There were no signs on the highway or at the trailhead the last time I was there.) The gravel road is passable by any vehicle, but it has some nasty water bars that could high-center a low-clearance vehicle so go very slowly over them.

Parking and trailhead facilities: Limited parking; no toilet; undeveloped camping sites at the trailhead and nearby.

The Hike

Lady of the Lake is an ideal choice for an easy day hike or overnighter with small children. Besides being a short hike, the weather isn't as critical as it is at the higher elevations.

Unfortunately, hikers might have to get their feet wet immediately upon starting this trip. The bridge over Fisher Creek washed out years ago, and until late in the year, the stream carries too much water to ford without wading.

After Fisher Creek, the trail goes by a small inholding with a cabin then heads down a well-maintained, forest-lined trail to Lady of the Lake. The Forest Service sign says 1 MILE to the lake, but it's probably more like 1.5 miles. The trail breaks out of the trees in the large marshy meadow at the foot of the lake.

Just before the lake, Trail 563 heads off to the right (south) to Chief Joseph Campground on U.S. 212. Trail 563 also offers fairly easy access to Lady of the Lake, but the route described here is much shorter and faster.

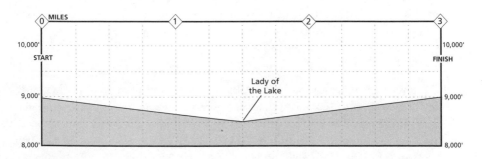

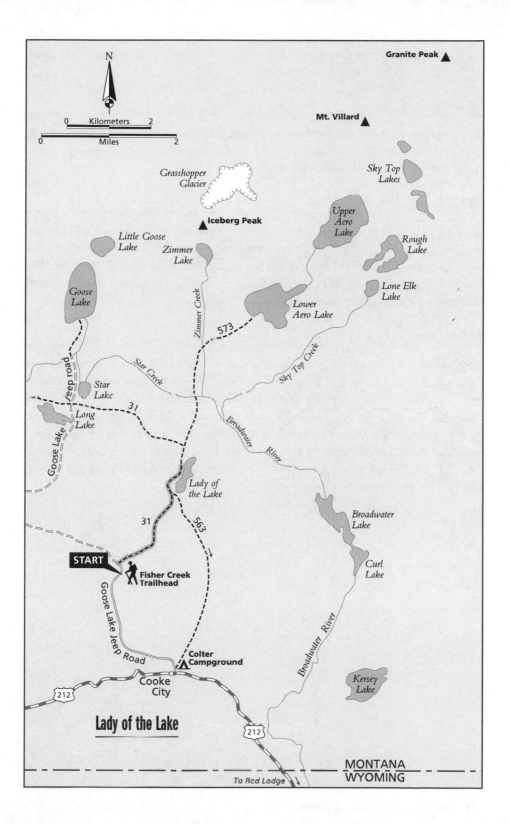

N

0 — Kilometers — 2
0 — Miles — 2

Granite Peak ▲

Mt. Villard ▲

*Grasshopper
Glacier*

Sky Top
Lakes

▲ **Iceberg Peak**

*Upper
Aero
Lake*

*Little Goose
Lake*

*Zimmer
Lake*

*Rough
Lake*

*Goose
Lake*

*Lower
Aero Lake*

*Lone Elk
Lake*

Zimmer Creek

573

Star Creek

Sky Top Creek

Jeep road

*Star
Lake*

31

*Long
Lake*

Goose Lake

Broadwater River

*Lady of
the Lake*

*Broadwater
Lake*

31

563

*Curl
Lake*

START

**Fisher Creek
Trailhead**

Goose Lake Jeep Road

Broadwater River

**Colter
Campground**

**Cooke
City**

212

*Kersey
Lake*

Lady of the Lake

212

To Red Lodge

MONTANA
WYOMING

The return trip involves more climbing than the way in, so allow extra time, especially if traveling with small children.

Options

You can also reach Lady of the Lake by taking Trail 563 from Colter Campground. You could also use this trail to make this a shuttle trip, which means leaving a vehicle at the Colter Campground.

Camping

This is a heavily used area, with some major wear and tear along the trail on the west shore of the lake. The Forest Service has prohibited camping at several overused sites to allow rehabilitation. For overnighters, the best campsite is about halfway along the lake on the left just after a cut in a huge log across the trail and through a small meadow. Campfires are allowed but discouraged.

Fishing

Lady of the Lake is a personal favorite of places to take kids for their first wilderness camping experience. The hike is easy, and the brook trout are always willing. For those with some wilderness experience, there are four small lakes nestled in the trees to the southeast. They're a bit tough to find, but they promise solitude. Grayling are stocked in Mosquito Lake when available, while the other lakes are scheduled for stocking with cutthroats. Don't bother to fish Fisher Creek. Acid effluent from mines abandoned before environmental protection laws were in place keeps this stream pretty sterile.

55 Aero Lakes

General description: A strenuous base-camp trip into the heart of the Beartooth's alpine country

Special attractions: The stark beauty of this high plateau area and a wide diversity of potential side trips

Type of trip: Out-and-back

Total distance: 12 miles, not counting side trips

Difficulty: Difficult

Traffic: Moderate

Maps: USGS—Cooke City, Fossil Lake, and Granite Peak; RMS—Cooke City-Cutoff Mountain

Starting point: Fisher Creek Trailhead

Finding the trailhead: To reach the trailhead from Cooke City, drive east on U.S. Highway 212 for 2 miles to a turnoff to the Goose Lake jeep road, less than a quarter mile before the Colter Campground. Turn left (north) and drive northeast 2 miles on this gravel road and pull into the inconspicuous trailhead on your right. (There were no signs on the highway or at the trailhead the last time I was there.) The gravel road is passable by any vehicle, but it has some nasty water bars that could high-center a low-clearance vehicle so go very slowly over them.

Parking and trailhead facilities: Limited parking; no toilet; undeveloped camping sites at the trailhead and nearby.

Key Points

1.5 Lady of the Lake Trail junction with Trail 563; turn left.

2.5 Junction with trail to Long Lake; turn right.

2.8 Stream coming in from Long Lake.

3.6 Star Creek.

4.8 Start of climb to Aero Lakes.

5.7 Base of Lower Aero Lake.

Recommended Itinerary

You could hike into Aero Lakes and out the same day, but this would be a shame. Instead, plan on a long day hike to get to the lakes and spend the time to find an idyllic campsite. Then, spend two or three days exploring this incredible high-country.

The Hike

This trailhead is slightly harder to locate than most others in the Beartooths, but this hasn't lessened its popularity. The area has lots to offer, and it receives heavy use both by locals and those who travel from afar for a chance to experience this spectacular wild area.

The trailhead lies on the eastern fringe of the section of the Beartooths that has been extensively mined, logged, and roaded. Even in the 2 miles of gravel road to the trailhead, the contrast between this area and the pristine wilderness is clearly evident. To get an early start, camp at the undeveloped campground at the trailhead.

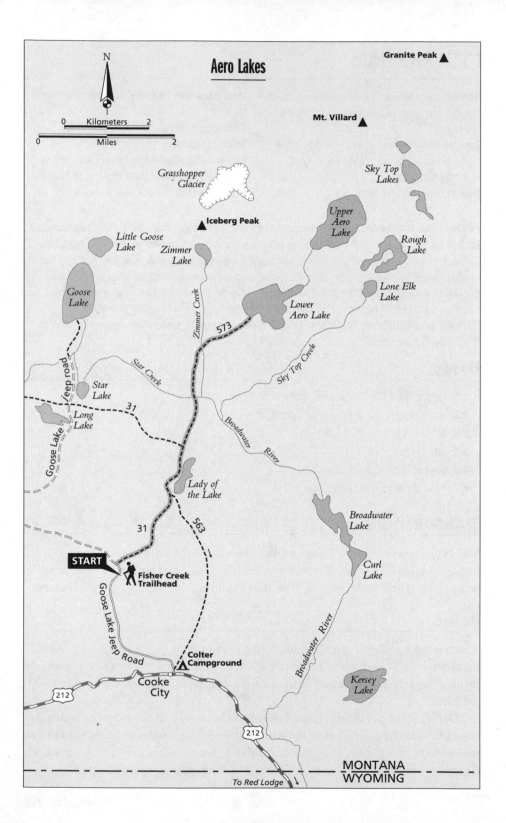

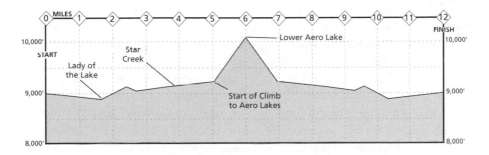

At Aero Lakes you're many miles from the nearest machine. At night no city lights nor smog block the view of the stars. Nearly one million acres of pristine land surround you here, more than enough for a lifetime of wandering. At this altitude, the summer season is very short. Ice may not free the lakes until mid-July. The moist tundra tends to produce a prodigious number of mosquitoes when the wind isn't blowing. Bring lots of bug dope.

The first leg of the trip takes you to Lady of the Lake, an ideal choice for an easy day hike or overnighter with small children. Unfortunately, they might get their feet wet immediately upon starting this trip. The bridge over Fisher Creek washed out years ago, and until late in the year, the stream carries too much water to ford without wading.

After Fisher Creek the trail goes by a small inholding with a cabin, then heads down a well-maintained, forest-lined trail to Lady of the Lake. The Forest Service sign says 1 MILE to the lake, but it's probably more like 1.5 miles.

The trail breaks out of the trees in the large marshy meadow at the foot of the lake. Just before the lake, Trail 563 heads off to the right (south) to Chief Joseph Campground on U.S. 212. (Trail 563 also offers fairly easy access to Lady of the Lake, but the route described here is much shorter and faster.)

Once at Lady of the Lake, follow the trail along the west side of the lake. At the far end of the lake, the trail heads off to the left for about a quarter mile to a meadow on the north side of the lake where two trails depart. The left trail heads northwest to Long Lake. Take the right trail, which leads almost due north less than a half mile to the confluence of Star and Zimmer Creeks. Ford the stream here and continue north along Zimmer Creek another mile or so until you see Trail 573 switchbacking up the steep right side of the cirque. If you see a major stream coming in from the left, you have gone too far up the drainage.

The scramble up the switchbacks is short but steep and requires good physical conditioning. Locals call this "Cardiac Hill," and for good reason. It climbs almost 900 feet in about a mile, close to a Category H on our hill rating chart.

At the top of Cardiac Hill, the trail suddenly emerges from the timber and pauses above Lower Aero Lake. Be sure to notice the dramatic contrast between the treeless plateau here and the timbered country below.

The shoreline around Lower Aero is rocky and punctuated with snowbanks. There are a number of places to camp. They all have great scenery, and the air conditioning is always on. Those planning to stay here for two or three nights should spend some extra time searching for that five-star campsite. Drop the packs and look around for an hour or so. Don't expect to have a campfire on this treeless plateau.

To proceed to Upper Aero Lake, follow the stream that connects the two lakes. Another good camping spot is just below the outlet of the upper lake. This provides a good view of the lake and prominent Mount Villard with its spiny ridges. It also makes a good base camp for fishing both lakes and for exploring east to Rough Lake and then north up the Sky Top Lakes chain.

Although most people visit Rough Lake or Lone Elk Lake on side trips, there's also good camping there. Both are large, deep lakes similar to Aero Lakes. Sky Top Lakes might look inviting on the map, but camping is very limited in this rocky basin.

After a day or two of exploring the high country, retrace your steps down Cardiac Hill to Zimmer Creek—and then, back to civilization.

Upper Aero Lake, the second deepest in the Beartooths.

Options

This trip could turn into a long (four or five days) shuttle for experts only by continuing east from Aero Lakes through the "top of the world" and exiting the Beartooths at the East Rosebud or Clarks Fork Trailheads.

You could also make a loop out of your trip by exiting on an off-trail route down Sky Top Creek, but be careful on the steep upper section of the stream where it tumbles off the plateau from Lone Elk Lake. Be forewarned: This route is only for the fit, agile, and adventuresome. It requires carrying your pack cross-country over to Rough Lake (probably named for how hard it is to reach) and then down to Lone Elk Lake. From Lone Elk Lake, it's a scramble down a steep route with no trail to a meadow where the stream from Splinter Lake slips into Sky Top Creek. This is a long, slow mile, and it can be hazardous, so be careful and patient. But it's also very beautiful, especially the falls where Sky Top Creek leaves Lone Elk Lake. At the meadow, there is an unofficial trail along Sky Top Creek all the way to the main trail. Follow cascading Sky Top Creek all the way until near the end when it veers off to the left to join up with Star Creek to form the Broadwater River. The track comes out into the same meadow (where Star and Zimmer Creeks join) you passed through on the way up Zimmer Creek on Trail 573. From here, retrace your steps back to Lady of the Lake and the trailhead.

Side Trips

Refer to Where to Go from Aero Lakes, on page 260.

Camping

There are no designated campsites in this area, but there are numerous possibilities. Please use zero-impact camping principles to preserve this fragile landscape.

Fishing

Lady of the Lake is a favorite place to take kids for their first wilderness camping experience. The hike is easy, and the brook trout are always willing. For those with some wilderness experience, there are four small lakes nestled in the trees to the southeast. They're a bit tough to find, but they promise solitude. Grayling are stocked in Mosquito Lake when available, while the other lakes are scheduled for stocking with cutthroats.

Don't bother to fish Fisher Creek. Acid effluent from mines abandoned before environmental protection laws were in place keeps this stream pretty sterile.

Fishing is generally slow in both Upper and Lower Aero Lakes, but the rewards can be worth it. Lower Aero has brookies that are large, occasionally approaching a pound or more. They are supplemented with cutthroats that have migrated down from Upper Aero and seem to be reproducing. Cutts can be seen trying to spawn between the lakes through most of July. Upper Aero is stocked with cutts, but a change in its current six-year cycle is being discussed. Fishing is tough here as the cut-throats tend to school, and they can be hard to find in a lake of this size.

Sky Top Lakes were once stocked with grayling, and these worked down into Rough and Lone Elk Lakes, but all seem to have disappeared, leaving just brook trout in Lone Elk and Rough. The Sky Tops will probably be stocked once again to maintain a fishery in this chain originating on the slopes of Granite Peak.

To the east of Sky Top Creek are a number of lakes, supporting mostly brook trout, although Weasel, Stash, and Surprise Lakes are stocked with cutts. For hearty souls Recruitment Lake holds a few extremely large brookies, but the chances of getting skunked are pretty good. Nevertheless, just one hefty fish from this lake would be the high point of a summer vacation.

WHERE TO GO FROM AERO LAKES While in the Aero Lakes area, set aside a day or two for exploring the "top of the world." Day trips in this area are generally more advanced than in other parts of the Beartooths. Here's a list of suggestions rated for difficulty as follows: Human (easy for almost everyone, including children), Semi-human (moderately difficult), or Animal (don't try it unless you're very fit and wilderness-wise). Also refer to more detailed rating information in the chapter Using this Guidebook.

Destination	Difficulty
Aero Lakes perimeter	Semi-human
Upper Aero Lake	Human
Leaky Raft Lake	Human
Rough Lake	Semi-human
Lone Elk Lake	Semi-human
Sky Top Lakes	Animal
Zimmer Lake	Animal
Iceberg Peak and Grasshopper Glacier	Animal
Mount Villard	Animal
Glacier Peak	Animal

56 Goose Lake

General description: An unusual hike partially on a jeep road

Special attractions: A large, fish-filled mountain lake in a treeless, high-altitude basin

Type of trip: Out-and-back

Total distance: 10 miles

Difficulty: Moderate

Traffic: Moderate

Maps: USGS—Cooke City, Fossil Lake, and Granite Peak; RMS—Cooke City-Cutoff Mountain

Starting point: Fisher Creek Trailhead

Finding the trailhead: To reach the trailhead from Cooke City, drive east on U.S. Highway 212 for 2 miles to a turnoff to the Goose Lake Jeep Road, less than a quarter mile before the Colter Campground. Turn left (north) and drive northeast 2 miles on this gravel road and pull into the inconspicuous trailhead on your right. (There were no signs on the highway or at the trailhead the last time I was there.) The gravel road is passable by any vehicle, but it has some nasty water bars that could high-center a low-clearance vehicle so go very slowly over them.

Parking and trailhead facilities: Limited parking; no toilet; undeveloped camping sites at the trailhead and nearby.

Key Points

1.5 Lady of the Lake.

2.0 Junction with trail to Long Lake; turn left.

2.8 Long Lake.

3.5 Star Lake.

4.5 Wilderness boundary.

5.0 Goose Lake.

The Hike

I purposely left this route out of the first edition of this book because, at the time, a Canadian mining company had proposed a massive open-pit mine near Goose Lake. Since then, the environmentalists defeated this mine. That doesn't make the area pristine, though, because the landscape around Goose Lake is still pockmarked with mining scars from the early 1900s. Thankfully, now, nature has made great strides in reclaiming many of the mine sites, and U.S government Superfund money has been used to hurry nature along. The end result is a reasonably attractive landscape dotted with trout-filled lakes.

Unfortunately, most of this area is not in the Absaroka-Beartooth Wilderness, withheld from the original legislation because of mining activity. This allows several old jeep roads to remain open to motorized travel, including the Goose Lake jeep road along the route described here, another reason I didn't include it in the first edition.

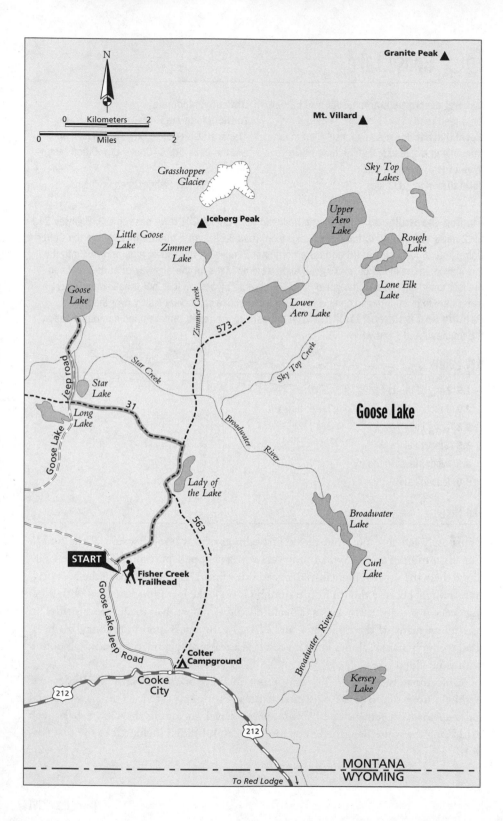

N

Kilometers 2
0
Miles 2
0

Granite Peak ▲

Mt. Villard ▲

Sky Top
Lakes

Grasshopper
Glacier

Iceberg Peak ▲

Upper
Aero
Lake

Rough
Lake

Little Goose
Lake

Zimmer
Lake

Lone Elk
Lake

Goose
Lake

Zimmer Creek

573

Lower
Aero Lake

Sky Top Creek

Star Creek

Star
Lake

31

Goose Lake

Long
Lake

Broadwater River

Goose Lake

Lady of
the Lake

563

Broadwater
Lake

START

Fisher Creek
Trailhead

Curl
Lake

Goose Lake Jeep Road

Colter
Campground

Broadwater River

Cooke
City

Kersey
Lake

212

212

MONTANA
WYOMING

To Red Lodge ↓

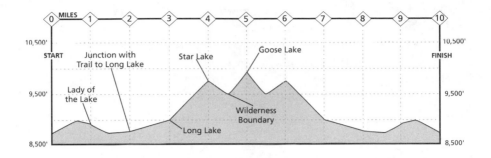

I recently hiked into Goose Lake again and with some reservation decided to include it in the revised edition, even though about half the route involves hiking on the Goose Lake Jeep Road. I found that hiking in the morning on a weekday meant I had the road all to myself. I enjoyed the hike and didn't encounter any all-terrain vehicles (ATVs). However, on the way out of Goose Lake that afternoon, I did meet a few, but even that didn't ruin the trip, mainly because this is such a scenic area that it's hard not to enjoy it.

The first part of the Goose Lake hike follows the route to Lady of the Lake. Unfortunately, you'll have to get your feet wet immediately upon starting this trip. The bridge over Fisher Creek washed out years ago, and until late in the year, the stream carries too much water to ford without wading.

After Fisher Creek, the trail goes by a small inholding with a cabin, then heads down a well-maintained, forest-lined trail to Lady of the Lake. The Forest Service sign says 1 MILE to the lake, but it's probably more like 1.5 miles. The trail breaks out of the trees in the large marshy meadow at the foot of the lake.

Just before the lake, Trail 563 heads off to the right (south) to Chief Joseph Campground on U.S. 212. Trail 563 also offers fairly easy access to Lady of the Lake, but the route described here is much shorter and faster.

Walk along the west shoreline about a half mile past the lake to a junction with Trail 31 heading up to the jeep road. There's a sign saying GOOSE LAKE JEEP ROAD, but it's set back away from the trail and is easy to miss. If you get to Star Creek, you've missed it, so backtrack about a quarter mile to the junction.

This section of trail has one confusing spot. Shortly after the junction, you reach a large meadow and the trail fades away. Don't take the logical route angling off to the right, which leads back to the Aero Lakes trail. Instead, the trail takes off up the hill at about two o'clock from the point where you enter the meadow. It's a steady climb with a few switchbacks for almost a mile until you reach the jeep road at Long Lake.

From here to Goose Creek about a half mile from the lake, you walk up the jeep road, passing Long Lake and Star Lake along the way. The jeep road is actually an easy trail and a rugged drive made for people who like to punish their vehicles. At Goose Creek, you enter the wilderness; motorized travelers must park here and walk the last half mile to the lake.

Goose Lake has a few mining scars, but the stunning scenery makes it easy to overlook them. The lake is ringed with some of the most precipitous mountains in the wilderness—Wolf Mountain, Sawtooth Mountain, and Iceberg Peak to the north; Mount Fox to the west; and Mount Zimmer to the east. Scenery doesn't get much better than this.

Options

You can make a loop out of this trip, sort of, by continuing down the jeep road at Long Lake instead of taking the trail back to Lady of the Lake. This bypasses the hill up from Lady of the Lake and takes you past Round Lake, but it also provides more opportunity to share your route with four-wheel-drives and ATVs.

Side Trips

At Goose Lake, cross the outlet stream and walk along an old mining road above the east side of the lake to Little Goose Lake. If you have some extra time on the way back to Fisher Creek, check out nearby Huckleberry and Ovis Lakes, both a short walk west of the jeep road.

Camping

You'll find limited camping at the lower end of Goose Lake and a slightly better selection of campsites at the upper end between the big lake and Little Goose Lake.

Fishing

Goose Lake and Little Goose Lake have good, self-sustaining cutthroat fishing, but because of the easy assess, they see lots of flies and lures and can be difficult to catch. You can depend on the other lakes in the area (Long, Huckleberry, Round, and Chris) to provide a catch of tasty brook trout for dinner. Ovis and Star Lakes have cutthroats.

57 Horseshoe Lake

General description: A long and difficult loop through some of the most remote and untamed country left in the continental United States

Special attractions: The wildest, most remote trip in this book

Type of trip: Loop

Total distance: 29 miles

Difficulty: Very difficult and demanding, strictly for the experienced hiker

Traffic: Extra light

Maps: USGS—Cooke City, Cutoff Mountain, Little Park Mountain, and Pinnacle Mountain; RMS—Cooke City-Cutoff Mountain

Starting point: Lake Abundance Trailhead

Finding the trailhead: Most trailheads in the Beartooths are quite accessible. This one is the other extreme. Just getting here can be quite the experience. The road to Daisy Pass leaves U.S. Highway 212 about 0.5 mile from the east edge of Cooke City. It's then about 8 miles to the trailhead. The first 4 miles are on a well-maintained gravel road that can be traversed by any two-wheel-drive vehicle. About a half mile after the top of Daisy Pass, turn left (west) on the Lake Abundance Jeep Road, which is not maintained. From this point on, don't proceed with anything less than a high-clearance, four-wheel-drive vehicle.

Parking and trailhead facilities: Plenty of parking; no toilet; an undeveloped campground at the trailhead.

Key Points

2.1 Goose Creek.

9.6 Junction with Horseshoe Creek Trail 34; turn left.

16.0 Lake of the Woods and junction with Trail 109; turn left.

16.5 Junction with trail to Peace Lake; stay left on Trail 109.

18.5 Trail to Horseshoe Lake.

21.2 Junction with Lake Abundance Trail 84; turn left.

27.7 Lake Abundance.

28.7 Lake Abundance Trailhead.

Recommended Itinerary

This route is about the right length for four nights out, but when considering good camping options, it works better for three nights out. If you decide on this recommended option, plan on a long last day to get back to your vehicle. If you decide on four nights, it's an easy decision to stay at Horseshoe Lake on the third night. If you decide on three nights out but don't want to hike 11–plus miles on the last day, bypass Horseshoe Lake and find a campsite somewhere along Rock Creek or Lake Abundance Creek. Regrettably, neither area has good camping areas.

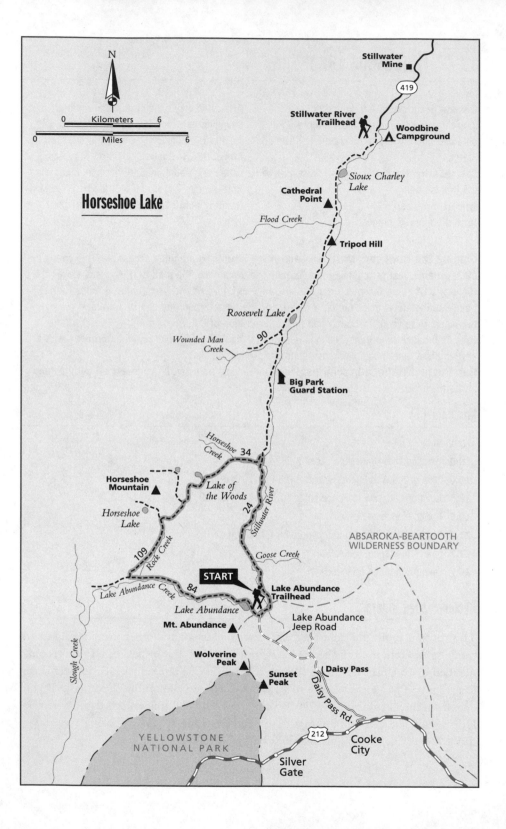

First night:	Along Stillwater River near Glacier, Octopus, or Horseshoe Creek
Second night:	Lake of the Woods or Peace Lake
Third night:	Horseshoe Lake

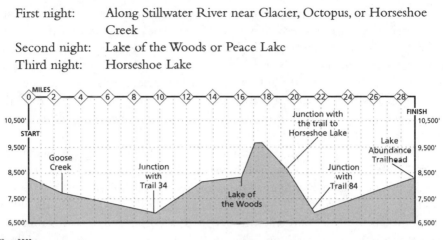

The Hike

This trip is not for the beginner or the faint-hearted. It goes through the wildest, most isolated country in the Beartooths, and most of the trail is poorly maintained and, in places, hard to find. Be sure to allow extra travel time for covering rough ground and for route-finding.

On the plus side, travelers here will think they have the entire universe to themselves because the area receives so little use. In this realm of solitude and untamed grandeur, you become immersed in the true spirit of the wilderness.

From the trailhead head down Stillwater River Trail 24, which takes off just across the little stream meandering through a large high-altitude meadow east of the trailhead. Goose Creek is the headwaters of the Stillwater River, though it doesn't look like much of a river at this point. That changes about 2 miles downstream when Goose Creek joins the upper Stillwater.

After a pleasant half-mile walk through the flat meadow, the trail drops over the end of the plateau and starts a steep downhill grade along the still small Stillwater River. When Goose Creek cascades in from the east, the gradient flattens out a bit and grows steadily more gradual all the way to the junction with Trail 34 up Horseshoe Creek. Cross the Stillwater where Goose Creek comes in—there's no bridge. It's safe to cross here, but plan on getting wet feet.

The first 4 miles of trail traverse a somewhat stark landscape, carpeted with flat, glaciated rock and punctuated like a pincushion with whitish snags. It was semistark before the fires of 1988, but one of the burns scorched its way down the Stillwater to finish the job. It's a lonely, cheerless stretch.

But then the landscape becomes more diverse and moist, supporting abundant wildlife populations, especially elk and deer. You should start looking for the first night's campsite somewhere along this reach of the upper Stillwater. There's no shortage of agreeable sites, so where to stop depends more on how far you want to go on the first day in.

A little more than 9 miles into the trek, start watching for the turnoff to Horse-shoe Creek. This junction is easy to miss, and it could be a long detour if you miss it. Refer to a topo map frequently to be sure you've crossed Horseshoe Creek. Shortly after the stream crossing, Trail 34 heads west out of a small meadow. There probably won't be a sign, but look for the post that once held the sign. The grassy meadow also tends to swallow up the trail as it departs, but attentive hikers won't miss it. After the first 50 yards, the trail becomes easy to follow, although from here on out the trail has received little trail maintenance.

Trail 34 climbs moderately to Lake of the Woods, following the creek all the way. About 1 mile before Lake of the Woods, the trail breaks out into a scenic subalpine landscape that burned only in spots. Lake of the Woods is a shallow pristine lake surrounded by marshy meadows. Those who camp here for the second night should set aside some time for the short side trip over to Peace Lake and, if there's time and energy to spare, the bushwhack up a short, 600-foot climb to Heather Lake, which is about 2 miles northwest of Lake of the Woods.

About 100 feet before hitting the shoreline at Lake of the Woods, Trail 109 takes off to the south. This junction can be difficult to find; backtrack from the lake if necessary and look carefully for the trail as it starts to switchback up a steep grade to the south. Again, the trail is easy to follow after the first 100 yards.

After the tough but short climb (gaining about 900 feet), the trail breaks out above timberline at 9,500 feet and follows a narrow ridge for a while. Set an easy pace and soak in the great scenery. Look west to 10,111-foot Horseshoe Mountain, north to 10,272-foot Timberline Mountain, and 8 miles south to 10,500-foot Wolverine Peak on the northwest boundary of Yellowstone National Park. As the trail drops off the ridge, keep the topo map and compass out—the trail fades away in several places.

Soon, you'll see a trail veering off the right to Horseshoe Lake. This is a nice side trip if you have the time, and you can camp there. The lake still bears a few signs of early-twentieth-century mining activity around its shores, but you'll still be overwhelmed by the wild remoteness of the place.

From Horseshoe Basin, descend gradually toward Lake Abundance Creek, following Rock Creek most of the way. This area escaped the 1988 fires and is loaded with wildlife, including a healthy bear population, so stay alert.

About 3 miles from Horseshoe Basin, turn left (east) on Trail 84 at the only easy-to-find junction on this trip. Then follow Lake Abundance Creek all the way back to the trailhead, about 7.5 miles total. This drainage is moist and lush, excellent wildlife habitat.

When I hiked this route, this trail needed to see a trail crew badly, and I spent the day climbing over downed trees. The trail skirts the north shore of Lake Abundance for about half of the final mile to the trailhead.

Options

The route could be hiked in reverse, but it wouldn't be any easier.

Side Trips

Peace Lake and Horseshoe Lake are easy side trips on trails, and if you're fit and adventurous (which you probably are or you wouldn't be on this trip), try Heather Lake.

Camping

It's always comforting to know that you can find a place that looks like you might be the first person to ever camp there. This is such a place, so when you set up your camp, please make sure you do your part to keep it that way.

Fishing

For anglers, the highlight of this trip is the possibility of catching aboriginal Yellowstone cutthroat trout. Peace and Heather Lakes have never been stocked and contain original cutthroats. It seems that someone took a few of these over the pass and placed them in Lake of the Woods, as the same stock is found there. While none of these fish are large, just catching them may be satisfying.

The entire Slough Creek drainage supports only cutthroats. Stocking of Yellowstone cutthroats has occurred in many places, including the creek itself. Currently only Lake Abundance (on a three-year cycle) and Horseshoe Lake (on an eight-year cycle) are stocked. Fish grow exceptionally well in Lake Abundance, and it's certainly worth the stop.

58 The Complete Stillwater

General description: A trans-Beartooth route following the Stillwater River all the way
Special attractions: It's all downhill
Type of trip: Shuttle
Total distance: 28 miles
Difficulty: Moderate, but long
Traffic: Extra light, except the last few miles around Sioux Charley Lake

Maps: USGS—Cooke City, Cutoff Mountain, Little Park Mountain, Pinnacle Mountain, and Cathedral Point; RMS—Cooke City–Cutoff Mountain and Mount Douglas–Mount Wood
Starting point: Lake Abundance Trailhead

Finding the trailhead: Most trailheads in the Beartooths are quite accessible. This one is the other extreme. Just getting here can be quite the experience. The road to Daisy Pass leaves U.S. Highway 212 about 0.5 mile from the east edge of Cooke City. It's then about 8 miles to the trailhead. The first 4 miles are on a well-maintained gravel road that can be traversed by any two-wheel-drive vehicle. About a half mile after the top of Daisy Pass, turn left (west) on the Lake Abundance Jeep Road, which is not maintained. From this point on, don't proceed with anything less than a high-clearance, four-wheel-drive vehicle.

Parking and trailhead facilities: Plenty of parking; no toilet; an undeveloped campground at the trailhead.

Key Points

2.1 Goose Creek.

9.6 Junction with Horseshoe Creek Trail 34; turn right.

14.9 Big Park Guard Station.

16.6 Wounded Man Creek.

16.8 Junction with West Stillwater Trail 90; turn right.

21.6 Tripod Hill.

22.3 Flood Creek.

24.8 Sioux Charley Lake.

27.8 Stillwater River Trailhead.

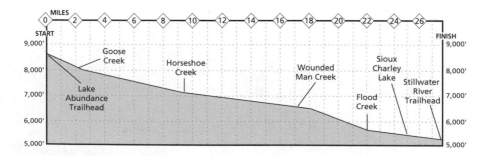

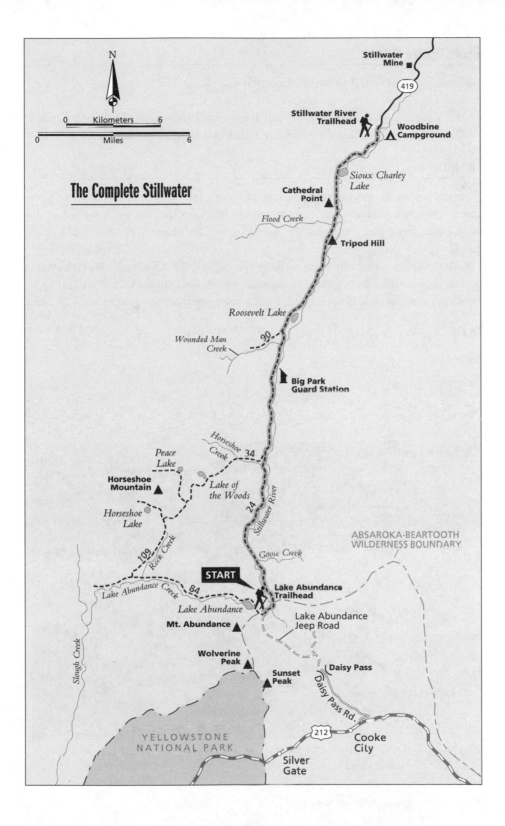

The Complete Stillwater

N

Kilometers 0 — 6
Miles 0 — 6

Stillwater Mine
419
Stillwater River Trailhead
Woodbine Campground
Sioux Charley Lake
Cathedral Point
Flood Creek
Tripod Hill
Roosevelt Lake
Wounded Man Creek
90
Big Park Guard Station
Horseshoe Creek
34
Peace Lake
Horseshoe Mountain
Lake of the Woods
Stillwater River
Horseshoe Lake
24
109
Rock Creek
Goose Creek
ABSAROKA-BEARTOOTH WILDERNESS BOUNDARY
START
Lake Abundance Trailhead
Lake Abundance Creek
84
Lake Abundance
Mt. Abundance
Lake Abundance Jeep Road
Slough Creek
Wolverine Peak
Sunset Peak
Daisy Pass
Daisy Pass Rd.
212
Cooke City
YELLOWSTONE NATIONAL PARK
Silver Gate

Recommended Itinerary

This route is best suited to two nights out.

First night: Along the Stillwater River near Octopus or Horseshoe Creek
Second night: Along the Stillwater River near Wounded Man Creek

The Hike

This trip can be traveled from either end, of course, but most people will prefer starting at Lake Abundance because, quite frankly, it's easier. In fact, it's downhill all the
way. There aren't many trails where hikers can go 28 miles without a single uphill
pitch.

Try to arrange for somebody to drop you off at Lake Abundance and then leave
a vehicle or arrange for a pickup at the Stillwater River Trailhead. The "trading keys"
option doesn't work well on this trail because one party has to agree to walk 28 miles

*The Upper Stillwater, just before it begins its long, steep plunge to the north edge of the
Beartooths.* Photo: Michael S. Sample

uphill so the other group gets 28 miles downhill. Arranging the shuttle may be a has-
sle, but it allows the rare chance to travel all the way through the Beartooths along
the Stillwater River. There are only two other ways to traverse the entire area and stay
on established trails. These are The Beaten Path, Hike 20, up the East Rosebud and
Slough Creek Divide, Hike 9, following East Fork Boulder River and Slough Creek
from Boulder River Road into Yellowstone Park.

From the marvelous, high-mountain park at the trailhead, this trail travels through
28 miles of forested river valley. The 1988 fires burned through the Stillwater, and the
first 4 miles still show the results. But now the forest is springing back, and the entire
area is lush and full of wildlife.

To some, the prospect of traveling 28 miles through one continuous valley forest
might sound monotonous. And granted, this route offers none of the thrills of "bag-
ging" a major peak or watching sunsets burnish the surface of some icy alpine tarn.
But it more than makes up for this by immersing the traveler in remote wilderness,
in a place at once peaceful and refreshing.

The trail is in good shape all the way and is well-traveled north of the junction
with Wounded Man Creek and Trail 90.

For descriptions of the route, refer to the Stillwater to Stillwater trip, Hike 12 and
the Horseshoe Lake trip, Hike 57. Be sure to take the time for the short side trip over
to Tripod Hill at mile 21.6. There's an obvious trail going east just before the Flood
Creek bridge. The point provides a spectacular view of the Stillwater River drainage,
including well-named Cathedral Point to the south just past Flood Creek. At Flood
Creek, a glance at the map shows that it isn't far to Flood Creek Falls. But this is an
extremely difficult bushwhack, which is really too bad because Flood Creek Falls is
one of the most spectacular sights in the Beartooths and one that very few people
will ever see.

Side Trips

Take a short side trip over to Tripod Hill for a nice view.

Camping

Potential campsites are abundant along the entire route, and there is plenty of wood
for thought-provoking campfires.

Fishing

The Stillwater above, or south of, Goose Creek doesn't support a fishery and probably never has. The steep cascades block upstream migration. Fish begin to appear in
the river at Goose Creek; below here there are brook trout as well as rainbows and
cutthroats. The farther downstream you go, the better the fishing.

Keep in mind, as you fish, that the steeper the terrain, the less hospitable it is for trout. Look for fish in the slower water. Rainbows and cutthroats are slightly more suited to faster, colder water, and they do better than brookies in the fast places.

Most anglers agree that brook trout are the best eating of the three types of trout found here, and eating them will only help the remaining fish to grow bigger. Plan on taking a meal with you when you leave; there will be plenty left for those who follow.

Sioux Charley Lake is really just a wide, slow spot in the river where many people choose to stop and catch a few brookies for dinner.

Absaroka Range

The Absaroka Range is circled with trailheads. Trailheads on the east side along the Boulder River Road are covered in that chapter. This chapter includes the rest of the trailheads on the west and south sides of the range. One trailhead, Hell-roaring, is actually in Yellowstone National Park but accesses a nice loop in the southern Absaroka Mountains.

Hiking is fun and a great way to build lasting friendships.

59 THE HELLROARING

General description: A trip starting inside Yellowstone National Park, hiking through the open terrain of northern Yellowstone and into the lush upper Hellroaring country in the Absaroka-Beartooth Wilderness in Gallatin National Forest

Special attractions: Open remoteness and abundant wildlife

Type of trip: Loop

Total distance: 20 miles

Difficulty: Moderate

Traffic: Heavy in first and last 2 miles; light for rest of the trip

Maps: USGS—Specimen Creek: RMS—Gardiner-Mt. Wallace; Trails Illustrated Maps—Mammoth Hot Springs and Tower Junction

Starting point: Hellroaring Trailhead

Finding the trailhead: Drive 14.3 miles east from Mammoth, Wyoming, on the Yellowstone Park Grand Loop Road, or 3.3 miles west from Tower, Wyoming, and pull into the Hellroaring Trailhead. The actual trailhead is 0.3 mile down an unpaved service road.

Parking and trailhead facilities: Ample parking, including room for horse trailers; no toilet.

Key Points

0.8 Junction with trail to Tower; turn left.

1.0 Suspension bridge over Yellowstone River.

1.6 Junction with Coyote Creek/Buffalo Plateau Trail; turn right.

2.1 Junction with trail to Buffalo Plateau Trail; turn left.

6.0 Backcountry campsite 2C1.

6.4 Backcountry campsite 2C2.

6.7 Park boundary.

7.2 Poacher Trail 98; turn left.

9.5 Coyote Creek Trail 97; turn left.

9.8 Hellroaring Bridge.

10.2 Hellroaring Guard Station and Horse Creek Bridge.

10.4 Junction with trail to Jardine; turn left.

13.0 Park boundary.

15.8 Backcountry campsite 8H9.

16.3 Junction with trail to campsite 8H8; trail down west side to creek and to campsites 8H5, 8H3, and 8H1; a foot bridge; and trail along Hellroaring Creek; turn left and cross creek on bridge.

17.8 Backcountry campsite 8H6.

18.1 Junction with Yellowstone River Trail and spur trail to campsites 8H4 and 8H2; turn left.

18.4 Junction with trail to Coyote Creek and Buffalo Plateau; turn right.

19.0 Suspension bridge over Yellowstone River.

19.2 Junction with trail to Tower; turn right.

20.0 Hellroaring Trailhead.

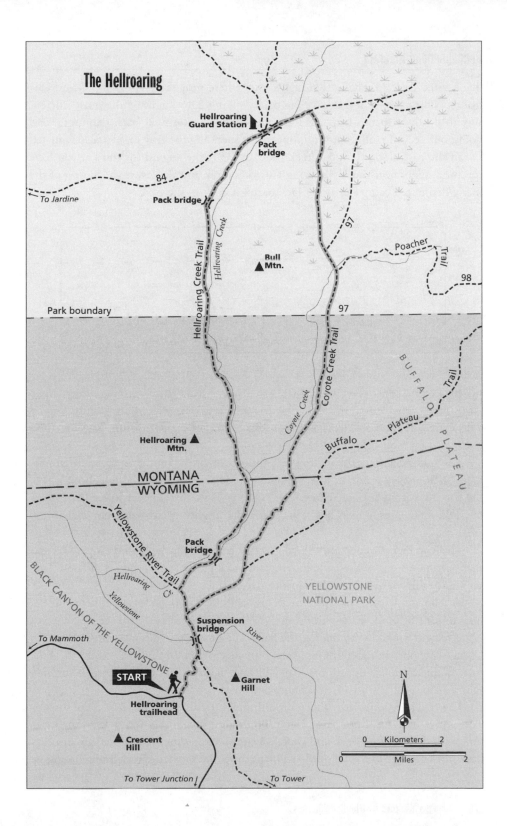

The Hellroaring

Hellroaring
Guard Station

Pack
bridge

84

← To Jardine

Pack bridge

Hellroaring Creek Trail

Hellroaring Creek

Bull
▲ Mtn.

97

Poacher
Trail

98

Park boundary

97

Coyote Creek

Coyote Creek Trail

B U F F A L O
Trail

Plateau

Hellroaring ▲
Mtn.

Buffalo

P L A T E A U

MONTANA
WYOMING

Yellowstone River Trail

Pack
bridge

Hellroaring

Yellowstone

Cr.

YELLOWSTONE
NATIONAL PARK

BLACK CANYON OF THE YELLOWSTONE

Suspension
bridge

River

← To Mammoth

START

Hellroaring
trailhead

▲ Garnet
Hill

N

▲ Crescent
Hill

0   Kilometers   2

0   Miles   2

To Tower Junction

To Tower

Recommended Itinerary

Try a three-day trip staying two nights somewhere near the Hellroaring Guard Station, spending the second day fishing or day hiking. This might be the most efficient way to do this trip, but it means long days with the overnight pack coming in and going out, so you could opt for a longer trip spending the first night at a designated site in the park along Coyote Creek (2C1 or 2C2), the second (or third, if you have the time) night near the Hellroaring Guard Station, and the last night in one of the many designated campsites along Hellroaring Creek in the park.

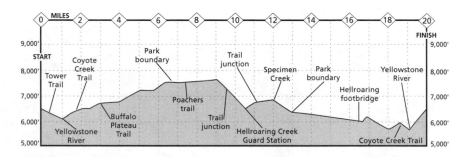

The Hike

This is not the most spectacular hike in this book, but it offers some special features not found on most other backpacking vacations.

The hike penetrates the uncrowded remoteness of the southern Absaroka Mountains. Such privacy is rare in today's popular hiking areas—even though about half of the trip lies within famous Yellowstone National Park. Also, expect to see large wildlife. Elk, moose, bison, and bears, including the mighty grizzly, are abundant in the area.

This trip makes a nice loop thanks to two trails (Hellroaring and Coyote Creek) that head north out of the park, looping around a grassy butte called Bull Mountain, which is easily viewed from the Coyote Creek Trail.

In Yellowstone the trails go through low-altitude, dry, open terrain where you can hike in June of most years with no snowbanks. Hit the trail early to see wildlife that often retreats to shady day beds as the landscape heats up in late morning.

In September hundreds of big game hunters crowd into the area just north of the park boundary, most using horses and staying in large outfitter camps. In summer months, however, the area is amazingly devoid of people.

The trail starts out with a steep drop through mostly open hillside to the suspension bridge over the Yellowstone River. From here, go another 0.6 mile to the junction with the Coyote Creek and Buffalo Plateau Trails. (Some maps for this area may have not been updated. The outdated maps show the Coyote Creek Trail coming up from Hellroaring Creek instead of branching out from the Buffalo Plateau Trail 0.5 mile after taking a right [north] at this junction.)

You can do this loop in either direction with little extra effort, but we took the counterclockwise route, so go right (north) at the Coyote Creek/Buffalo Plateau junction.

About a half mile after leaving the Yellowstone River Trail, the Buffalo Plateau Trail goes off to the right. You go left (north) on the Coyote Creek Trail. In another half mile or so, you might see the abandoned trail coming up from Hellroaring Creek (abandoned but still visible on the ground and shown on many maps).

Before and after the park boundary, the trail goes into a partially burned forest and stays there for about a mile. I couldn't help notice that during this forested leg of the trip, the trail seemed to serve as a fire line, with the trees on the west side of the trail green and unburnt and those on the east side victims of the 1988 fires.

After you go left (north) at the junction with the Poacher Trail (about a half mile north of the park), the trail breaks out on the east edge of a huge, marshy meadow. This is a very easy place to get on the wrong trail. Note on the map that the trail crosses this meadow and goes up the west side even though an excellent trail (not on most maps) continues up the east side of the meadow, tempting you to follow it. If you do, you won't be completely lost, but you'll add about a mile to your trip. Both trails intersect with the Coyote Creek Trail 97, about a half mile apart. Whichever trail you follow, turn left (west) when you reach the Coyote Creek Trail.

This section of the trip goes through a more lush forest than the lower stretches of Coyote and Hellroaring Creeks. Just before crossing Hellroaring Creek, the trail drops steeply for about a half mile, making you happy you didn't do the trip in reverse.

Hellroaring is a huge stream even this far from its eventual merger with the Yellowstone River, and the Forest Service has constructed a great bridge to handle the heavy horse traffic this area gets during the hunting season.

After the bridge, you pass through a large meadow and by the Hellroaring Guard Station. If you're staying overnight outside of the park, pick from the many nice campsites in this area. Four FS trails take off to the north and west from this area, but you keep turning left at all the junctions and follow Hellroaring Creek back to the park. After the guard station, the trail stays out of sight of the creek up on the west hillside and passes through mature lodgepole.

After the park boundary until just after campsite 8H9, the trail stays away from the creek in timber. However, when we hiked this trail, we came through a live forest fire burning on both sides of the trail, including 8H9. Later, this fire burned north up to Hellroaring Guard Station. Since this lightning-caused fire was a natural part of the Yellowstone ecosystem (just like rain and wind), the National Park Service (NPS) rightfully let it burn.

After breaking out into a series of large meadows, you reach the junction with the bridge over Hellroaring Creek. Unless you want to ford Hellroaring Creek, take a left

Massive bridge over Hellroaring Creek near the guard station.

(east) here. On the other side of the bridge, a spur trail to campsite 8H8 goes off to the left and you go right (south), following the stream for 1.5 miles back to the Yellowstone River Trail where you go left (east) and retrace your steps back to the trailhead.

The trail is in excellent shape the entire way, but the many trail junctions (some not on maps) can be confusing, especially when you're outside of the park.

Options

You can do this loop in reverse, but it might be slightly more difficult because of the hill east of the Hellroaring Guard Station. You can also skip the loop option and go out-and-back along either Coyote or Hellroaring Creek.

Side Trips

Several trails juncture at the Hellroaring Guard Station, so you have plenty of options for side trips. We only had one extra day, so we took the Carpenter Lake loop. It's about 13 miles around the loop, including some confusing spots on the little-used

Carpenter Lake Trail. The 1988 fires burned the Carpenter Lake area, including the lakeshore.

Camping

This route has designated campsites within Yellowstone National Park along Hellroaring and Coyote Creeks and undesignated camping areas outside the park. All campsites in Yellowstone allow campfires unless otherwise indicated, and you usually can have a fire outside the park, too. Likewise, all campsites in the park have bear poles, but outside the park, you'll have to hang your food in trees.

Fishing

Cutthroats abound throughout Hellroaring Creek and in lower Coyote Creek. If you have time, hike a mile or two down to the Yellowstone River for some superb cutthroat fishing. Carpenter Lake is loaded with cutthroats, but the tree-lined shoreline makes fly casting difficult.

Camping just north of Hellroaring Guard Station.

60 ELBOW LAKE

General description: A long day hike or overnighter

Special attractions: Mt. Cowen, an incredible mass of rock and the highest point in the Absaroka Range

Type of trip: Out-and-back

Total distance: 16 miles

Difficulty: Difficult

Traffic: Moderate

Maps: USGS—Knowles Peak, The Pyramid, and Mt. Cowen; RMS—Mt. Cowen Area

Starting point: East Fork Mill Creek Trailhead

Finding the trailhead: Drive south from Livingston, Montana, on U.S. Highway 89 for 26 miles and turn left (east) at a well-marked turn onto the Mill Creek Road. You cross the Yellowstone River after 0.8 mile. Continue driving southeast on Mill Creek Road (Forest Road 486), which turns to gravel after 6 miles. You can cut about 2 miles off the route by taking the East River Road south from Livingston and turning left on the well-signed Mill Creek Road. For the East Fork Mill Creek Trailhead, go 9 miles from U.S. 89 and turn left (northeast) on FR 3280, which is well-signed, for 1.5 miles to the trailhead, which is located a quarter of a mile before the Snowy Range Ranch. Snowbank Campground, an FS vehicle campground, is on the main Mill Creek Road 1.3 miles past the West Fork Road.

Parking and trailhead facilities: Limited parking, so be careful not to block the road; no toilet.

Key Points

1.2 Junction with Upper Sage Creek Trail 48; turn left.

2.7 Sage Creek.

4.0 Junction with major social trail; turn right.

6.5 Elbow Creek.

8.0 Elbow Lake.

The Hike

The rugged north Absaroka Range forms the east wall of the Paradise Valley south of Livingston, Montana, along the Yellowstone River. Of all these formidable peaks, 11,206-foot Mount Cowen is the highest.

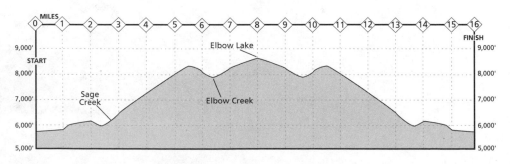

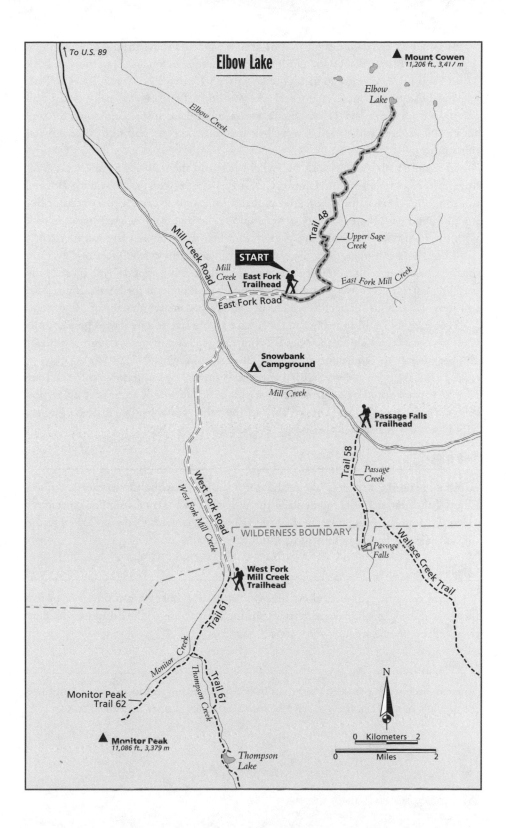

As you leave the trailhead on Trail 51, it stays high and skirts around the south side of the Snowy Range Ranch for a little more than a mile before crossing the East Fork Mill Creek on a new bridge to the junction with Upper Sage Creek Trail 48. Turn left and head north along Sage Creek. As you cross the bridge, a major social trail comes in from the Snowy River Ranch. Don't go left here. Instead, go down the trail about 200 yards and take a left at a well-defined junction (no trail sign when I hiked this route).

The trail climbs steeply with no switchbacks and then crosses Sage Creek. After the creek, it continues an unrelenting, Category 1 climb (with good switchbacks, i.e., not too long) across a dry hillside. You probably will want to carry extra water for this stretch. Otherwise, there is plenty of water along the trail even in late August. Check with the Forest Service about snow conditions before trying an early summer trip.

Elbow Lake is 8 miles from the trailhead. You gain almost 3,500 feet of elevation, making this a tough hike even for the extra-fit. The trail is in good shape most of the way. The last 2 miles to the lake get rough, muddy, and difficult for horses. If you hike to Elbow Lake in July, expect to see lots of wildflowers, including a sea of balsamroot.

Start early and plan to make the entire hike to the lake in one day, as good campsites are nonexistent along the way. Starting early helps you get through the major climbing before the afternoon sun starts beating you down.

Elbow Lake is very scenic, with a gorgeous waterfall crashing down into the lake. Mount Cowen does lure a fair number of climbers, but do not attempt it unless you know what you are doing. Unlike most of the other peaks in the Absaroka Range, Mount Cowen is a technical climb.

Side Trips

Explore the nearby nameless lake to the northeast by following the stream that enters Elbow Lake's eastern side. Incidentally, the unnamed lake has no fish. For spectacular views of Mount Cowen, hike up the little valley on the eastern side of Cowen to the top of the ridge. You may spot some mountain goats.

Camping

There are no great campsites along the way to the lake, but you can find four or five nice sites at the lake. This lake receives surprisingly heavy use, so the campsites are quite overused; be sure to set up a zero-impact camp.

Fishing

You can catch some pan-size cutthroats in Elbow Lake and in Elbow Creek, but these fish see lots of artificial flies, so have beans and rice for dinner instead of trout.

61 THOMPSON LAKE

General description: A moderate day hike or overnighter

Special attractions: A beautiful mountain lake, a rare occurrence in the southern Absaroka Range

Type of trip: Out-and-back

Total distance: 10 miles

Difficulty: Moderate

Traffic: Moderate

Maps: USGS—Mineral Mountain; RMS—Gardiner-Mt. Wallace

Starting point: West Fork Mill Creek Trailhead

Finding the trailhead: Drive south from Livingston, Montana, on U.S. Highway 89 for 26 miles and turn left (east) at a well-marked turn onto the Mill Creek Road. You cross the Yellowstone River after 0.8 mile. Continue driving southeast on Mill Creek Road (Forest Road 486), which turns to gravel after 6 miles. You can cut about 2 miles off the route by taking the East River Road south from Livingston and turning left on the well-signed Mill Creek Road.

For the West Fork Mill Creek Trailhead, go 1.2 miles past the East Fork Road and turn right (south) on the West Fork Road. Go 5.8 miles to the end of the road and the trailhead. There was no sign at this turn onto the West Fork Road when I was there, but turn where signs point to the Yellowstone Bible Camp. Snowbank Campground, an FS vehicle campground, is on the main Mill Creek Road 1.3 miles past the West Fork Road.

Parking and trailhead facilities: A large trailhead with room for horse trailers; no toilet.

Key Points

2.2 Junction with Monitor Peak Trail 62; turn left.

4.0 Thompson Creek.

5.0 Thompson Lake.

The Hike

For me, Thompson Lake was a pleasant surprise, a gorgeous little gem nestled in the southern Absaroka Range, which has a shortage of lakes. It's also an easy hike on a well-maintained and well-traveled trail. The heavy stock traffic has helped keep this trail very distinct. There were no mileage signs, but based on my normal hiking pace, it's close to 5 miles to the lake.

The route starts out in a forest burned by the 1988 forest fires, but after about a mile, it heads into a mature, unburned forest for the rest of the way. The route is undulating but has no hills worth writing about. Watch for the Monitor Peak Trail junction in a large meadow on the top of a ridge, the only meadow on this route. About a mile before the lake, you cross Thompson Creek, but unofficial log bridges built by earlier hikers allow you to cross without getting your feet wet.

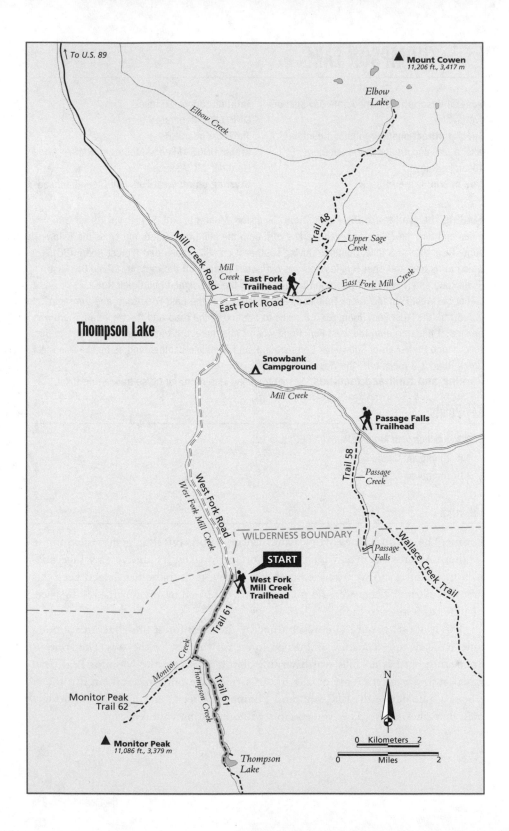

Thompson Lake

To U.S. 89

▲ **Mount Cowen**
11,206 ft., 3,417 m

Elbow Lake

Elbow Creek

Trail 48

Upper Sage Creek

Mill Creek Road

Mill Creek

East Fork Trailhead

East Fork Road

East Fork Mill Creek

▲ **Snowbank Campground**

Mill Creek

Passage Falls Trailhead

Trail 58

Passage Creek

West Fork Road

West Fork Mill Creek

WILDERNESS BOUNDARY

Passage Falls

Wallace Creek Trail

START
West Fork Mill Creek Trailhead

Trail 61

Monitor Creek

Thompson Creek

Trail 61

Monitor Peak Trail 62

N

▲ **Monitor Peak**
11,086 ft., 3,379 m

Thompson Lake

0   Kilometers   2

0   Miles   2

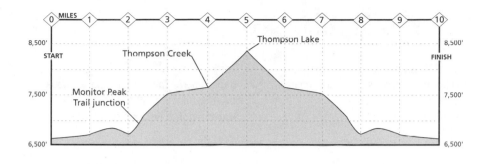

Options

If you are ambitious and wilderness-wise, you can make Thompson Lake part of a long, adventurous loop by continuing past the lake to the junction with Trail 64, possibly taking the spur trail up to Charlie White Lake for the second night out. Turn right (west) on Trail 64 and right again on Trail 67, spending the third night at Fish Lake before heading back to the trailhead on Trail 67. I haven't done this route, but the Forest Service tells me it's open but not well-maintained. I strongly suggest checking with the FS before attempting it.

Side Trips

If you stay two nights at Thompson Lake, you can use the extra day to check out Charlie White Lake.

Camping

The south end of the lake has several good campsites, but some of them have been trashed by stock parties tying horses to trees too close to the lakeshore and campsites. This ruins it for everybody. The FS has a prominent notice on the trailhead information board prohibiting this, but some stock parties have obviously ignored the regulation. This lake receives surprisingly heavy use, so be sure to set up a zero-impact camp and help undo some of the damage done by others.

Fishing

Thompson Lake has a nice cutthroat population, but the fish have seen lots of flies so they can be fussy and can send you home skunked.

62 PASSAGE FALLS

General description: An easy day hike
Special attractions: A gorgeous waterfall
Type of trip: Out-and-back
Total distance: 4 miles
Difficulty: Easy

Traffic: Heavy
Maps: USGS—The Pyramid and Mt. Wallace;
RMS—Gardiner-Mt. Wallace
Starting point: Passage Falls Trailhead

Finding the trailhead: Drive south from Livingston, Montana, on U.S. Highway 89 for 26 miles and turn left (east) at a well-marked turn onto the Mill Creek Road. You cross the Yellowstone River after 0.8 mile. Continue driving southeast on Mill Creek Road (Forest Road 486), which turns to gravel after 6 miles. You can cut about 2 miles off the route by taking the East River Road south from Livingston and turning left on the well-signed Mill Creek Road. For the Passage Falls Trailhead, continue 4 miles past the West Fork Road or 2.7 miles past Snowbank Campground.

Parking and trailhead facilities: A large trailhead with a one-way road through it and ample parking, including room for horse trailers; no toilet.

Key Points

1.2 Junction with Wallace Creek Trail; turn right.

1.8 Boundary of private property.

2.0 Passage Falls.

The Hike

This is a delightful, short hike to the magnificent Passage Falls on Wallace Creek, a fairly large stream. The falls is most spectacular in the spring but worth the trip any time.

The trail is double-wide except for the last 0.2 mile where you turn left onto a single track for a small drop down to the waterfall. This last section has a few steep spots, so hang onto the kids. The route follows the stream until the junction. It's quite heavily traveled, so don't plan on being alone. The trail goes right down to the falls for an up-close and personal view.

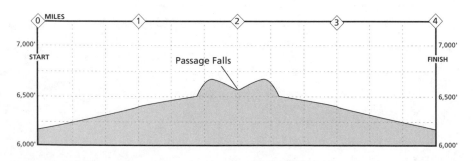

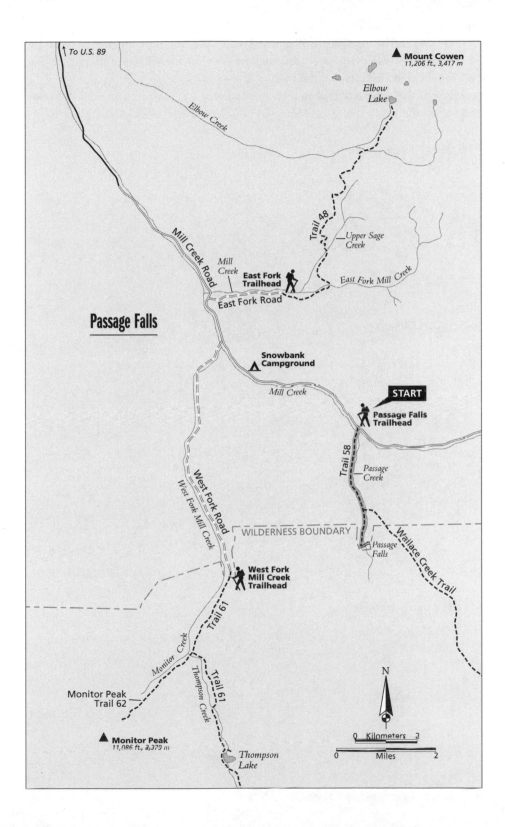

Passage Falls

↑ To U.S. 89

▲ **Mount Cowen**
11,206 ft., 3,417 m

Elbow Lake

Elbow Creek

Mill Creek Road

Trail 48

Upper Sage Creek

Mill Creek

East Fork Trailhead

East Fork Mill Creek

East Fork Road

Snowbank Campground

Mill Creek

START

Passage Falls Trailhead

Trail 58

Passage Creek

West Fork Road

West Fork Mill Creek

WILDERNESS BOUNDARY

Passage Falls

Wallace Creek Trail

West Fork Mill Creek Trailhead

Trail 61

Monitor Creek

Trail 61

Thompson Creek

Monitor Peak
Trail 62

N

▲ **Monitor Peak**
11,086 ft., 3,379 m

Thompson Lake

0   Kilometers   2

0   Miles   2

The waterfall is on Gallatin National Forest land but right on the edge of an inholding that's being developed for wilderness cabin sites. Be sure to respect the landowners' rights and stay on the trail.

Unfortunately, this trail is open to motorized vehicles, so you might see a dirt bike or ATV on the trail.

63 Pine Creek Lake

General description: A moderate day hike or overnighter

Special attractions: A beautiful mountain lake with attractive side trips

Type of trip: Out-and-back

Total distance: 10 miles

Difficulty: Moderate

Traffic: Heavy

Maps: USGS—Emigrant and Mt. Cowen; RMS—Mt. Cowen Area

Starting point: Pine Creek Trailhead

Finding the trailhead: Drive south from Livingston, Montana, on U.S. Highway 89 for 5 miles. Then turn left (east) on East River Road (Highway 540) and head south for 9 miles; 0.7 mile past the cabin community of Pine Creek, turn left (east) onto paved Forest Road 202. Go to the end of this road (2.5 miles, paved all the way) where Trail 47 starts at the far end of the campground. For an alternate route from U.S. 89, take the Pine Creek Road between mile markers 43 and 44.

Parking and trailhead facilities: Ample parking; toilet; FS vehicle campground at trailhead.

Key Points

0.2 Junction with George Lake Trail; turn left.

1.0 Pine Creek Falls.

5.0 Pine Creek Lake.

The Hike

From the trailhead, the first mile of Trail 47 is deceptively flat. At the end of the flat stretch, you stand at the foot of beautiful Pine Creek Falls. This is far enough for some hikers who have heard about the next 4 miles. In those 4 miles, the trail climbs more than 3,000 feet. However, for others, the allure of a mountain lake held in a glacial cirque is too much to resist. The trail is usually dry, so draw some water at the falls. Be sure to treat it. Water from anywhere in the Pine Creek area is not recommended for untreated drinking due to the threat of *Giardia*.

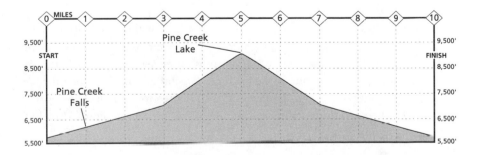

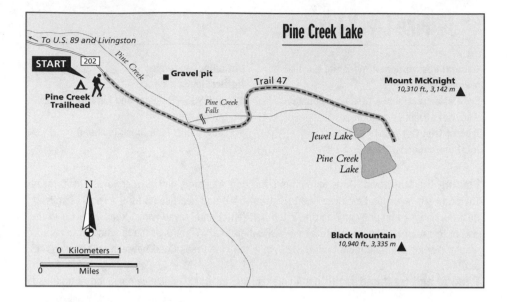

Pine Creek Lake

To U.S. 89 and Livingston

START 202

Pine Creek

Pine Creek Trailhead

Gravel pit

Pine Creek Falls

Trail 47

Mount McKnight
10,310 ft., 3,142 m

Jewel Lake

Pine Creek Lake

N

0 Kilometers 1

0 Miles 1

Black Mountain
10,940 ft., 3,335 m

Because the trail climbs 1,000 feet per mile, most people take between three and four hours to reach the lake. On the bright side, coming out takes only two hours. Therefore, this could be a day hike.

The lake lies beneath 10,940-foot Black Mountain in an obvious glacial cirque. On the north side of the lake, the bedrock shows pronounced striations where the glacier shoved its rocky load across the granite. At the outlet, a broad slab of granite impounds the lake. Overly friendly ground squirrels, marmots, pikas, and a few mountain goats are common around the lake.

The best time to visit Pine Creek Lake is between July 15 and September 30. To attempt it any earlier will mean wading through snowdrifts on the last part of the trail; in October those drifts may reappear quickly. If you prize solitude, wait until after Labor Day. Before school starts, youth camps use the trail heavily.

If you have extra time, hike around to the east end of the lake and climb the divide to look into Lake McKnight and the Davis Creek drainage. There is no trail into Lake McKnight, and the country is so rough and remote that few hikers ever walk its shores.

One of the pleasures of camping at Pine Creek Lake is the possibility of seeing alpenglow on the peaks. As the sun moves lower in the west and begins to set behind the Gallatin Range, the atmosphere deflects a portion of the color in the spectrum, leaving a pronounced reddish hue in the last few moments of sunlight. When the conditions are right and this red light bounces off the polished rock surfaces just north of the outlet, the effect is startling. With only a little poetic license, one could say it looks like the peaks are on fire.

Side Trips

Experienced hikers will like the off-trail trip over to Lake McKnight.

Camping

Good campsites are scarce, but you can find one at the lower end of Pine Creek Lake or at the small tarn below the lake.

Fishing

Pine Creek Lake has a nice population of cutthroats, but these fish see lots of flies and lures, so they can be difficult to catch.

Afterword: The Value of Guidebooks

It has been whispered here and there—usually by "locals"—that books like this are a bad idea. The theory goes something like this: Guidebooks bring more people into the wilderness; more people cause more environmental damage; and the wildness we all seek gradually evaporates.

I used to think like that, too. Here's why I changed my mind.

I wrote and published my first guidebook in 1979 (*Hiking Montana*); some of my hiking buddies disapproved. Since then, I've written nine more hiking guides and published more than a hundred for other authors, and I'm very proud of it. I also hope these books have greatly increased wilderness use.

Experienced hikers tend to have a lofty attitude toward the inexperienced masses. They think anybody who wants to backpack can buy a topo map and compass and find their own way through the wilderness. But the fact is, most beginning backpackers want a guide. Sometimes new hikers prefer a living, breathing guide to show them the way and help them build confidence, but most of the time, newcomers can get by with a trail guide like this one.

All FalconGuides (and most guidebooks published by other publishers) encourage wilderness users to respect and support the protection of wild country. Sometimes, this is direct editorializing. Sometimes, this invitation takes the more subtle form of simply helping people experience wilderness. And it's a rare person who leaves the wilderness without a firmly planted passion for wild country—and waiting for a chance to vote for more of it.

In classes on backpacking taught for the Yellowstone Institute, I have taken hundreds of people into the wilderness. Many of them had on a backpack for the first time. Many of them were not convinced that we need more wilderness, but they were all convinced when they arrived back at the trailhead. Many, many times, I've seen it happen without saying a single word about wilderness preservation efforts.

It doesn't take preaching. Instead, we just need to get people out into the wilderness where the essence of wildness sort of sneaks up on them and takes root, and before you know it, the ranks of those who support wilderness have grown.

Yes, overcrowding is already a problem in some places and will be in others. But the answer to overcrowded, overused wilderness is not limiting use of wilderness and restrictive regulations. The answer is more wilderness. A trampled campsite is ugly, to be sure, but it can be rested and reclaimed. Overuse is a short-term problem. Once roads are built and cabins go up, the land no longer qualifies for wilderness designation.

How can we convince people to support more wilderness when they have never experienced wilderness? In my opinion, we can't. Without the support of people who experience wilderness, there will be no more wilderness, so, it follows, the more people who experience wilderness, the more support for wilderness.

That's why we need guidebooks. And that's why I changed my mind. I believe guidebooks have done as much to build support for wilderness as pro-wilderness organizations have done through political and public relations efforts.

And here's another key value of guidebooks. All FalconGuides (and again, most guidebooks from other publishers) contain sections on zero-impact ethics and wilderness safety. Guidebooks provide an ideal medium for communicating such vital information.

In thirty years of backpacking, I have seen dramatic changes in how backpackers care for wilderness. I've seen it go from appalling to exceptional. Today, almost everybody walks softly in the wilderness. And I believe the information contained in guidebooks has been partly responsible for this change.

Having said all that, I hope many thousands of people use this book to enjoy a fun-filled vacation backpacking in the Absaroka-Beartooth Wilderness—and then, of course, vote for wilderness preservation the rest of their lives.

—*Bill Schneider*

Hiker's Checklist

Consider checklists as general guides only. You should carefully consider each item you take, and keep weight in mind during all of your trip-planning. Standardized checklists, such as the following, can be helpful, but it's better for each person to modify the standard lists for different seasons and environments. Keep the checklist in the top of your pack, and take notes when you notice something missing. Keep in mind that equipment does not have to be new or fancy (or expensive), but make sure you test everything before you leave home.

Equipment for day hiking:
- [ ] Day pack or fanny pack
- [ ] Water bottle(s)
- [ ] First-aid kit
- [ ] Survival kit
- [ ] Compass
- [ ] Maps
- [ ] Plastic trowel
- [ ] Toilet paper
- [ ] Sunscreen and lip lotion
- [ ] Binoculars (optional)
- [ ] Camera and extra film (optional)
- [ ] Flashlight and extra batteries
- [ ] Pocketknife
- [ ] Sunglasses

Added equipment for overnight trips:
- [ ] Tent and waterproof fly
- [ ] Sleeping bag (20° F or warmer) and stuff sack
- [ ] Sleeping pad
- [ ] Cooking pots and pot holder
- [ ] Extra water bottle
- [ ] Full-size backpack
- [ ] Pack fly or lightweight poncho
- [ ] Cup, bowl, and eating utensils
- [ ] Lightweight camp stove and adequate fuel
- [ ] Trash compactor bags
- [ ] Zip-locked bags
- [ ] Small ditty bags
- [ ] Paper towels

☐ Nylon cord (at least 50 feet)
☐ Small cloth towel
☐ Personal toilet kit
☐ Notebook and pencil

Clothing

In general, strive for natural fibers such as cotton and wool and "earth tones" instead of bright colors. Dig around in the closet for something "dull." Your wilderness partners will appreciate it. Try out the clothing before leaving home to make sure everything fits loosely with no chafing. In particular, make sure your boots are broken in, lest they break you on the first day of the hike.

Clothing for day hiking:
☐ Large-brimmed hat or cap
☐ Sturdy hiking boots
☐ Light, natural-fiber socks
☐ Lightweight hiking shorts or long pants
☐ Long-sleeve shirt
☐ Waterproof coat and pants
☐ Mittens or gloves

Additional clothing for overnight trips:
☐ Warm hat (i.e., stocking cap)
☐ Long underwear
☐ Sweater and/or insulated vest
☐ Long pants
☐ One pair of socks for each day plus one extra pair
☐ Underwear
☐ Extra shirts
☐ Sandals or lightweight shoes for wearing in camp

Food

For day hiking, bring high-energy snacks for lunching along the way. For overnight trips, bring enough food, including high-energy snacks, but don't overburden yourself with too much food. Plan meals carefully, bringing just enough food, plus some emergency rations. Freeze-dried foods are the lightest and safest in bear country, but expensive and not necessary. Don't forget hot and cold drinks.

What to keep in the top of your pack:

- ☐ Bug repellent in sealed bag
- ☐ Extra batteries
- ☐ Extra bulbs in film case
- ☐ Headlamp with fresh batteries
- ☐ Keys attached to inside of pack
- ☐ Map (each member of group should have a copy)
- ☐ Money, credit card, and driver's license
- ☐ Sunglasses in break-proof case
- ☐ Sunscreen
- ☐ Plastic trowel and toilet paper and any needed feminine hygiene products
- ☐ Waterproof notebook
- ☐ Duct tape rolled on pencil

First-Aid kit

For more information on wilderness first-aid kits, see *Wilderness First Aid* by Gilbert Preston, MD (Falcon 1997).

- ☐ Ace bandage
- ☐ Adhesive bandages (Band-Aids)
- ☐ Adhesive tape
- ☐ Antibiotic ointment packets or small tube of Neosporin®
- ☐ Triangular bandage
- ☐ Gauze pads (four 4"x4")
- ☐ Gauze rollers
- ☐ Medications (laxative, antidiarrhea, allergy, aspirin or Ibuprofen)
- ☐ Nonadhesive bandage for burns
- ☐ Nylon bag
- ☐ Rubber or vinyl gloves
- ☐ Safety pins
- ☐ Scissors
- ☐ Tweezers or forceps
- ☐ Wound closure strips
- ☐ Moleskin or Molefoam
- ☐ Personal medicine as required, i.e., allergy pills
- ☐ Snake bite kit if in snake country

Survival kit

Always bring a survival kit with these items:

- ☐ Candle
- ☐ Cigarette lighters (two, in waterproof wrapper)
- ☐ Compass with signal mirror
- ☐ Emergency fire starter in film case
- ☐ Emergency food bars (two)
- ☐ Iodine water purification tablets
- ☐ Matches (with strike strip in waterproof container)
- ☐ Plastic whistle
- ☐ Space blanket
- ☐ Pocketknife or multipurpose tool

Post-trip Checklist

- ☐ Call or notify those with whom you left your itinerary and tell them you returned safely.
- ☐ For your safety and the safety of others, report any hazards you encountered.
- ☐ Clean gear and repair any items damaged during the trip.
- ☐ Take sleeping bags out of stuff sacks; put them in loose storage bags or hang them.
- ☐ Dry out your tent, fly, and rain gear before storing.
- ☐ Dump garbage, but don't fill trailhead garbage cans. Drive it in, drive it out.
- ☐ Replenish survival and first-aid items.

About the Author

Living Life One Mile at a Time

Whenever Bill Schneider isn't out in the wilderness, he wants to be. He has spent more than thirty-five years hiking the trails of Montana and other western states.

In the beginning, during college in the 1960s, he worked on a trail crew in Glacier National Park. Then he spent the 1970s publishing the *Montana Outdoors Magazine* for the Montana Department of Fish, Wildlife & Parks and covering as many miles of trails as possible on weekends and holidays.

In 1979 Bill, along with his business partner, Mike Sample, established Falcon Press Publishing and published two guidebooks the first year. Bill wrote one of them, *The Hiker's Guide to Montana,* now titled *Hiking Montana,* which is still a popular guidebook. Since then, Falcon has become a premier national publisher of recreational guidebooks and other outdoor books with well over 700 titles in print.

He has also written sixteen other books and many magazine articles on wildlife, outdoor recreation, and environmental issues. Along the way, on a part-time basis over a span of twelve years, Bill taught classes on bicycling, backpacking, zero-impact camping, and hiking in bear country for the Yellowstone Institute, a nonprofit educational organization in Yellowstone National Park.

In 2000 Bill, who lives in Helena, Montana, left Falcon to start a career as a publishing consultant and concentrate on a long list of writing projects.

To learn more about Bill Schneider's books, visit www.billschneider.net.

Help Us Keep This Guide Up to Date

Every effort has been made by the author and editors to make this guide as accurate and useful as possible. However, many things can change after a guide is published—trails are rerouted, regulations change, techniques evolve, facilities come under new management, etc.

We would love to hear from you concerning your experiences with this guide and how you feel it could be improved and kept up to date. While we may not be able to respond to all comments and suggestions, we'll take them to heart and we'll also make certain to share them with the author. Please send your comments and suggestions to the following address:

> The Globe Pequot Press
> Reader Response/Editorial Department
> P.O. Box 480
> Guilford, CT 06437

Or you may e-mail us at:

> editorial@GlobePequot.com

Thanks for your input, and happy travels!